Katie Roiphe is a writer and journ~~alist~~
including the *New Yorker*. Her books
Still She Haunts Me. She is a professo~~r~~

'*Uncommon Arrangements* is a vibrant,
inner lives, and positively fizzes wi~~th~~ ~~emotion~~ . . . This is a
marvellous parade of old-fashioned British eccentricity . . . Their trials
make for the most deliciously addictive reading. Is this a form of intrusive
literary voyeurism? Probably. But when it's this good, who cares?' Viv
Groskop, *Observer*

'*Uncommon Arrangements* is a book that combines high gossip – the very
highest – and deep insight to a degree that is wholly dazzling . . . It stays
with you for months and months, wheedling its way into your thoughts
about your own relationships long after you have returned it to the shelf'
Rachel Cooke, *Observer*

'Katie Roiphe is a sort of literary oyster. She can absorb masses of gossipy,
ephemeral background and turn it into a pearl of distilled wisdom.
Uncommonly enjoyable . . . Roiphe executes this group portrait with
grace' Hermione Eyre, *Independent*

'Shrewd and entertaining . . . This graceful and impeccably researched
book . . . is a delight' Miranda Seymour, *Guardian*

'*Uncommon Arrangements* brilliantly captures the self-consciousness of
the Modernist age . . . An elegant and pacy narrative' Kate Colquhoun,
Daily Telegraph

'Riveting . . . Roiphe's aim, in which she succeeds triumphantly, is to go
inside the marriages she documents' Lucasta Miller, *Sunday Times*

'Acutely empathetic, pithily written portraits . . . Read it and you'll want
to go out immediately and buy it for all the couples you know' *Time Out*

'A fascinating and gorgeously written insight into the unconventional
marriages of the Bloomsbury set' *London Paper*

UNCOMMON ARRANGEMENTS

SEVEN MARRIAGES IN LITERARY LONDON

1910–1939

Katie Roiphe

virago

VIRAGO

First published in Great Britain in 2008 by Virago Press
This paperback edition published in 2009 by Virago Press

First published in the United States in 2007 by Dial Press

Copyright © Katie Roiphe 2007

The Acknowledgements on pp. 333–334
constitute an extension of this copyright page.

Book design by Lynn Newmark

The moral right of the author has been asserted.

A CIP catalogue record for this book
is available from the British Library

ISBN 978-1-84408-271-1

Printed and bound in Great Britain by
Clays Ltd, St Ives plc

Papers used by Virago are natural, renewable and recyclable
products sourced from well-managed forests and certified
in accordance with the rules of the Forest Stewardship Council.

Mixed Sources
Product group from well-managed
forests and other controlled sources
www.fsc.org Cert no. SGS-COC-004081
© 1996 Forest Stewardship Council
FSC

Virago Press
An imprint of
Little, Brown Book Group
100 Victoria Embankment
London EC4Y 0DY

An Hachette UK Company
www.hachette.co.uk

www.virago.co.uk

For my mother and for Violet

Contents

MARRIAGE À LA MODE

"Dear Princess Bibesco, I am afraid you must stop writing these little love letters to my husband while he and I live together. It is one of the things which is not done in our world," wrote Katherine Mansfield to her husband's determined mistress in the first cool days of spring in 1921. Mansfield was groping her way toward a new etiquette, at a time when the couples she knew both were and weren't married, and affairs both were and weren't tolerated. That same month Dr. Marie Stopes opened London's first birth control clinic on Marlborough Road; and the streets were filled with the new knee-length skirts.

I have borrowed the title of this introduction from Katherine Mansfield's short story "Marriage à la Mode," which is a brutal send-up of a fashionable marriage of the time, and she borrowed it from John Dryden's restoration comedy of the same name. When I talk about a "marriage à la mode," I mean a certain type of progressive marriage, occurring in literary circles in England, in the period from roughly 1910 to the beginning of the Second World War. This book offers a series of unconventional domestic portraits. The couples I have chosen were more than usually involved in questions of freedom and attraction. Their relationships were depraved or innovative, depending on one's point of view, and they tried to solve the problem of intimate relations in more or less creative ways.

I admit that my interest in these lives is not purely the interest of a scholar. Rather, it is largely selfish: What can they tell me? What can they teach? In some sense, what I am after is the distilled wisdom of decades lived, of mistakes made, of love stirred by time. There is, after all, something majestic in witnessing the entire sweep of a marriage, in seeing a note sent in the mail, a hidden passage scrawled into a diary, a photograph of a couple drinking coffee in their garden. There were moments, in the course of my research, when I sat in the mahogany rooms of the library, immersed in letters and journals, pages so delicate now that pieces of them can crumble off in your hands if you are not careful, that I felt myself come close to something almost alive. I was watching misunderstandings bloom into bigger misunderstandings; I was watching friendship move inside of a marriage; I was watching early enchantments age. Granted, this is a way of reading that I learned in graduate school was unsophisticated, childish. This is a trick that we were taught to use on narcissistic young students to rope them in: to let them milk a text for what personal understanding they could, to ask greedily, What does it mean to me? And yet that is precisely what I wanted from the lives chronicled in this book. That is what I have always wanted from biographies. That is, no doubt, the real reason that I have read my favorite biographies three, four, even five times. And for this book, I wanted to go inside of a marriage, to look at the oily mechanism, to feel it in my hands, and see how it worked. When for instance I read Katherine Mansfield's astonishing journal entries about her serious illness at the age of thirty-four, and how it taxed her ethereal, childlike relationship with John Middleton Murry, I felt myself approaching a piece of information that seemed important, a practical piece of knowledge I could use.

Out of a slew of possible "marriages à la mode," I have chosen as my subjects writers and artists, and one hostess with artistic leanings—in other words, those inhabiting the fringe of respectable citizenry—in part because their marriages are interesting, and in part because they obsessively record and narrate their inner lives in ways that some people may find bizarre, and even distasteful. I have chosen some figures who are still quite well known, like the writer and social critic H. G. Wells, and the painter Vanessa Bell, who was Virginia Woolf's sister, and others, like Vera Brittain and Elizabeth von Arnim, who are less well known now but were bestselling authors and influential figures of the time. In the end, many of the couples in this book raised their personal lives to the level of philosophy. They felt that their love affairs and marriages were themselves creative acts.

Some of the figures under consideration had radical theories about love, like H. G. Wells who saw himself "in revolt against the definite sexual codes of the day"; and others like Vanessa Bell, fell into strange arrangements out of emotional necessity. Some like the bestselling memoirist Vera Brittain wrote newspaper articles about what she labeled her "semi-detached marriage," and others like the famous hostess Ottoline Morrell simply tried to do the best she could with a compromised situation. The figures I have chosen were all part of loosely overlapping social circles, reading each other's work, attending each other's parties, and shrewdly observing each other's relationships.

Wherever possible, my research draws on the memoirs and letters and articles of the children of these marriages, as well as friends, acquaintances, and casual observers, in order to flesh out the accounts of the people involved. Certain observers, like Virginia Woolf for instance, appear throughout, with a dry running commentary on nearly everyone I have described. At times, the candid exchange of information and opinion which might be dismissed as sheer gossip under normal circumstances, contains small gems of insight for anyone with a biographical interest in a marriage. On occasion, it has been tempting to condemn these messy, often unorthodox attachments, but I have tried to approach them with as much fairness as possible: Do some of these unusual arrangements work? Can the pain of betrayal be channeled into something that strengthens the tie between two people? Is it possible that some of these extraordinary arrangements are admirable, and more enduring than many ordinary marriages? That they were, as the art critic Roger Fry said of Vanessa Bell's unusual ménage, "a triumph of reasonableness over the conventions"? Or were their efforts to romanticize unconventionality simply a defense against the limits of love? Was all of their free thinking simply a highly articulated cover for consummate selfishness? Or could it be said that they were trying to bang out a new, fairer contract between the sexes? In a series on marriage published in the *Daily Express* in 1929, Warwick Deeping wrote: "I believe this period of ours is one of those seasons of questioning and of stress through which we shall come to a fairer conception of comradeship."

I have not attempted to encompass and exhaustively narrate an entire marriage in any of the chapters that follow. In his own group biography, *Eminent Victorians,* which was published in 1918, Lytton Strachey argued against typically baggy biographies "with their slipshod style, their tone of tedious panegyric, their lamentable lack of selection, of detachment, of design," and aspired instead to "a becoming brevity which excludes everything that is redundant and nothing that is significant." For him the art of group portraits was the art of selection, and I have taken that as my model, along with Phyllis Rose's brilliant tour de force of domestic archeology, *Parallel Lives.* Of course, condensing decades of marriage is challenging, making sense out of an enormous barrage of emotional information is finally an act of interpretation, as is sorting through conflicting accounts; it may be important to say that I am telling these stories as they appeared to me. Each chapter is structured around a crisis in a marriage and how it is resolved or not resolved. In some cases the crisis is as large as life-threatening illness, and in others it is as small as a slightly drunken conversation over dinner that threatens the balance of carefully submerged emotions.

Several of the marriages in this book were to one degree or another open marriages: or at least marriages in which affairs were quietly tolerated. Several of the writers harbored powerful private mythologies, like Vera Brittain, whose brief, adolescent love affair with a boy who was killed in the Great War haunted her and shadowed her marriage for decades. My interest is in exploring what these sorts of private mythologies do to a flesh-and-blood relationship, and how the imagination itself works on a living marriage, how the stories we tell ourselves impose themselves on our days. There were in many of these marriages romantic idées fixes, or idealized visions of other people, that complicated and distorted the relationship with a real husband or wife.

Many of the marriages I have written about were stretched and tested by triangles of various varieties and configurations. Both Katherine Mansfield and Vera Brittain had intimate female friends who shouldered some of the work of a marriage and complicated the conventional structure of two people alone in a relationship. And when the controversial lesbian writer Radclyffe Hall fell in love with another woman, she encompassed her into her household along with the woman she had thought of for nearly two decades as her wife. Hall solved the problem of waning sexual attraction by importing someone new into the relationship, and the three began to move through the world in what the Paris gossip columns called a "trio lesbienne." H. G. Wells invented what he festively labeled a "modus vivendi" in which he was allowed to seek out affairs, and the only condition was that he would confide in his wife, Jane, and that he would never leave her entirely. And when her own marriage faltered, Vanessa Bell established an extraordinary constellation of intimate friends and lovers and ex-lovers to provide her with the family structure she needed. That so many of the couples I describe were willing to remain in a shell of a marriage, sometimes a marriage that existed in name only, says a great deal about the enduring power of the institution, even during a time when that power was actively being questioned.

Though these "marriages à la mode" are more extreme than

most, in their dramatic betrayals and unexpected fidelities, they mirror in bits and pieces the strains embedded in every marriage, and the debates they embodied echo contemporary debates. The wilder solutions or more colorful arrangements lay bare the deeper issues at stake in all relationships: the fluctuations and shifts in attraction, the mysteries of lasting affection, the endurance and changes in love, and the role of friendship in marriage.

At times one feels the natural prurience of the subject matter—like a houseguest who has lingered in a hallway and overheard a quarrel between her hosts. But why should it be prurient to study other people's marriages? We do it all the time in less explicit ways: we flip through magazine articles about celebrity breakups at the dentist's office, or carefully deconstruct the tension between a couple at a dinner party. We sift through the minutiae of a domestic squabble with our friends on the phone, or read novels about adultery while half immersed in a bath. It is nearly impossible to see behind the lacquered surface of almost any marriage, and yet it seems valuable too. How does one manage the ordinary and extraordinary unhappiness that comes up in the course of a long life together? How does one accommodate the need for settled life with the eternal desire for freshness? Marriage is perpetually interesting; it is the novel that most of us are living in.

I was drawn to the period spanning the two world wars in part because it was as richly conflicted as our own. The lives of the writers and artists emerging from the Edwardian period bridged an enormous gap in attitude: their earliest education was infused with the exquisite restraint of the Victorians, and they came of age amidst the seductive freedoms and sexual frankness promised by the new century. Reading their own accounts, one almost feels that they carried lodged within them two complete worlds. They watched the streets fill with the first automobiles. They listened to the gossip about King Edward VII and his mistress, Mrs. Keppel. They visited the first Post-Impressionist Exhibition, which scandalized the art world with the paintings of Matisse, Gauguin, Cézanne, and Picasso. They read the first navy blue editions of *Ulysses*, which were printed in Paris. They watched as the novels *Lady Chatterley's Lover* and *The Well of Loneliness* were banned for obscene content. They jettisoned the clutter and wallpaper and heavy drapes of the Victorian interior and created fashionably stark spaces in their homes. And the clash between the two very different sensibilities, the Victorian and the Modern, would be written into their most personal decisions, their marriages subject to the same tensions, the same electric contradictions. They were destined to construct their personal lives on that highly unstable spot, poised between an intense nostalgia for traditional ways of doing things and a great hunger for equality and progress. As the economist John Maynard Keynes put it, the peculiar quandary of their generation was that "we all want both to have and not to have husbands and wives." They believed in improvising the old form, in creating relationships like art, in experimenting in love in all sorts of colorful and dubious ways, and yet they could not entirely elude the primal allure of the past. At least three of the women who appear in these pages lived with a rather large amount of sexual disorder, and maintained a secret passion for Jane Austen.

The period of romantic experimentation I am describing occurred against a very specific cultural backdrop. The devastation of World War I had transformed the social landscape: it had expanded the role of women while severely depleting an entire generation of men, shaking comfortable Edwardian England from some of its certainties. In the years after the war the liberation that had already begun—the shorter skirts, brighter lipsticks, franker talk, cigarettes—extended into a wider examination of equality, and a rapid rethinking of the institutions of the last century. The war, in its strange, disorienting way, had begun to put sexual mores into perspective. How, for instance, should the country view the proliferation of illegitimate war babies, born out of terrified reunions and desperate attempts at carpe diem? This was a dilemma that filled newspaper columns and preoccupied dinner party conversations. And then, some of the residual rituals of old-fashioned morality seemed, after the tremendous loss of life, oddly trivial: how could one force chaperones on soldiers who had dragged their dead friends through the trenches, or on nurses who had bathed the wounds of naked men? After everything that had happened, it would not be possible to go back.

For relations between the sexes, in particular, the 1920s was an intense, questioning time. "What ever happened to married pairs? They are almost extinct," wrote Katherine Mansfield in 1921, with typical overstatement. But she was right in suggesting that a fierce examination of the institution of marriage was under way. Throughout the twenties, "The Marriage Question" had become particularly vexed: with newspaper series examining the state of modern marriage, a proliferation of debates about divorce law, and countless books on the rejuvenation of the institution. To many intellectuals, the whole conception of marriage as it existed seemed bankrupt—the repository of defunct, repressive ideas, about women in particular. The social critic Rebecca West complained about the "dinginess that has come between us and the reality of love" and the "gross, destructive, mutual raids on personality which often form marriages." Many of the writers and thinkers of the day looked at the marriages of their parents and saw all of the petty oppressions that they were determined not to reproduce. In his essay on divorce, Theodore Dreiser included the following line: "Consider the farce that marriage practically the world over has become."

An early and influential contribution to the popular discussion came from Dr. Marie Carmichael Stopes. In 1918 she published *Married Love,* a highbrow self-help book that approached marriage in the brisk, benevolent spirit of scientific improvement, to enormous popular success. "There is rottenness and danger at the foundations of the State if many of the marriages are unhappy," she declaimed. "To-day, particularly, in the middle classes in this country, marriage is far less really happy than its surface appears." In its distinctive, flowery way, the book preached the necessity and mechanics of sexual pleasure for both sexes. The isolation and ignorance of young couples were not, she argued, natural. She elaborated on the importance of having close friends outside of the marriage, and she chronicled the secret unhappiness and sexual disappointments of married couples. In fact, this was a subject that Dr. Stopes knew about firsthand. Her own life exemplified the famed obscurity and sexual mystification bequeathed by the late Victorian years: she had married a man who never consummated the marriage, and she was so innocent that she did not realize, at first, what was wrong. After leaving the relationship, and educating herself on sexual matters, she was committed to the absolute necessity of spreading sexual knowledge. Her impassioned, loopy book was ubiquitous, as were its sequels. And Dr. Stopes herself rose to prominence as a popular authority on the relatively new, frank subject of marital happiness.

There was a spate of books on marriage published over the next decade, like Bertrand Russell's *Marriage and Morals* and Annie Keen's *Women and Marriage in Modern England,* and many of them argued for trial marriage and a general relaxing of the absolute taboos against extramarital sexual relations. The novel idea of trial marriage was that people would live together and test out their relationships before committing themselves to legal marriage. The fairly revolutionary, and almost entirely theoretical, idea was that if people were more experienced there would be less divorce and less unhappiness. (I say that it was almost entirely theoretical because it must have seemed unlikely even to its proponents that trial marriages would gain widespread acceptability at any point in the near future.) But in imagining healthier, fairer unions, this new generation of writers and philosophers and journalists were using words that their parents' generation had not: *freedom, honesty, equality.* They were determined to live differently, to import the ideas of political progress into their most personal relations.

Many of the writers and artists under consideration approached the most intimate facets of their personal lives in a pioneering spirit. Their loves were freighted with social importance. Their sexual liaisons were part of a grand social experiment that would end in greater equality and understanding between the sexes, and this belief imbued their most intimate relationships with a reforming energy, with the palpable excitement of a culture transforming itself in front of their eyes. They were confident that if they could do away with the mystification and obfuscation that clouded Victorian marriages, then future generations would be more contented and relationships would be more rational, would make more sense. They believed in progress even in the murkier realms of romantic happiness. To an impressive extent, they had intimations of some of the changes that the century would deliver—equality for women, for instance. But they imagined the institution of marriage radically transformed in ways that never came to pass. The fundamental assumptions of marriage—monogamy, proprietary feelings, and, often, economic dependence—are still with us, as are many of the conflicts and difficulties that the couples in this book thought belonged to the hypocrisies and inequities of the past. The perfect clarity, the revolutionary stirring they saw in relations between the sexes, never entirely materialized. The sexual freedom, the openness they had foreseen, brought with it its own complexities, which they could not have predicted; and at the same time those tattered, sentimental, Victorian images of marriage that they were so eager to cast off proved more stubbornly entrenched than they would have thought possible.

Their earliest educations, steeped as they were in Victorian values, seemed to many writers to have put them at a distinct disadvantage in their personal lives. "Is it prejudice, do you think, that makes us hate the Victorians," wrote Lytton Strachey, "or is it the truth of the case?" Many of the women under consideration were married before they were prepared for marriage by experience. They were married before they knew themselves. The writer Vita Sackville-West, for instance, felt that she had been pressured by convention to marry too early, and too innocently. She wrote in a letter to her husband: "Women, like men, ought to have their youth so glutted with freedom that they hate the very idea of freedom." Her intriguing implication was that if women had sexual adventures before they married, they would know their own minds and their marriages would be stronger. On the face of it, this seems extremely sensible. But now that so many of us do spend our youths glutted with freedom—and glutted does seem to be the right word—are our marriages any happier? It appears from the divorce rate, and from the robust business of marriage counselors and couples therapists everywhere, that they are not: some marriages are still happy, and some marriages still fail in similarly spectacular ways. The potent freedom Sackville-West envisioned has not delivered the greater wisdom and clarity she predicted; it did not transform our personal relations into any of the utopian constellations that were so fashionable to predict and ruminate on in the twenties. All of our experience seems to have led to its own peculiar forms of bewilderment, and the ostensible revolution in our personal lives may not have changed as much as it should have. Do we still marry because it is time to get married, in somewhat the same spirit as Sackville-West's generation? Does the rush to settle down simply take a slightly different form, and occur at a slightly later age, than it did for her generation? For many women marrying at the turn of this new century, the impetus to marry has been influenced by the outer limits of their biological capacity to have children. The novelist Lorrie Moore once wrote that marrying seemed to her like a game of musical chairs that you played till the music stopped, and then married whomever you were with so as not to be the last one left standing.

Many of the couples in this book had perhaps too much faith in the honesty that had become so fashionable in the twenties. D. H. Lawrence articulated this philosophy in his own inimitable, mad way: "If [your wife] seems to you in any way false, in any circumstance, tell her so, angrily, furiously, and stop her. Never mind about being justified. If you hate anything she does, turn on her in a fury. Harry her, and make her life a hell, so long as the real hot rage is in you. Don't silently hate her, or silently forbear. It is such a dirty trick, so mean and ungenerous. . . . With a wife or husband, you should never swallow your bile. It makes you go all wrong inside." Few of the people I have written about were as expressive as D. H. Lawrence—almost no one was—and yet many of them took the idea of honesty, of a sort of rational consistency, very much to heart. Many of them believed that if they told the truth— often ugly, cutting truths—then nothing they actually did could be considered wrong. In this, they were reacting against what they saw as the hypocrisy fostered by their parents' generation, and their parents' parents' generation, but they may have placed too much faith in the redemptive power of communication for its own sake. Over and over in the pages of this book, a husband or wife elaborates on the details of an attraction, or an affair. They feel the need to talk it through. But to narrate and reveal an affair or an attraction does not necessarily make it any more palatable to a spouse; and in the end some truths are perhaps best left unnarrated. John Updike would write decades later that most marriages are ruined by too much communication, and this certainly holds true in some of the marriages described here: they are ruined, at least, by the wrong type of communication.

To any contemporary reader, it is striking how absent children are from any consideration whatsoever in the forming and breaking of the unusual domestic arrangements in the chapters that follow. The children of these modish marriages are repeatedly shunted off to nurses, and even, in the case of one unlucky little boy described here, to boarding school before the age of four; and there seems to be remarkably little hand-wringing or guilt surrounding these minor abandonments. Is it difficult for a child to watch a parent vanish into a love affair for weeks at a time? Do complicated family constellations require a special sort of explanation, or a translation into the child's world? The answer to these questions seems not to have interested the writers and artists of the milieu I have described. The delicate childish psyche is simply not considered in the conduct of one's personal life. Nowhere does anyone stop to think "what will this arrangement do to the children?" This is perhaps a little surprising given the rise of popular Freudianism during the same period, but then, maybe it is not. Parents still believed that children would raise themselves, that they would, in a sense, grow like houseplants, with the considerable help of nannies, governesses, and nurses along with a slew of family friends who drifted in and out of the household. The idea of tailoring one's personal life to suit the children was alien to them. In some cases, there did seem to be elements of true neglect, but in others, it simply had not occurred to otherwise loving parents to take their children's development into consideration. There was certainly no sense that family life, or the parents' pursuit of love, in particular, should in any way revolve around the child.

As many critics of the day pointed out, women's emancipation itself put an unprecedented strain on marriage. In the nineteenth century, the idea of complete equality between spouses was extremely rarefied, confined only to a handful of intellectuals and bohemians; but by the 1920s it had created a more widespread stress on the institution. The modern marriage had a whole new power dynamic to contend with, as the wife was no longer necessarily subjugated to the husband's will. The intimate script consequently remained unwritten: Who would be more powerful in the world outside of the home? Who would make decisions? Who would have the consummate authority? If the man was no longer the master of the home, the scene was set for an epic power struggle, one that we may, in fact, still be enacting. D. H. Lawrence once sent a drawing to his wife, Frieda, from Capri: it showed a little Jonah confronting the whale, with the handwritten caption, "Who will swallow whom?" This seems for many of the powerful personalities that I am writing about, an apt summation.

The other, murkier issue raised by equality in marriage is that even the most progressive men and women under discussion often seemed profoundly ambivalent about it. Though male writers like H. G. Wells were ideologically committed to equality, they could not in the privacy of their own homes entirely stomach it. While spouting a fashionable egalitarian language in their writing, or at cocktail parties, they were at the same time constantly reproducing traditional structures of female dependence. As much as they enjoyed the outspoken, independent New Woman whom they encountered everywhere, with her cigarettes and her cropped hair, they did not entirely trust her, and the old-fashioned wife devoting her entire life to her husband's comfort and care somehow retained her eternal glamour. Perhaps more surprisingly, for many of the New Women under discussion the same deep conflict toward equality held true: the allure of the dominating male, the fantasy of surrendering themselves to a stronger male personality, had not entirely faded with their enlightened ideals. Instead, there was a deep, almost erotic appeal in the act of subjugation. Even formidable feminists like Rebecca West and Elizabeth von Arnim, who devoted a great deal of thought to the power relations between men and women, were enraptured and nearly defeated by traditional, almost brutal displays of male power. I have tried here and elsewhere to understand and not to judge: this is, after all, a phenomenon that is with us still.

In spite of the most progressive, forward-thinking intentions of the couples in this book, it is astonishing what a stubborn hold the most archaic ideas of marriage had on their imaginations. It was impossible, even for artists as cynical as Katherine Mansfield, as promiscuous as H. G. Wells, as fiercely critical as Rebecca West, or as determinedly bohemian as Ottoline Morrell, to evade the freighted values of their Victorian—or Victorian-influenced—childhoods. Their most progressive, most outrageous desires clash with the retrograde yearning for traditional roles, and in each case, the dissonance produced is interesting in its effect.

In the intimate process of immersing myself in other people's marriages, I found that it is extremely tempting to see victims and aggressors, and sometimes, as in the case of Elizabeth von Arnim, it is impossible not to, but I have tried whenever possible to resist this scenario, as it is the least interesting prism for viewing any relationship. There is also no doubt, in each of these stories, that both members of the couple have colluded in the creation of a romantic dynamic. Where a man has been monstrous, the woman has almost always had some hand in creating her particular monster.

In certain instances, one wonders, as in the case of Ottoline Morrell or Jane Wells, why they didn't simply pack their bags and walk away from their marriage. Divorce, in their circles, would not have been an insurmountable taboo. In fact, in the case of Jane Wells, in particular, the scandal centered around how calmly she seemed to tolerate the rather flamboyant humiliations of her marriage. But the supreme importance of habit, the inertia of accumulated life, the fidelity toward one's former self, cannot be underestimated. "Marriage is time," Joan Didion wrote recently, and this seems irrefutably true. To leave a marriage is to lose time: it is like voluntarily shaving years off one's own life. And then, of course, there is the other maverick, inexplicable substance holding seemingly unhappy people together: love.

Our own dreary debates about marriage—see, for instance, *The Bitch in the House*—tend to take relentlessly trivial forms. They seem to be entirely summed up in the question of who has cleaned up the smattering of Legos scattered across the floor of the baby's room. *The New York Times* recently saw fit to run a front-page article on marriage in the Style section entitled: "You Want It Clean? You Clean It!" In this petty bickering the larger questions of romance and power must lurk. One has to assume that while the kids were piling into the car, and the lunches and juice boxes and diaper bags were being packed, there has been a monumental disappointment; a painful shift in expectations that has left a residual, low-burning rage.

If it weren't for the fact that so many women seem to connect with this anger, that these books *resonate,* in the words of their publishers, it would be tempting to dismiss them as whining from a few overly sensitive writer types with too much time on their hands. But there does seem to be some current of anger reflected in this prose, some widespread outrage: *This is my life?* From all of this bitterly articulated disappointment we must extrapolate: Are our expectations too high? Why should there be so much fury attached to the most insignificant drudgeries of domestic life? Instead, they should be part of the point, part of the pleasure, part of the chaos, part of what Winifred Holtby, a journalist in the twenties, called "the rich unrest of family life." But it seems we are nonetheless mired in this unproductive resentment. Why when women have so many choices, are we still as angry as gloved suffragettes hurling bricks through windows? What unmitigated bliss, one does wonder, were we expecting?

Our disappointment in the progress we ourselves have sought out mirrors that of the 1920s. The "marriages à la mode" were torn as we are torn: between tradition and innovation, between freedom and settled life, between feminist equality and reassuring, old-fashioned roles. Elizabeth von Arnim once wrote that "a civilized husband is a creature who has ceased to be a man," and she herself was torn between that civilized husband and the dominating, old-fashioned brute;

just as we seem to be torn between the man who supports his wife and the man who carries the baby in the BabyBjörn. The conflict is so prevalent, so widespread, that it is almost hard to comment on the larger cultural ramifications: it is in the fertile ground of marriage that these elusive questions of masculinity and femininity, of who we are and what we want from each other, resolve themselves.

Absolutely central to many of these "marriages à la mode" is the question of affairs. If one ceases to believe in the sacredness of marriage, if one begins to think of it as a more humble, imperfect arrangement meant to further our happiness in the brief period allotted to us on earth, the idea of fidelity becomes more vexed. There was also, in the first decades of the twentieth century, a burgeoning interest in sexual happiness, forwarded in the work of sex theorists like Havelock Ellis and Edward Carpenter, taken up by novelists like D. H. Lawrence and H. G. Wells, refined by the new Freudians, and popularized in the mainstream press. For many of the writers under discussion, the highest value was to be faithful to their own *feelings,* to act transparently according to their own desires: it was hypocrisy that they were most afraid of; it was living according to conventions that did not reflect their true selves. Take the following description of an adulterous encounter. Rebecca West wrote a letter to her friend Violet Hunt confessing her affair with the married H. G. Wells: "I think it was the only honest thing I could do, and not to have done so would have been an evasion, a sham adherence to standards I don't hold." This was the language of the day. This was the logic many of the couples under consideration subscribed to: one had something resembling a responsibility to act on one's feelings, whatever they might be. This was what it meant to live reasonably. This was what the "rational" behavior they often spoke of boiled down to. And yet, for most of them, a constant stream of affairs would not prove a practical, workable way to live.

And, of course, once one decides to have affairs the question quickly becomes, where does the affair lead? What is the ideal outcome? In one of H. G. Wells's enormously popular novels, a woman says to her lover: "If I were to come away with you and marry you in just a little time I should cease to be your lover, I should be your squaw. I should have to share your worries, and make your coffee—and disappoint you." This is, of course, the eternal quandary of *Anna Karenina*: if you run off with your lover, he or she is subject to the same household irritations and wearing routines as a spouse. The kind of perfect, condensed love that exists in an affair cannot, by its very definition, be sustained in a marriage over the long term.

As a culture we are preoccupied, still, with affairs, and with sexual boredom: it emerges in our novels and short stories (see books by Tom Perrotta, John Updike, Alice Munro, Iris Murdoch, Richard Ford, Claire Messud and Philip Roth, to name only a few), and it emerges in the pages of magazines like *Redbook,* read by vast swaths of the country ("So you've settled into a bedroom routine that's comfy but—dare we say it—a bit dull?"). We are still haunted by the narrative of lost excitement in our relationships. We still face what Radclyffe Hall rather elegantly called "the infinite sadness of fulfilled desire." In many ways, the anxiety about the natural evolutions of love is central to many of the marriages I have described. Can the person who makes your coffee remain an object of desire? Will the person of romantic temperament be forced to seek out affairs because the routines of marriage will not contain him or her? Dryden's original play, *Marriage à la Mode*, included the lines: "Why should a foolish marriage vow/ which long ago was made/ Oblige us to each other now/ When passion is decayed?" This, crudely put, is one of the dilemmas that the modish marriages in this book sought to address: how should marriage itself, the structure of one's most intimate relationship, encompass the changes in love? Many of the marriages I have written about sought to address these concerns, to create a more flexible form of union that would take these issues into consideration, that would allow for and adapt to the natural ebb and flow of affection; but in this, they met with varying degrees of success.

One of the more surprising themes of the lives chronicled in this book is how dangerous a romantic turn of mind can be, how destructive it can be in daily life. Many of them illustrate the principle that if we set up impossible expectations for ourselves, then we condemn ourselves to unhappiness in the more ordinary domestic arrangements that we usually find ourselves in. The romantic who is always searching, who is always yearning to exist on a heightened plane of emotion, is a profoundly unstable force in a marriage. Like the famous hostess Ottoline Morrell, they often fail to see the world clearly, amidst the illusions, the candlelit stories, that they create for themselves. And there is a search for intensity, as in the case of Vera Brittain, among others, that makes settled life with one person difficult to sustain. In *Marriage and Morals,* Bertrand Russell wrote: "In romantic love the beloved object is not seen accurately, but through a glamorous mist; undoubtedly it is possible for a certain type of woman to remain wrapped in this mist even after marriage provided she has a husband of a certain type, but this can only be achieved if she avoids all real intimacy with her husband." Russell writes against the desire for romantic love; he goes so far as to argue that a good marriage should be based primarily on stronger stuff, that affection and friendship should be transcendent in a betrothal, which reads even now as a radical suggestion. We cannot live, he argues, in a state of constant passion. And yet, in the popular literature of marriage, at least, we continue to long for and mourn precisely that: the intensity of romance.

Some of the hand-wringing about marriage in the twenties remains eerily relevant to today's marriages. Our increasing immersion in work, and longer hours for both men and women, refracts on relationships in ways that we have barely begun to explore. With work so ascendant in our lives, where does that leave our personal lives? In *I Don't Know How She Does It,* the bestselling novel of exhausted working motherhood, the heroine thinks to herself: "So it's come to this. Richard and I actually lay in bed last night discussing whether we were too tired to have sex." In the same vein, three quarters of a century earlier, Bertrand Russell wrote in one of his tracts on marriage: "Consider the life of a typical business man of the present day: from the time when he is first grown up he devotes all his best thoughts and his best energies to financial success: everything else is merely unimportant recreation; presently he marries, but his interests are totally different from his wife's, and he never becomes really intimate with her. He comes home late and tired from the office. His wife's interests appear to him essentially feminine, and while he approves of them, he makes no attempt to share them. He has no time for illicit love, any more than for love in marriage."

Many of the women in these pages thought extensively about the importance of economic equality in marriage, about how necessary it was to the emotional balance of a marriage for the wife to have her own economic power. Almost all of them concluded that it was crucial to their relationships, to their own romantic happiness, that they have their own source of income, that they achieve independence in the eyes of the world. But it is interesting to note that we are now approaching this same issue again from a new direction: What does it mean for all of the educated women who have "taken time off" to raise children within their marriage? Are there deeper reverberations to choosing not to be in the world? Is there a submerged price to be paid for economic dependence, for being the caretaker of the children, the cheerful provider of gourmet dinners, and shopper and arranger of flowers placed on a table? I recently overheard an ex-banker, who makes her husband an elaborate meal every night as part of the deal they struck, admit that she has to beg him for a pair of shoes or for a double stroller, and it made me wonder if writers like Vera Brittain, Rebecca West, and Elizabeth von Arnim were right, and one actually has to pay for equitable marriage. Or is it possible that this form of dependence is somehow romantic for some women, that it fills some deeper need? It seems that we are still negotiating this same intricate problem, the subtle emotional meaning of traditional economic dependence.

Many of the couples under discussion felt a certain pride in their uniqueness, in their failure to rely on accepted conventions. Vita Sackville-West once said of her open marriage, in which she and her husband, Harold Nicolson, pursued affairs with people of the same sex while maintaining their connection to each other: "I suppose that ninety-nine people out of a hundred, if they knew all about us, would call us wicked and degenerate. And yet I know with absolute certainty that there are not 99 people out of a hundred *less* wicked and degenerate than we are. I don't want to boast, but we are alive, aren't we? And our two lives, outside and inside, are rich lives—not little meagre repetitions of meagre cerebral habits." And while their union may have been more complicated, and less purely happy than she reports, there is in the improvisation, in the sheer effort of inventing a form, something heroic. One cannot fall into "meagre repetitions," one cannot live automatically, one cannot simply live the way everyone else is living: one has to have the constant energy, the constant imagination, the constant, refueling affection, because one is making up a life as one goes along.

In observing the whole sweep of a marriage, I was also struck by the million minor ways in which people fail to communicate, and the ways in which these minor moments of miscommunication, often startlingly trivial in themselves, can balloon into much bigger, irrevocable misunderstandings. On sifting through conflicting accounts of several relationships, I was fascinated by how much can be misinterpreted by two people who live together under the same roof and eat meals together. I was also struck by how differently a fairly innocuous situation can be read, how something as small as the set of a face over breakfast can determine an enormous emotional disappointment: a wife can wish desperately that her husband would come and talk to her, and her husband can desperately want to approach her but find her expression too cold and forbidding. The moment passes and is lost. And, then, I found that many of these sorts of misunderstandings are notable in how invisible, how stealthy, they are. Many of the couples in the pages of this book did not recognize the shifts, and slowly accumulating distances, until it was too late. One gets from these stories a definite sense that important things happen while one is in bed with a stomach virus, or while one is straightening up and placing a pile of letters into a drawer: much of what happens in a marriage occurs when you are not looking.

Finally, I emerged from these portraits with a new respect for the ferocious ability of the individual to get and seize what he or she needs. As a union falters or fails, these writers and artists create vivid alternatives for themselves: they imagine another form of family, including friends and lovers and siblings and ex-flames, and take from the outside world what emotional sustenance they need. Where the usual, nuclear family will not hold, they invent a structure—singular, new, innovative, often mad—that sometimes, in rare and magnificent moments, works.

JANE WELLS

H. G. WELLS

REBECCA WEST

> *"Between the ages of thirty and forty I devoted a considerable amount of mental energy to the general problem of men and women . . ."*
>
> —H. G. WELLS

AUGUST 5, 1914. A few minutes after midnight as Britain was entering the war, an illegitimate baby was born in a conspicuously anonymous redbrick house on the northern coast. His mother, Rebecca West, whose real name, which nobody used, was Cicily Fairfield, held the sleeping bundle in her arms, while her sister and a friend perched on her bed. The baby's father, H. G. Wells, was one hundred miles away, sitting up late in his llama-wool pajamas, in the second-floor study of his large comfortable house in Essex, putting the finishing touches on an essay for the *Daily Chronicle,* which he was planning to call "The War That Will End War." He poured himself a cup of tea, which he had brewed himself on the small stove nestled in the fireplace, and nibbled a dry biscuit. His wife, Jane, was asleep in the bedroom, her dark blond hair fanned out against the pillow. He loved his wife, and he loved his young mistress. He loved his ivy-covered Georgian house, Easton Glebe, which was a gracious symbol of how far he had come from his hardscrabble origins. Unlike nearly everyone he knew,

Wells was feeling optimistic about the war, exhilarated by the possibilities of the world in flux. Through his window he could see the familiar outline of a fig tree in the darkness.

Wells prided himself on the fact that there had been no deception. Jane knew all about the affair. This was not the first one, and it would not be the last. Jane was his anchor, his foundation, his sanity—there was no question of his living without Jane—but he suffered from a sexual restlessness that he had long ago ceased to resist. This particular manifestation of it had been set in motion in September of 1912, in the drawing room of Easton Glebe. Rebecca West was a rising nineteen-year-old journalist who wrote fierce, witty pieces for the suffragette paper *The New Freewoman* and the *Clarion*. H. G. Wells was already a world-famous author with influential friends, a classically pretty wife, and two small sons. At this point, Wells was best known for scientific romances like *The Time Machine,* but he had recently written a series of scandalous novels examining the relations between the sexes, several of which were banned from circulating libraries, denounced from pulpits, and attacked in newspaper editorials for poisoning the minds of young people with their promiscuous morals. In her role as professional provocateur, Rebecca had just written a taunting review of the latest: "Of course, he is the old maid among novelists; even the sex obsession that lay clotted on *Ann Veronica* and *The New Machiavelli* like cold white sauce was merely an old maid's mania . . ." Somehow this critique had amused or intrigued him—who was this young woman?—and he invited her to lunch.

As soon as she walked in, she was overwhelmed by his unlikely magnetism: a small, round, middle-aged man, with extraordinary light blue eyes, thickets of eyebrows, and a mustache, he emanated the energetic confidence of a man highly valued by the world. For his part, Wells admired her wide brow, dark expressive eyes, and "splendid *disturbed* brain." As always, Rebecca arrived looking bright and disheveled, as if to broadcast that there were other, more pressing things on her mind than grooming; it was perhaps this tendency that inspired Virginia Woolf to write rather meanly: "Rebecca is a cross between a charwoman and gypsy, but as tenacious as a terrier, with flashing eyes, very shabby, rather dirty nails, immense vitality, bad taste, suspicion of intellectuals and great intelligence." At a certain point in the afternoon, Wells's wife, Jane, discreetly withdrew, leaving the two writers alone, and was, the young feminist noted, "charming, but a little bit effaced." Their lunch lasted for more than five hours.

The next time Rebecca visited Wells at his London house they found themselves kissing in front of his bookshelves. With her usual boldness, Rebecca appears to have asked him to sleep with her and relieve her of her innocence. In this, she may or may not have been influenced by Wells's infamous young heroine, Ann Veronica, who threw herself at a married man, proclaiming in what now seems like an absurd piece of dialogue: "I want you. I want you to be my lover. I want to give myself to you." In any event, Wells wrote to her shortly afterward: "Dear Rebecca, You're a very compelling person. I suppose I shall have to do what you want me to do." But then, entangled with a long-term mistress, Elizabeth von Arnim, and fearful of the damage yet more scandal would do to his reputation, he changed his mind. He and Rebecca wrangled back and forth over his decision, until he disappeared on a trip abroad. He had told Rebecca that even friendship between them would be impossible. The abrupt break launched Rebecca into great storms of melodrama. She had a theatrical streak, had in fact trained to be an actress before turning to writing. "You've literally ruined me," Rebecca wrote. "I am burned down to my foundations. I may build myself up again or I may not . . . I know you will derive immense satisfaction from thinking of me as an unbalanced young female who flopped about in your drawing room in an unnecessary heart attack." Rebecca emerged from the attenuated flirtation so distraught that her mother whisked her off on a restorative tour through Spain and France.

After reading her published accounts of the trip, Wells wrote to her: "You are writing gorgeously again. Please resume being friends." They began to see a little more of each other, and months later, when Wells quarreled with Elizabeth von Arnim, whom he called "little e," he and Rebecca became lovers. The leisurely affair that might have ensued was cut short by a moment of carelessness, a rushed afternoon encounter in his London flat during which she conceived a child. By both accounts, it would appear to have been an accident, though Rebecca would later write wildly to her son that H. G. wantonly impregnated her "because he wanted the panache of having a child by the infant prodigy of the day." Given Wells's caution in approaching the affair and his fervor for secrecy this seems highly unlikely, but throughout her life Rebecca remained, on the subject of Wells, partial to colorful distortions and interesting slurs. As soon as he heard the news of her pregnancy, Wells's response was to tell his wife immediately. Wells told his wife everything. That was part of their pact. But for all three of them, the wartime baby would be a test of their forward-thinking ideas.

Wells's unorthodox relation to his wife had already become the subject of much public speculation. The prominent literary hostess Ottoline Morrell would later remember discussing it with Bertrand Russell over lunch in her town house on Gower Street, both expressing their disapproval: not at the adultery, which they had engaged in themselves, but at the openness of it. The scandal was Jane Wells's quiet tolerance of her husband's carryings-on. Beatrice Webb, the founder of the Fabian Society, theorized that Jane couldn't criticize Wells's philandering because of the murky origins of her own relationship with him. When Jane met him he had been married to another woman. In the carnivorous, gossipy circles they moved in, accustomed as they were to dissecting character, Jane's reticence, her grace, some might call it, was maddening. "In all this story," the flamboyant lesbian writer Vernon Lee wrote to Wells, "the really interesting person seems to me to be your wife. . . ." And something about her position did seem to arouse curiosity—who was Jane Wells?

This would not be an easy question to answer. For one thing, Jane wasn't really Jane. In an improbably domineering gesture, Wells had renamed his wife, Amy Catherine Wells, "Jane." When Mrs. Wells was younger she had always gone by Catherine, which she preferred to Amy. But Wells wanted to conjure a competent, sensible helpmate, and the proper name for this admirable and upstanding young woman seemed to be Jane. All of their friends called her Jane, and she herself willingly adopted the plain, serviceable name; but what did she think of a man who took creative liberties with fundamental pillars of her identity? And what did it say about that man that all of his fantasies of uxorious harmony and romantic perfection should converge in the name "Jane"?

There is no doubt that, to the world, Jane presented a composed and contented exterior. There are several photographs of her with her fine profile, her wavy, ash-blond hair swept into a voluminous bun, bent over a Remington typewriter as she typed up her husband's manuscripts, looking, in her striped button-down shirt, the epitome of the dignified secretary. In addition, she managed all of his business affairs, shepherding his significant fortune into prudent investments and corresponding with his legion of agents, translators, and editors. At the same time, she was adept at the more traditionally feminine arts. She was a member of the Royal Horticultural Society and kept an extensive journal to improve her gardening technique. She organized amateur theatricals and games of tennis for their weekend guests with great enthusiasm, altogether creating the pleasing and comfortable environment that made it possible for the fussy and sensitive Wells to sit down and do his work. On a deeper level, Jane answered some chord of self-doubt in him in a way that no one else could. She soothed the fits of rage and melancholy that sometimes paralyzed him, and gave him the constancy and peace he needed. When his self-image faltered, she reflected back a confident, glowing version of who he was. "She stuck to me so sturdily," he put it, "that in the end I stuck to myself." She was his ideal companion, a consummately wifely wife. But there had always been a lack of sexual sympathy at the heart of the marriage. Wells rarely described her without using certain words, like "fragile" or "delicate" or "innocent" or "Dresden china." Though he admired her enormously, she lacked the vitality that attracted him: he couldn't imagine being rough or playful with her in bed.

There was a certain irony to the fact that Jane had become the perfect housewife. When Wells and Jane began their association in the 1890s neither of them believed in the institution of marriage. He was in the process of leaving his first wife, and with fifty pounds between them, the two of them moved into modest rooms together. They had a double bed, and folding doors opening out into a living area with a tin bathtub, and a dining room table that doubled as a desk. Wells was struggling to cobble together a living from articles and reviews, which he produced in enormous volume, and it was only the constant irritant of the reaction of neighbors, landladies, and servants that finally convinced them it wasn't worth expending all of their energy on not being married. In 1895 they went to the registrar's office and became man and wife. In these early years together, Jane had become a ballast to him. He wrote, "It was a good thing for me that behind the folding doors at 12 Mornington Road slept a fine and valiant little being, so delicate and clean and so credulous of my pretensions, that it would have been intolerable to appear before her unshaven or squalid or drunken or base." This valiant little being was the wife of the writer he wanted to be, somehow finer than the rest of the fallen world.

Wells would later look back on this period on Mornington Road as their happiest. Their landlady would bring up coffee on a tray, and Jane would sit in her blue nightdress and long blond braids, buttering her toast, the slate sky framed by large bay windows. The only thing marring the cozy scene was his inchoate sense of sexual disappointment. Something appeared to him to be missing in her responsiveness. As he put it, Jane "regarded my sexual imaginativeness as a sort of constitutional disease; she stood by me patiently waiting for it to subside." During this time he began to draw what he called "pischuas" for her: elaborate cartoons of their life together that seemed in their infantile humor, their odd visual language, to replace a more adult form of intimacy or communication, as if he were a very clever child presenting his imaginative offerings as a frantic and troubled tribute to a mother. This would be his first effort to scribble over the reality of their life together.

In the beginning, when he was struggling with his career, Wells didn't think much about women; but later, after the publication of his scientific romances *The Time Machine* and *The War of the Worlds,* as he became famous and sought after, the subject appeared to raise itself. Intriguing, intelligent, liberated women seemed to emerge from the chatter of every cocktail party, and the newly celebrated author was interesting to them. He had always had the kind of intellectual arrogance that drew women to him, and now he had the worldly success to back it up. He also emanated an unapologetic hedonism that rarely escaped the notice of the women in a room. He would later offer this extraordinary formulation: "I was not under such prohibitions as we impose upon lawyer, doctor, or schoolmaster. Except in so far as affection put barriers about me, I have done what I pleased; so that every bit of sexual impulse in me has expressed itself."

An early turning point in their marriage was the harrowing birth of their first son, George Philip, whom they called "Gyp," in the summer of 1901. For twenty-four hours, both mother and baby were in serious danger. H.G.'s curious response to the ordeal was to run off to the south for several months, leaving Jane to convalesce with the baby in the care of two doctors, a nurse, and the servants. For at least a few weeks, it seems, she wasn't sure where he was, and their entire relationship was thrown into question. This was one of those rare, fluid moments when a marriage opens itself to change, and the terms begin to define themselves. Instead of responding to her husband's sudden absence with anger, Jane wrote H.G. a warm, understanding letter in which she blamed herself for being too possessive when he left, and set their relationship on its stable new course. In her own way, she conveyed that she was going to allow him the absences he needed. She would even go so far as to understand those absences. She would purvey the perfect, infinitely flexible, unconditional love he craved, and create a stable family home he could leave and return to at will. The arrangement she seemed to be offering was quite extraordinary, and one can only guess at her motivations. Would she have acted differently if he had remained the impoverished biology teacher he was when they met? Was the license she granted him somehow connected in her mind to his literary genius? Was she, as Rebecca and others suspected, interested in the things she had accumulated, and their rising material success? Or was it simply that she loved him so much she couldn't risk losing him? It is hard to say, but we do know that Jane was not unadventurous. After all, she had traded the safety of her mother's home for an ambiguous connection with an impecunious married man. She was willing to give up her chances, as an attractive and educated young woman, for a more stable marriage for the sake of his personal magnetism. Altogether, it seems more likely that she was acting out of love, rather than the grasping materialism or unnatural passion for security that she would later be accused of, but we can't know for certain. We do know that by the time Rebecca came along a decade later, H.G. and Jane had worked out what he called a "modus vivendi" whereby he could have his affairs, which he lightly referred to as "passades," and she could be assured of his highest regard.

2

PANTHER AND JAGUAR

In the spring of 1914, Wells established the conspicuously pregnant, twenty-one-year-old Rebecca in a bleak, semidetached, redbrick house in a small seaside town. The setting was appropriately dramatic with its steep, windy cliffs leading down to the sea. As their son, Anthony, would later observe, the only recommendation of his birthplace was "that it was so far off the socially beaten track, so desperately without conventional allure, that nobody who was anybody . . . was likely to be encountered there." One of Rebecca's doctors said that she was in danger of a miscarriage, which she appears to have interpreted as a veiled offer to help her along with one. In fact, Wells was still holding out some hope that she would give the child up for adoption. He had written, a few years earlier, that bearing a baby by a lover "in the present state of public opinion, in almost every existing social atmosphere, would be a purely anarchistic course." But Rebecca was determined to keep the baby. She was considering sending him to "foster" somewhere for a year so that she could devote herself to her work, but she did not want to give him up.

The drastic change in her circumstances must have been hard for Rebecca to take in. All of a sudden she herself had become one of the engrossing social problems she and her feminist colleagues had analyzed so energetically in their discussion circles. A year earlier, as an ardent social critic, she had written indignantly that an out-of-wedlock mother was "the most outcast thing on earth." (Ironically, she had also made fun of one of the feminists from *The New Freewoman* "who was always jumping up asking us to be kind to illegitimate children, as if we all made a habit of seeking out illegitimate infants and insulting them!") H.G. had impressed on her the need for discretion, writing that it would leave them freer with each other and save Jane enormous embarrassment if she could keep her condition a secret, and so the frank and voluble Rebecca managed to hide her pregnancy from nearly everyone outside her family, referring to the mysterious ailment that kept her in isolation as a "lung inflammation."

Once the baby was born, Rebecca wrote a spirited letter to her friend Violet Hunt, the glamorous writer, socialite, and consort of Ford Madox Ford, who herself had been involved with Wells, explaining the reasons for her secrecy. "My illness is finally over," Rebecca began, "and I am quite definitely not dead." She claimed that she had no choice but to become involved with Wells once her feelings became clear to her. Like Wells, Rebecca believed that not acting on one's sexual impulses was the height of hypocrisy—it was a moral imperative to follow through on one's attractions. Nonetheless, the idea that she would be judged by her affair with a hugely prominent man was still daunting to her. She was apprehensive about the monumental impact it would have on her nascent reputation, and the bewildering intricacies of her moral position at that precise moment in time: "I knew that if it was talked about there was a sporting chance that I would become a heroine. Pale Fabians would say that I was the Free Woman, and wanted to be the mother of the Superman, and the older school left over from the nineties might say I was his wife in the sight of god, and similar clichés." Altogether the letter made a show of sophisticated gaiety, with the whole episode coming off as a kind of interesting lark, but Rebecca also revealed a certain amount of anxiety about what she was already calling the polygamy of the situation.

When the baby was born, Rebecca had been with her friend Mrs. Carrie Townshend, who had become a trusted confidante of both parents. Faced with the tableau of mother and nursing child, Mrs. Townshend was skeptical that Rebecca would accept the divided life Wells was offering her, and sent him a warning note: "She isn't the kind that keeps sex in a water-tight compartment. She's not a bachelor-woman but all that there is of the most feminine . . . I don't think R. is really suited for polygamy though I admit that she would like a 5th of you better than the whole of anyone else." At this point, Rebecca was still caught up in the grandeur of her gesture, and had not yet begun to absorb the daily realities of her life. She was also, in spite of her biting, worldly writing voice, extremely young. As usually happens in these sorts of situations, Wells assured Rebecca that he would create a home for the three of them that would be the center of his life, and as also usually happens in these situations, he did not.

Over the next few months Rebecca began to feel more and more the insecurity of her position. She wanted to write. She was working on a polemic calling for harsher book reviews for the first issue of the American periodical *The New Republic*. Her physical isolation may have contributed to the new independent edge in her writing voice, and she began to hone her feminist position into increasingly subtle and brilliant permutations. She started an essay on how women's love of luxury kept them from being geniuses. Inflamed by what she saw as the weakness of even the most intelligent women in their relations with men, she ranted against the traditional feminine goals of elegance and desirability. Love, she wrote, should be entered into only reluctantly. Here one gets a taste of her frustration with herself. She denounced women "keeping themselves apart from the high purposes of life for an emotion that, schemed and planned for, was no better than the made excitement of drunkenness." One senses in this essay's electric passages a disappointment with her own choices: she was giving up some of her wildness, some of her outrageous, chattery self, for that same unreliable emotion. Was love worth everything she had already given up? And why should she give up more than Wells? The extraordinary essay was entitled "The World's Worst Failure," and by this failure she meant women. "Since men don't love us nearly as much as we love them that leaves them much more spare energy to be wonderful with," she complained in one of her novels, and one can't help seeing in those words some reflection of her increasingly tangled relation with Wells.

The last thing the ambitious young feminist wanted was to be the concubine to a great man, but ironically, locked up with a new baby, in a remote cottage by the sea, dreaming of parties in London and beautiful clothes in the windows of the stores

on Bond Street, that is precisely what she seemed to have become. She found herself frittering huge swaths of time waiting
for "the Great Man." As she wrote to a friend, "I hate domesticity. I don't want to stay here and I don't want to go to
Westcliffe. I can't imagine any circumstances in which it would
be really amusing to order 2 ounces of Lady Betty wool for
socks for Anthony . . . I want to live an unfettered and adventurous life."

With all of their radical ideas, Wells and Rebecca seem to
have fallen into a life of fairly traditional hypocrisy. Their fragile new ménage was based on the usual lies. He visited her as a
fictional "Mr. West" who was either in the movie business or a
roving journalist. The servants were told that Rebecca was not
the child's mother, and Wells snuck down the hall into her
room at night to keep up appearances in front of them. In order to maintain the integrity of this flimsy series of untruths,
they moved houses several times. For a while, the baby
Anthony was taught to call Wells, "Wellsie," and his mother,
"Auntie Panther." Wells brooded about his already besmirched
reputation, and what effect it might have on his literary career.
He believed that his earlier, highly public affair with a girl
named Amber Reeves, with whom he had also had an illegitimate child, had shaken his general standing in the literary
world and endangered his livelihood. Later he would say that
he deplored Rebecca's transparent deceptions, but he himself
was not ready to claim Anthony as a son: his bold rhetoric, as
always, matched by startling flashes of conservativism in his
personal life. And so, the baby lived in a strange, shifting household, in which his mother and her friend drifted past, and
changed forms.

Wells was convinced that the world was evolving before their eyes, that his new ideas about sexuality were taking hold, with university students eagerly passing around his books, and a new youthful cachet adhering to his middle-aged efforts. As he proclaimed in *The Fortnightly Review* in 1911, after the attacks on his racier books: "We are going to write, subject only to our own limitations, of the whole of human life. We are going to write of wasted opportunities and latent beauties until a thousand new ways of living open to men and women." Unlike his rival Henry James and many of his contemporaries, Wells had never been interested in art for art's sake; as he says, his literary purpose was no less than to invent for a generation "new ways of living." He viewed himself as a political visionary whose imagination could be set to work in the practical business of the revolution. But in the small towns Rebecca inhabited, and in vast swaths of London, the near-Victorian sensibilities of the larger populace remained virtually intact. Wells wrote Violet Hunt, asking, "Do you—in all of your knowledge of London— know some amusing, fairly clean little hotel, that wouldn't bother its head about who we are?" He and Rebecca often dined in obscure restaurants in Kensington where they would not be seen. And years later, when Wells went to pick up Anthony at school instead of his nurse, the boy was expelled, with the curt explanation that the school had already tolerated too much scandal on Anthony's behalf.

The truth is that even in their liberal, artistic circles, Wells and Rebecca couldn't move with complete freedom. Rebecca's good friend Sylvia Lynd met her at a dinner party at her favorite restaurant in London, Le Petit Riche. The small group ate and chattered in the candlelight. And in the middle of the meal Wells strolled in with his friend Arnold Bennett. The two writers had dined at the Reform Club and drunk a good deal of champagne. Bennett proceeded to spear the end of a cigar with a pocket knife and smoke it while Wells launched into a stream of his charming, contrarian talk. Sylvia Lynd was appalled by his arrival. She said later that her sense "of propriety believed in neat compartments . . . besides I like Janie, and all the non-jealousy business is humbug—it's the price they pay for Pasha's company—converting all of their sounds of woe to Hey nonny nonny."

At least on the surface, both women did seem to tolerate each other's existence. Jane cabled her "dear love" to Rebecca when she had her baby. Whatever her deeper feelings, Jane, who was now in her early forties, had internalized Wells's desire that she treat his mistresses with pleasantness and affection. Paradoxically, it had come to be part of her wifely supremacy that she tolerated, and even helped, the women he was involved with. With each benign gesture she confirmed that she was unconcerned, above the fray. And when Jane was ill, Rebecca also wrote a mannerly get-well note: "Dear Mrs. Wells, I have just heard from H.G. how ill you have been and I wanted to tell you how sorry I am to hear that you have had such a distressing time and how glad I am to hear that you are getting on well." Privately, though, Rebecca complained bitterly about Jane throughout her life. With her considerable, sometimes unchecked imaginative powers, she began to transform Jane into a controlling virago who dominated H.G. with "appalling fantastic wickedness." And Jane in her own ineffectual, private way may have expressed her difficulties with Rebecca. She used to take the letters she received from Wells's paramours, and either underline in pencil or write faint exclamation marks next to the most insincere portions of their letters: extracting and recording for herself a bitter humor from the situation. She would in her own quiet, schoolteacherish way, have the last word.

Wells, meanwhile, found the baby unromantic. He enjoyed visiting Rebecca and taking her for rides in his new motor car, which he called "Gladys," in the surrounding countryside. But he did not enjoy the baby's crying, or the nursery, or the waiting around, which he referred to in a stern letter to Rebecca as a "severe test" of his love for her. With her clever housekeeping and sprawling homes, Jane managed to insulate him from the daily noise of childrearing. And it galled him particularly that he should be confronted with the evidence of babies in the home of his mistress, the place he expressly intended as a flight from all the noise and clutter of domesticity. In fact, the impinging of domestic cares on love was one of Wells's great themes. In his novel *The Passionate Friends,* one of his characters says to her lover that if she marries him they will cease to be lovers, and their relationship will devolve into her making him coffee. This is a striking encapsulation of his romantic philosophy: in Wells's world, even making coffee is incompatible with the erotic flare of a grand amour; the wearing, practical concerns of daily life are not to be mingled with the sacred frivolity of sex. He found it particularly galling to surrender the unreal, wine-soaked atmosphere of a semi-illicit love to the tangible, unlovely demands of a baby.

For her part, Rebecca was finding it hard to do the work she very much needed to do. In 1916 she had published an irreverent book on Henry James in which she called his trademark sentence "a delicate creature swathed in relative clauses as an invalid is in shawls." But she was still doing too much of what she thought of as the hackwork of journalism, and couldn't carve out enough time for her real writing. A photograph from this period shows a fairly stout Rebecca in a white dress, her hair rolled into two untidy buns over her ears, looking somehow more shapeless and uncertain than usual, and an alert, anxious little boy impeccably dressed in a white sailor suit and patent leather shoes. In one of her feminist essays, Rebecca condemned women who "took up work not because they loved the work but in order that they might affect an appearance of strength which some man would find a virile satisfaction in breaking down into weakness, an appearance of independence which some man would be proud to exchange for a dependence on him." And Rebecca was determined not to exchange her work for a dependence on Wells, no matter how tempting the prospect might seem. And so, they sent the baby away to board at a Montessori school in London, before he turned four. Rebecca consoled herself that Anthony was thrilled to see that there were "little girlies" in the school, and ran off to join the other children without looking back. But when he grew up, Anthony Panther West would find much to complain about in his odd, uprooted childhood. In a simmering screed in *The New York Review of Books,* he would describe in furious detail what he saw as his mother's "passionate desire" to do him harm.

During their long and frequent separations, Rebecca and H.G. wrote each other letters filled with an affectionate patois in which they referred to each other as "Panther" and "Jaguar."

He wrote to her, "I shall roll you over and do what I like with you. I shall make you pant and bite back. Then I shall give you a shake and quiet you and go to sleep all over you and if I snore, I snore. Your Lord. The Jaguar." But the two frolicking, dangerous cats they created often seemed poised to rip each other to shreds. For one thing, Wells was jealous. He admitted that all of his elaborately articulated theories about free love fell apart when faced with the realities of his obsession. He found even her mildest flirtations or friendships with men unbearable. He insisted that it was much worse for a man if a woman was unfaithful. And on her side, Rebecca was beginning to sense that one-fifth of Wells might not, after all, be enough. During one of his increasingly long absences Rebecca, then twenty-three years old, wrote, "My life is simply empty and I am possessed by a terrifying sense that I am growing old and that there are no more peacocks and sunsets in the world."

As time went by, Rebecca was increasingly bewildered by Jane's tenacity. She had only to open a copy of the literary review *The Bookman* to read an account of Wells's idyllic family life at Easton, with its stylish, impromptu soccer parties, complete with rolling tea carts. It had become clear not just to Rebecca but to the reading public that Wells's center of gravity had not shifted. And then, Rebecca also resented the eagerness with which Wells received Jane's letters while he was with Rebecca. Even at the height of his absorption with Rebecca, he wrote to Jane every day. In fact, he once wrote to her from his perch with Rebecca: "I love you very warmly. You are, in so many things, bone of my bone, flesh of my flesh and my making. I must keep you." To the modern ear, the words "of my making" are jarring, but his attachment to his wife is clear. To Rebecca's surprise, Wells continued to view Jane's role as inviolable, her position in his life as non-negotiable. At one point, he wrote crankily to Rebecca of "this growing mania of yours about the injustices of my treatment of you in not murdering Jane."

Wells and Rebecca were also beginning to have the kind of domestic quarrels that generally only overtake people who are living together or married. Wells found himself constantly aggravated by Rebecca's dramatic problems with her servants. His temperament demanded a smoothly run house, but he didn't want to have to think about the minutiae involved in running one. To an outside observer this seems like a fairly trivial issue, but for Wells it was not. He was enormously concerned with being properly looked after. After one of Rebecca's many crises in managing her servants, he and Jane sent an older woman who had nursed one of their friends at Easton to look after the household. This Miss North installed herself in Rebecca's living room, drinking endless cups of tea and complaining and clucking and criticizing, until Rebecca threw her out. Anthony later interpreted Miss North as a human message from Jane to Rebecca, an embodiment of her patronage and condescension. He believed that she had been placed there to exacerbate the situation and to make the contrast with Jane's own well-ordered home more pronounced. Whether or not this was literally true, the fracas over Miss North was a sign of a certain irritability, a palpable, electric current of rivalry between the two households.

In January of 1922, Rebecca planned to meet Wells in Gibraltar for a two-month holiday in the south of Spain. Wells was on his way home from a tremendously successful lecture tour in America, where his fame had swelled to the point that people recognized him in the street. Rebecca couldn't wait to see him. On the boat, she noted in her diary: "heart beating fast with love." But Wells arrived in Gibraltar in a state of dangerous exhilaration and nervous exhaustion. After a few walks on the beach and a quick tour of the sites, he took to his bed. He had nosebleeds. He had a sore throat. Rebecca had to make her meals out of sandwiches and fruit because the sound of a knife or spoon scraping a plate irritated him. His apocalyptic attitude toward his minor ailments particularly irritated her because he had criticized her so often for her digestive problems, bronchial ailments, and frequent infections.

At one point, in the lobby of their hotel, he told Rebecca to fetch his coat from upstairs in front of other people, and she exploded. Why should she have to be his maid? Who did he think he was? She believed the adulation of audiences in the States had gone to his head. She later claimed he was behaving so badly that several strangers, hotel owners, and chaplains offered to help her escape him and get home. Whatever the literal truth of this claim, Rebecca was undoubtedly feeling trapped. They toured the mountains and marigolds of Ronda, and the orange trees and cathedrals of Seville, but the clash of wills was now all-consuming. Wells wanted someone to care for him, and Rebecca wanted someone to fuss over her. He wanted nurturing; she wanted romantic excitement. The little difficulties of traveling gnawed at them, and toward the end of the trip, they argued bitterly about losing the way back to their hotel in Paris, and whose responsibility it was to guide the other. They both arrived home disgruntled, and after receiving her litany of his flaws by mail, Wells wrote to her: "The old male pusted (i.e. cat) has read her letter attentively and declines to plead guilty to an enlarged egotism. He objects to the Better Jaguar movement." As the tension between them mounted, both writers turned their considerable critical powers on each other. There had always been an element of teasing in their relationship—one of the qualities they admired most in each other was their ability to push and prod at the weaknesses of a façade. But now they began to take each other's character apart in cruelly effective ways. Wells attacked Rebecca for the relentless darkness of her perspective; Rebecca attacked Wells for being a "nagging schoolmaster." They quarreled over Anthony. They quarreled over quarreling. And finally, Wells wrote rather cruelly to Rebecca, "For ten years I've shaped my life mainly to repair the carelessness of one moment. It's no good and I am tired of it." In the year that followed, they repeatedly broke things off and came back together. They found each other maddening, compelling, brilliant, difficult, attractive, and neither was able to break the dark, magnetic force field between them.

At around this time, when his relationship with Rebecca was at its most tenuous, Wells became involved with Hedwig Verana Gatternigg, a slight Austrian translator with, he thought, a face like the Mona Lisa. As usual, he found it hard to resist a pretty female fan and he did not, at first, pay much attention to her obvious instability. She quickly became deluded about the seriousness of the affair, and he backed off. He told her he wouldn't see her and asked his servants not to admit her to any of his residences. She visited Rebecca and apparently tried to persuade her that Wells had seduced her. And then one June evening, Hedwig somehow slipped into Wells's flat, virtually naked under a raincoat, and threatened to kill herself if he didn't love her. He went into the hallway to call the hall porter, and as soon as he stepped out of the room she slashed her wrists and armpits. His rug and shirt were covered with blood, and he called to cancel his dinner with the secretary of state to India. She wasn't seriously hurt, but the whole imbroglio ended up on the front pages of the world's newspapers, where he could not immediately exercise his influence, like *The New York Times:* "Woman Tries Suicide in Flat of H. G. Wells." The next morning Rebecca met Wells for a long talk in Kensington Gardens, where he seems to have given her a somewhat white-washed version of the basic facts, which downplayed the extent of his involvement with Hedwig and placed Jane at the scene of the suicide attempt. On the advice of his lawyer, Wells and Rebecca later lunched together at the Ivy to publicly show their solidarity. Rebecca intended to be supportive. But the incident brought home to her the impossibility of the situation. Wells's life was simultaneously too operatic and too inert: she was beginning to think about running off to America.

3

THE VALIANT LITTLE BEING

At some point in the delicate creation of their triangle, Wells, Jane, and Rebecca each believed they could overcome the petty jealousies that plague ordinary people. But tradition ended up exerting too great a pull on all of them. The classical model of husband and wife cast too great a shadow for them to resist. During the last years of their relationship, Rebecca's yearnings for a fairly mundane respectability began to take over. *Hearst's International Cosmopolitan* would call her "the personification of all of the vitality, the courage, and the independence of the modern woman." But the daring, provocative Rebecca West, the same Rebecca West who penned an article called "I Regard Marriage with Fear and Horror," wanted to be Mrs. H. G. Wells. And the hedonistic Wells couldn't, in the end, contemplate leaving his wife. He had never seriously considered it. Jane offered him a security, an unconditional, unthreatening, unimpassioned love that he could not live without. The lure of his comfortable home nestled in its beautiful gardens, and his wife, who was an integral part of that home and that comfort, were too great for him to resist.

After her mother died in 1921, Rebecca slipped into the language of married couples when she wrote to Wells, "Thank you for being such a good husband—I will try to be a good wife to you." The primal power of marriage began to exert more of a hold on her imagination as she found herself relying more and more deeply on him. In her later years, she wrote that she wished she could have pleased her mother by never meeting Wells, and marrying young. And when she eventually married a banker named Henry Andrews in 1929 she seemed almost to revel in the little tokens of surrendered identity, sending a note to Virginia Woolf signed "Cicily Andrews" and sending out Christmas cards with printed greetings from "Mr. and Mrs. Henry Andrews." She went on to travel alone through Yugoslavia and write *Black Lamb and Grey Falcon,* and publish the pioneering investigation *The Meaning of Treason* after the Second World War. She went on to be featured on the cover of *Time* as the world's single most famous woman writer and was granted the honorary title Dame Rebecca West by the crown. But she also wrote a playful article for *The New Yorker* about a housewife's trials during the Second World War, and continued to enjoy the feminine trappings of an old-fashioned marriage.

As for Wells, his domestic fantasies always seemed to circle back to his spacious Georgian house. It may seem strange that a house should be so important to an avowed socialist, but for Wells, Easton Glebe was a tangible symbol of everything he had accomplished. Unlike some of the more free-spirited writers and intellectuals he associated with, Wells's home with its tennis courts and weekend visitors was as important an invention to him as his novels were. After a visit there Sir Sydney Waterlow, literary gadfly and highbrow gossip, wrote in his diary:

> I feel that every day he chuckles with renewed energy over the fact that here he is, saved by his own energy out of the misery of the underworld. . . . The reflection that he has a good house with comfortable beds and pretty furniture and is able to drink as much burgundy as he likes, seems to give him constant thrill and delight.

What Waterlow was getting at, with fairly undisguised snobbery, was that Wells's mother had been a housekeeper and lady's maid, and his father had been a gardener. Wells harbored rather extreme, Dickensian memories of the house he grew up in, with its unspeakable odors, smashed cockroaches, and potato-heavy meals, and the even more Dickensian memory of being apprenticed off to a draper. His mother ended up leaving the family and living out her days in a small cottage in the shadow of Up Park, the great house she worked in, yearning toward its moneyed tranquility. And it may be because of this that Wells did not take bourgeois comfort and respectability entirely for granted: it may be that he invested more in his home, and the affluent security of his family, because of the poverty and insecurity of his childhood. Whatever outlandish arrangements he made in his private life, his house stood inviolate, with his wife and children inside. Easton was his dream of domestic security incarnate, a physical embodiment of his steadfastness and achievement. But even if Wells were inclined to leave Easton and Jane, would he have left them for Rebecca?

The truth is there was a competitive spark in his relationship with Rebecca, an inflammatory equality he found unnerving. He was enormously attracted to the New Woman, as his affairs with noted feminists like Rebecca West and Margaret Sanger attested to, but only up to a point. He admired but didn't quite trust their vaunted independence. As he said to Rebecca: "Jane is a wife. But you could never be a wife. You want a wife yourself—you want sanity and care and courage and patience behind you just as much as I do." There was, in his ostensibly strange relationship with Jane, something sweet and sustaining, at least for Wells.

Occasionally, Wells admitted that his arrangement with Jane was not perfect. He was willing to concede that she may have spent a few painful evenings alone. But he continued to see their originality as a couple as a feat of intellectual bravura: they had to think up a new way to live, like writers inventing a new style, or socialists penning a manifesto, or anthropologists conducting an experiment. How could two people who weren't sexually compatible live together? They were no longer sleeping together, but the affection and cumulative history remained. As he put it, "two extremely dissimilar brains were working very intelligently at the peculiar life problem we had created for each other." And in the end, he felt that their attachment was stronger and more enduring than the more mundane, constricted marriages he saw around him.

But was their union as balanced and happy as Wells would have us believe? Is it possible that Amy Catherine Wells was content being her husband's business manager, and puttering around her garden with its blue cedars and apricot roses, scrawling entries in her gardening journal while he was off with a string of fascinating mistresses? When he was gone she sometimes went to the theater with friends. She loved her boys, and involved herself in their upbringing before they went off to boarding school. She curled up and read *Remembrance of Things Past*. But was that enough? It's difficult to know. Wells wrote: "We two contrived in the absence of a real passionate sexual fixation, a binding net of fantasy and affection that proved in the end as effective as the very closest sexual sympathy could have been in keeping us together." In the end, Wells's version of events was so powerful, so charismatically set out, and disarmingly honest that it was taken up and echoed in chorus by nearly all of the observers of their relationship. Everyone from his own son to Julian Huxley to his servants would parrot his phrases in describing the marriage: Jane was like "Dresden china," too "fragile" for his sexual demands, his affairs were "passades," and their arrangement a "modus vivendi." His account of his marriage was so enchanting in its apparent frankness, so lively in its quasi-scientific investigation of rakishness, that it would eclipse any other version of the relationship that might have emerged.

Mathilde Meyer, the Swiss governess of the two Wells boys, wrote a telling description of her first impression of Jane in her memoirs: "Who was Mrs. Wells? I wondered. I thought that there was a certain wistful melancholy about her. Was she a widow left with two sons?" And then there is a photograph of the family—the two little boys in sailor suits, kneeling on the floor with a train set, Wells hovering restlessly in the doorway, and his wife slumped in a rocking chair in an unmistakable posture of defeat—that hints at a different family portrait than the one Wells so painstakingly paints.

When Wells was off in France or Italy with one of his mistresses, he liked to picture Jane cheerfully tending the garden at home. He told himself that these wafting feminine charms of hers, like her "love of beauty," would somehow provide an occupation for her. He saw the two of them united in a common purpose as they "defied the current wisdom and won." But who exactly was winning? The closest he ever came to saying that Jane did not entirely embrace their arrangement is the following: "Though she helped and sustained me with her utmost strength and loyalty, I do not think she believed very strongly in my beliefs. She accepted them but she could have done without them." This is not a very strong statement of discontent, and it was crucial to Wells's self-image, to the meticulous, almost clinical investigation of his romantic life he conducted in public, that he had not caused her too much pain. It was crucial that he not see her suffering as a source of remorse, that he not be forced to examine his affairs too closely in relation to her. In fact he felt confident enough in his blamelessness to write cheerfully: "I never get the slightest regret out of any of my sexual irregularities. They were amusing and refreshing and I wish there had been more of them."

In April of 1906, when he was lecturing in America, Jane offered a much darker assessment in one of her letters:

> I am thinking continually of the disappointing mess of it, the high bright ambitions one begins with, the dismal con-cessions—the growth, like a clogging hard crust over one of home & furniture & a lot of clothes & books & gardens & a load dragging me down. If I set out to make a comfortable home for you. . . . I merely succeed in contriving a place where you are bored to death . . . Well, dear, I don't think I ought to send you such a lekker, (sic) it's only a mood you know.

That she would entertain a mood like this argues against the cheerful hostess and eternally happy gardener Wells presented to the world, along with the materialistic hausfrau others ex-trapolated. The letter continued: "I feel tonight so tired of play-ing wiv making the home comfy & as if there was only one dear rest place in the world, & that were in the arms & heart of you." This small snippet of domestic dialogue expresses a more intense, physical longing, and a more consuming, anarchic sad-ness than Wells ever admits in his cool, sensible Jane.

There is also the fact that a few years after the war, before Virginia Woolf delivered the first version of her famous *A Room of One's Own* as a lecture, Jane Wells took rooms of her own in Bloomsbury. She admired Marcel Proust and Virginia Woolf and Katherine Mansfield, and she wanted to write. H.G.—fairly remarkably for someone used to controlling everything—never saw those rooms. Jane wanted a hidden place of her own, away from him. Her desk in Bloomsbury seems to have been her great rebellion, her own retreat from the well-oiled domesticity of their home at Easton. She kept the rooms until a year before she died.

Jane submitted the stories she was working on to various periodicals without her famous last name, and for the most part they were rejected. She was not a natural writer. Her sentences tended toward lifelessness and cliché. But unlike many aspiring writers, she had something to say. Her stories, which Wells calls "wistful" and "very charming" and "sweet," are in fact filled with straightforward expressions of pain. They are populated with wives comfortably abandoned, tactfully ignored, "enshrined" in charming houses. "The Beautiful House," which ran in *Harper's Magazine* in March of 1912 under the name "Catherine Wells," is about the ache of a woman watching her beloved with a lover. Reading its feverish pages, one can't help imagining Jane's anxiety with each of her husband's new liaisons—would this one break up her marriage?—and then her relief when it settled into the same pattern as all of the rest. While from the outside their marriage seemed stable after so many years, it must have felt precarious to her each time one of these excitable young women drank a cup of tea in her house.

Another surprise of Catherine Wells's fiction is its elaboration of sexual fantasy: in one of her stories, a handsome young photographer who comes to photograph a famous husband sets in motion an overwhelming longing in his wife, which is described with all the pulpy heat of a novelette. In fact, the honeyed, sexually charged prose makes one wonder if its author could be as dry and devoid of sexual energy as Wells would have us believe. He wrote that she was "immune" to the fevers of sexual desire, that she lacked the sensual strength and imagination to have a vivid sexual life. Was Wells deliberately playing up this aspect of her character? Was it one of those exaggerated characterizations that rise up between a married couple, agreed upon in some unspoken way out of expedience or tact? Jane seems to have allowed him the convenient fiction that she was sexless, or somehow too fragile and good to withstand his advances. But why? Could it be that she was afraid to admit to the sexual feelings she elaborates in these stories? The bestselling meditation on the sexual quandaries of British marriage, *Married Love* by Dr. Marie Carmichael Stopes, explained, "Most women would rather die than acknowledge that they do at times feel a physical yearning, indescribable, but as profound as the hunger for food." One wonders if Jane Wells would have come across this book, as it was so much discussed, and sold so many copies. It seems likely that she would have. But Wells claimed that the "Catherine" who penned these stories was a stranger to him; and it seems unlikely that the Jane he lived with voiced any of her frustrations or fantasies directly to him.

Mrs. Wells's story "Walled Garden" comes tantalizingly close to the details of her own situation. It describes a healthy, vivacious woman whose rather effete literary husband announces that he is going to rename her "Rosalind." She says flirtatiously, "Baptize me then!" and imagines them splashing each other with water, but instead he kisses her solemnly on the forehead. Their wedding night contains a revelation: "Bray made love to her delicately and reverently, and Rosalind, after an interval of puzzled discovery, settled down to her married life with a feeling of faint disappointment which she could hardly justify." Reading this, one wonders if the delicacy H. G. Wells regretted in their sexual life was coming from her or from him. Was the reverence she laments here a product of his view of her, rather than something innate in Jane's character? Wells tells us that Jane loved to ski and climb mountains, which makes the physical "fragility" he often complains about a little hard to credit. (In fact, it was he whose "bad lungs and kidneys" made it impossible for him to join her in these exertions.) It seems possible that Wells, in his self-conscious rebellion against "the definite sexual codes of the time," his deliberate throwing off of Victorian constraint, was himself prey to more than one Victorian idea: perhaps his innocent wife had to be treated delicately, and couldn't fulfill his sexual demands, simply by virtue of being his wife. (His first wife, Isabel, coincidentally, also failed to manage his sexual needs, forcing him to look elsewhere. And one can't help noting that his sexual disappointment within the institution of marriage is matched only by his uninhibited joy outside of it.) In *Married Love,* Dr. Marie Carmichael Stopes argued, "The idea that woman is lowered or 'soiled' by sexual intercourse is still deeply rooted in some strata of our society." She most likely would not have intended by this one of the great libertine thinkers of the era, but this seems to be precisely how he felt. In spite of his advanced theories and risqué novels, Wells seemed to believe that the women he married were somehow above the baseness and physicality of the rest of the world.

Ironically, Wells may have found himself in a Victorian

quandary of his own making and psychology: it wasn't Jane who couldn't keep up with him, but he who couldn't allow her to.

In his autobiographical writings, Wells claimed that no other woman entered as deeply or intimately into his emotions. Of his ten-year interlude with Rebecca West, he concedes only that "I was always very near loving Rebecca, as she was often very near loving me." And in his own mind, Jane remained his one true companion. When he heard that she was sick with cancer in the winter of 1927, while on a motoring holiday in France, he wrote to her immediately, "My dear, I love you much more than I have loved anyone else in the world and I am coming back to you to take care of you and to do all I can to make you happy." Over the next few months, he immersed himself in work and tried to stay close to her, remaining at Easton for longer stretches than he was accustomed to, though he did manage to escape for a few weekends in France with his current mistress, Odette Kuehn. When Jane finally died that fall he was utterly lost, and wrote great paeans to the fineness of her character. He found it hard to believe that he couldn't gather up huge armfuls of white and purple daisies and bring them to her.

That week, Rebecca wrote to a friend she was worried that now that Jane was dead, Wells would become tiresome to her. The two had maintained an intermittent and touchy friendship since their separation, and Wells had stayed in touch with their son, but Rebecca still bore traces of the decade-long affair, which Virginia Woolf called "the hoofmarks" of Wells. Twenty years later, when Rebecca heard Wells had died in the middle of the night, she would still muster a stream of violent, contradictory feeling: "He was a devil, he ruined my life, he starved me, he was an inexhaustible source of love and friendship to me for thirty-four years, we should never have met, I was the only person he cared to see to the end, I feel desolate because he has gone."

In the days after Jane's death, Wells crafted a formal oration for her funeral that was delivered by a professional actor. Jane emerged from this ornate oratory as such a saintly, patient figure, such a pale Victorian angel, that there was almost no place for authentic human grief. George Bernard Shaw's wife, Charlotte, who was a close friend of Jane's, complained: "He drowned us in a sea of misery and as we were gasping began a panegyric of Jane which made her appear as a delicate, flower-like gentle being surrounding itself with beauty, and philanthropy, and love. Now Jane was one of the strongest characters I ever met." Wells was beginning to write their relationship, as he would one of his novels, and in the process Jane's character was abstracted into a fluttering female archetype. One wonders how aware he was of the fiction he was crafting. In the clever, comic "auto-obituary" he wrote for himself in 1943, the same obituary in which he referred to himself as "one of the most prolific literary hacks of his era," he said, rather tellingly: "When he dealt with passion he was apt to write insincerely." The gentle, tolerant femininity of his Jane strained credulity. And her humorless perfection, so carefully established and prettily described, did not ring true to those who knew her best. Arnold Bennett, an intimate of both Wellses, who was close enough to Jane to begin his letters to her "My Sweet Jane," also took exception to the strong element of mythmaking in Wells's elegy. That evening, he commented dryly in his journals: "The oration was either not well done, or too well done."

The October day was clear and sunny. The chapel opened onto the garden with its brilliant flowers, and several mourners had the unsettling impression that Jane might walk in at any moment, with her red gardening shears and basket dangling over her arm. Charlotte Shaw wrote, "There came a place where the address said, 'She never resented a slight; she never gave voice to a harsh judgment.' At that point the audience, all more or less acquainted with many details of H.G.'s private life, thrilled, like corn under a wet north-wind, and H.G.— H.G. positively howled."

Accompanied by his sons, Wells followed the coffin into the crematorium. He saw the white-gold flames lick the sides of the coffin. Did he suddenly see his finely wrought arrangement with Jane in a different light? Did he feel a great untruth surge behind his words "she bore no resentment"? Did he feel the pain he knew he had caused her, and see her words, in her girlish, curly writing: "I feel tonight so tired wiv making the home comfy"? One cannot know the answer, of course, but he bowed to his own failures when he wrote: "The best and sweetest of her is known only to one or two of us, subtle and secret; it can never be told."

KATHERINE MANSFIELD AND
JOHN MIDDLETON MURRY

> *"What is happening to 'married pairs'? They are almost extinct. I confess, for my part, I believe in marriage. It seems the only possible relation that really is satisfying."*
>
> —KATHERINE MANSFIELD, 1921

MAY 3, 1918. Katherine Mansfield shivered outside the marriage registry office in South Kensington. Her rings were sliding off her fingers. Her neck was damp from fever. Her hair was cut as it always was, in black bangs straight across her forehead and the bob she had pioneered long before everyone else had one, but her appearance was somehow diminished from her publicity photograph: her face looked tiny and drawn; she had dark circles under her eyes. Her groom, John Middleton Murry, whom she called Jack, was helping one of their witnesses, Lady Dorothy Brett, whom everyone called Brett, on with her coat. They were all on their way to a lunch to celebrate the marriage. But Katherine was occupied, instead, with what didn't happen that day. She would always remember Jack turning away from her and putting a handkerchief to his mouth. She would also remember that when the binding words were spoken, six long years after they met, her new husband did not take her in his arms. Their troubled, immature bond, which they privately referred to as their "child love," was finally taking on an adult formality, and yet the public gravitas would not change anything between them. "Our marriage," Katherine wrote to him later. "You cannot imagine what that was to have meant to me. It's fantastic, I suppose. It was to have shone apart from all else in my life and really it was only part of the nightmare after all. You never once held me in your arms and called me your wife."

But Katherine was not one to allow private disappointments or secret, girlish sentimentalities of which she harbored quite a few, to affect her public bravado. A few days later, Virginia Woolf wrote after lunching with her: "For some reason she makes out that marriage is of no more importance than engaging a charwoman. Part of the fascination of her is the obligation she is under to say absurd things." In fact it was precisely this obligation that caused an inordinate number of people to distrust Katherine. Lytton Strachey described her as "an odd satirical woman behind a regular mask of a face . . . she was very difficult to get at; one felt it would take years of patient burrowing, but that it might be worth while." In fact she would often be described as having a face like a mask: with the innate pallor of a geisha, and thick black bangs cut straight across her forehead, there was a kind of natural theater to her looks that accentuated the shadier aspects of her personality. The creation of a persona was to her a serious business, and honesty had never been one of her higher values.

For several weeks after the wedding, Murry stayed up at night listening to his new wife's hacking cough, feeling each cough in his spine. In fact, if he were honest, he had barely recognized her when he met her at the station after she had been abroad for four months because she was so changed; his first thought was that her black eyes looked like the eyes of someone who had been in prison. Telling himself that his basement rooms, with grating over the windows and almost no light during the day, were inadequate for a lengthy convalescence, he sent her off to the countryside with a friend until he could finish renovating "the elephant," the tall gray house on Hampstead Heath that would be their home.

By this time Katherine Mansfield was a successful short story writer of some repute. She had published two books, and her stories appeared in prestigious literary journals like *New Age* and *Signature*. Her personal reputation was mixed. Many people found her terrifying, and others insincere. Even by the accounts of those who loved and admired her, she was theatrical, brilliant, and wildly manipulative. John Middleton Murry was one of those intellectuals who makes his way largely on charm and desperation. He had great literary aspirations but had not yet written anything that matched his ambitions; he was the kind of sensitive, artistically inclined man who milks the idea of being "promising" well into his forties. He was a talented critic and an impressive writer, and he eventually found a niche as an editor, freely traversing several overlapping literary circles, but he would never be satisfied with the literary expressions of what he privately believed to be his genius. The two had shared a free-form, experimental relationship for so long that the idea of a conventional, adult marriage loomed large for both of them. They had elaborate fantasies of a perfect, bookish domesticity, but fantasy is what they were both most proficient at—ordinary life they found harder.

John Middleton Murry first glimpsed Katherine Mansfield

over plum soup at an elegant dinner party in December of 1911. The dramatically pretty twenty-three-year-old writer arrived late, in a dove gray evening dress pinned with a red flower and draped with a gauzy silver wrap, and she was quieter and marginally less terrifying than he thought she would be. Having just published a quirky book of stories, *In a German Pension,* to a certain amount of critical acclaim, she was already part of the glamorous literary world he felt himself hovering on the verge of, and he was drawn to her innate confidence. Murry himself was still a student at Oxford; his own tiny bit of anxious cachet came from being the editor of the avant-garde literary review *Rhythm* which would later become *The Blue Review.* He wanted to be a great writer, a great editor, a great literary figure of some amorphous, as of yet undefined, variety. He had the charisma of a self-made man: having come to Oxford from a drab, working-class background, he had remade himself in the university's image. He was also, in his elegantly disheveled tweeds, exceptionally attractive to both men and women, with scalloped, slicked-back hair over a high forehead, prominently arched eyebrows over large hazel eyes, angled cheekbones, a cigarette dangling from his mouth—"that lovely, terrifying mouth," Katherine would call it—and an oddly potent air of insecurity and ambition.

Several months later, Murry came down to London to see Katherine for tea. Her rooms were flamboyantly sparse, with no table, no dining room chairs, and nothing as bourgeois as a teacup. She served their tea in giant bowls as they sat cross-legged on the bamboo mats that covered her floor and above them on the mantle sat an elaborate hookah. She often liked to receive guests in a kimono, but on this particular day she was more conventionally dressed. Did she somehow sense Murry's timidity? As she squatted to pour the steaming tea, Murry felt queasy at the sudden physicality of the gesture. There was a view of slanted rooftops out the window. And sprawled across the divan in the corner was a small Japanese doll in ruffled clothes.

Murry, who was prone to slightly hysterical bursts of intimacy with near strangers, found himself offering up his future to Katherine and placing himself entirely in her hands. He confessed that after slaving all his life to get to Oxford, he now found it unendurable, and he wasn't sure if he should stay for the next few months and complete his degree. This was a defining conversation for both of them. There was something decidedly seductive in his willingness to offer her the stewardship of his burgeoning career. Katherine was perfectly happy to take charge of his life. She told him it would be wrong to stay at Oxford if he felt that way, and that he should move to London and edit *Rhythm* from there. He treated her like an oracle, and immediately took her advice, which would launch them into a decade-long habit of her providing the momentum in his life. "We are both abnormal," Katherine would later write to him. "I have too much vitality—and you not enough."

Murry informed his tutors that he was leaving Oxford, moved back to his parents' spare room, and began writing articles for the *Westminster Gazette*. He was poor but excited about his new London life. One warm spring night he and Katherine went out to dinner with one of his Oxford friends, Frederick Goodyear, who himself fell a little in love with Katherine. Afterward, flushed and tipsy from the wine, they all three walked around a fountain to prolong the evening, and out of the blue Katherine invited Murry to come and be a boarder in her spare room for seven shillings a week. He accepted without hesitation, and the next week he moved his few possessions into her small sitting room, which previously had been occupied by a piano and a stone Buddha. The first morning she put out his breakfast of brown bread, butter, honey, and an egg, with a little sign that said, "This is your egg. You must boil it." They lived for a while in this pleasant, companionable state, eating cheap meat pies for dinner, writing all evening, and then talking until two in the morning over yet more giant bowls of tea. They called each other "Murry" and "Mansfield," and before going off to bed in their separate rooms they shook hands.

On one of these late nights, Murry was sitting on the floor, leaning against her rolltop desk in his tattered navy blue fisherman's sweater, his hands around his legs, chin resting on his knees like a small boy. "Why don't you make me your mistress?" Katherine asked suddenly. Murry said nothing. He lay down on the floor with his hands behind his head to think, the silence thick between them. And then he did a sort of scissor kick with his legs that she would never forget, and said, "I feel it would spoil—everything." Katherine tried to hide how hurt she was, but even if she hadn't, Murry would most likely not have noticed. Murry did not go out of his way to notice things about other people. He was feeling comfortable for the first time in his life. He believed that during these "golden days," as he would later call them, they had inadvertently stumbled on a utopian arrangement. Why complicate their perfect rapport? On some level he must have known that the suspended state between having and not having, this elaborate, scholarly form of playing house, suited him much better than a more conventional union.

As he revealed in one of their late-night talks, Murry had already proved himself too delicate for love affairs. His first relationship, with a pretty, dark-haired Frenchwoman named Marguerite, that he'd met in a café, had been nearly overwhelming. He had been shyly drawn to her, and somewhat overawed by her voluptuous physical presence. The relationship only progressed to sexual intimacy because she pretended to be ill and summoned him to her bedside, leaving him frankly dismayed that he was expected to sleep with her, his feelings being too tender and exquisite to be consummated in the gross physical act. The affair ended with a dubious engagement and his running off and leaving her without a word. As he put it, "There was the same strange inertia in me as a lover as in all my other doings."

Katherine kept her own less innocent past largely to herself. She had grown up Kathleen, or "Kass," Beauchamp, an affluent banker's daughter in New Zealand, who spent much of her bespectacled girlhood curled up in her room—with bowls of flowers scattered around, a cello leaning against the wall—devouring volumes of Flaubert and Oscar Wilde and George Bernard Shaw, and dreaming vaguely of an artist's life. Shortly after arriving in London, she began an affair with a reedy nineteen-year-old violinist who smoked cigarettes out of a holder, and she ended up pregnant. Before she began to show, she became engaged to a good-natured music instructor named George Bowden, with salt-and-pepper hair and round tortoiseshell glasses, whom she had known for only a few weeks. She wore a black suit and black hat to the wedding registry office, which her groom seemed not to find strange, and that night when they went to consummate their marriage at a hotel with satin furniture and satin-tasseled lamp shades, she lost heart and ran away without a word of explanation. Her new husband had not known she was pregnant with another man's child.

Eventually, traveling under the name Käthe Beauchamp–Bowden, she settled in a small hotel in Bavaria, with a garden where the guests drank coffee in their dressing gowns. Her state of mind during this time is unclear, as she burned all of her notebooks from these months and told her closest confidante from school to burn all of her letters, but at some point in June or July she had a miscarriage after lifting a heavy suitcase on top of a wardrobe. Afterward, presumably to console or distract herself, she arranged to take care of an English boy who was recovering from pleurisy. She also struck up an affair with a Polish translator, Floryan Sobieniowski, who gave her the gonorrhea that may have caused the rheumatism and heart trouble that would plague her for the next decade. Here was the extreme worldliness, the exquisite richness of feeling that she had sought out. But she wrote later, "It hasn't ALL been experience. There is waste—destruction, too."

Throughout all of this tumultuousness with men, Katherine also had, hovering ambiguously on the outskirts of her life, a woman: a plain, affectionate school friend named Ida Baker, whom she called "L.M." or "Jones," or in crueler moments "the Mountain." Katherine had experimented sexually with girls when she was younger, but her relations with Ida appear to have been entirely chaste. Instead, the two were involved in something much more eccentric and intimate than a love affair—a complicated, lifelong entanglement in which Ida would periodically drop everything and devote herself to Katherine in whatever capacity she was needed—as house-keeper, seamstress, confidante, companion, cook, or nurse. "The truth is friendship is to me every bit as sacred and eternal as marriage," Katherine wrote to her in one of her kinder moods. But as soon as Murry agreed to move in as a boarder, Katherine made it clear that for the time being Ida's services would not be required. Ida, who felt rather trampled, nonetheless helped Katherine prepare her rival's room for his arrival. She even donated the five pounds Katherine planted there as an immediate supplement to Murry's meager income.

Eventually Murry succumbed to Katherine's stronger will, and the two continued to live together, much as before, except that they now slept together. Katherine was happy. Murry burned with the thwarted intelligence, the unfulfilled promise that makes for excellent companionship. He put all of his un-channeled energy, his intellectual desire, into talk. He read her work with the careful, critically astute, deeply admiring attention that all writers crave. He was a gratifying reader, and Katherine found it convenient to have such a qualified critic-in-residence. Together they edited the magazine, Katherine tinkered with her stories and reviews, and Murry indulged in his histrionic intellectual passions; as Katherine put it, "Murry couldn't fry a sausage without thinking about God."

What followed over the next few years was an essentially nomadic existence of bankruptcy, moving house, and elaborately contrived yet wildly impractical false starts. In September of 1912 they moved to a rustic cottage near

Chichester, printed stationery with letterhead, took a three-year lease, imagined raising their children there, and then, after devastating financial difficulties with *The Blue Review* and several tussles with unwanted visitors—including Floryan Sobieniowski, Katherine's Polish lover—they moved back to a one-room flat in London. They had been gone a little over a month. Later that year, after decamping to several other residences, including one apartment in Chelsea infested with bugs, they moved to Paris, with barely any hope of making a living, because Katherine loved Paris, and Murry felt it would be conducive to his finally sitting down and writing his great novel. They borrowed money to ship Ida's furniture across the channel, and found a pretty, affordable apartment on the rue de Tournon. A few months later, Murry declared bankruptcy, and they had to sell all of their furniture, or rather Ida's furniture, to brothels in order to raise the money for their return trip. As they were leaving Katherine's overcoat was stolen by the housekeeper, and a disheartened Murry wrote bleakly to one of his patrons: "We shall probably manage it but we shall have to sell everything and start naked as we came into the world." In fact, during the two-year period between 1912 and 1914, Murry and Katherine moved no less than thirteen times. To neither of them did it occur that this astonishing restlessness had something to do with each other. To neither did it occur that their perpetual pursuit of the perfect home, their constant yearning toward a shimmering oasis of domesticity somewhere in the middle distance, was in some way an avoidance of the present: they couldn't get on with the business of living and working together.

Contributing to their dazzling impracticality was a mutual

infatuation with childhood. From very early on, they conceived of their relationship as a "child love," and in many ways they managed to stave off the usual responsibilities of adult life: bills, parenthood, stability. Between them they developed a baby patter, in which Katherine was "Tig" and "Wig," and Murry was "Bogey," and they referred to each other as "my darling precious child" and "tiny child" and "my playfellow." The ensuing imaginary games were elaborate. As Katherine began to suspect that they would never have children of their own, the many mentions of her doll and cats in her letters became more extravagant and affectionate; at one point, she even sent a letter to her doll care of Murry. The childishness of this gesture captures something charmed and stunted in their relation: at their best, they were playful, radiant, romantic; at their worst, they were irresponsible and moody. It also explained their bewildering array of addresses: they played house as children tend to do, and they tired of playing house as children also tend to.

But as the years went on Katherine began to toy with the idea of a more complete, adult love. She didn't like the element of renunciation and misanthropy in Murry's character; it was beginning to wear on her that he was, as she put it, "a monk without a monastery." In some women there is the romance of rousing an untouchable, distant man to passion, and Katherine seems to have been one of those women, but she also felt the chill of a permanent, low-level rejection. In August of 1914 she confided in her journal, "I do not trust Jack. I'm old tonight. Ah I wish I had a lover to nurse me, hold me, comfort me, to stop me thinking." In this mood of disenchantment, she began to correspond with Murry's warm, high-spirited friend Francis

Carco, who was in Paris, and in the spirit of total honesty they subscribed to, she told Murry about this correspondence but he didn't seem particularly interested. "I was a strange creature," he observed. "There was little indeed of the conquering male about me."

In October they moved to the Rose Tree cottage near where their friends D.H. and Frieda Lawrence were staying in Chesham. Lawrence came over to help Murry with the preparation and painting of the cottage, and Murry's languid, ineffectual strokes with his paintbrush were so irritating to him that Lawrence finally growled, "*Get it done*."

That fall Lawrence and Frieda were not at their best. They often burst into violent, theatrical quarrels, and "the Murrys," as Lawrence called them, absorbed some of the tension (one of Lawrence's oddly archaic tics was that he liked to call unmarried couples by a fictional married name; he referred to himself and Frieda as "the Lawrences" long before they were legally married). Both Katherine and Murry were put off by what they saw as Lawrence's sex obsession; they didn't like to talk about and analyze sex constantly, the way Lawrence did; and they derisively nicknamed the Lawrences' cottage "The Phallus." Katherine explained primly, "I *shall never* see sex in trees, sex in running brooks, sex in stones and sex in everything." Some of her vehemence may have stemmed from jealousy of Murry's intense, almost worshipful attachment to Lawrence; both men were adamantly heterosexual, and both admitted to fascinations with men that bordered on the romantic. Murry generally liked to see other men as attracted to him, and himself as the passive, bewildered recipient of their interest, though this is how he liked to see all of his relations with the outside world.

Whatever its precise emotional composition, Lawrence and Murry's warm, volatile friendship, at that stage, absorbed them, and Katherine felt increasingly alone.

By Christmas, the strains in Katherine and Murry's relationship were beginning to show: it had been three years since they had met. They went to a Christmas party at the house of their mutual friends the Cannans. Everyone drank excessively, and no one was sober enough to carve the suckling pig. Cannan played the pianola, and the gathered company began to act out a play about "The Murrys." Katherine was to leave Murry for a man played by the striking Jewish painter Mark Gertler, who had black curly hair and the open, sensual face of a Roman statue. In the course of the drama, the actors' involvement became a little too convincing, and the two started kissing as everyone looked on. Katherine refused to leave Gertler and go back to Murry, as she was supposed to, according to urgent stage direction of the gathered playwrights. Frieda Lawrence took a drunk, tearful Gertler outside, under the stars, and told him that Katherine was wrong to seduce him. Lawrence then dragged Murry outside to ask him why on earth he allowed himself to be treated this way, which was a question the rumpled Katherine may have been asking herself as well. Murry's passivity *was* staggering; he was, after all, a man who called his own autobiographical novel *Still Life,* and admitted to "analyzing my own inward life to immobility." The Murrys were reconciled later that night—they were always reconciled—but Katherine was already planning to run off to France to see Francis Carco.

Katherine must have found it maddening that throughout this entire episode Murry's authentic response seemed to hover somewhere between indifference and the friendly concern that she might be disappointed by Carco. None of her provocations aroused anything more virile or possessive in him. He was very obviously willing, if not suspiciously eager, to let her go. On the day she got her passport, she met him in a café, aglow with guilt and excitement. But in his journal, Murry noted dryly: "It is curious that I wasn't jealous of her happiness nor inclined to wet-blanket it." After spending four pleasant but ultimately unremarkable days with Carco at his army base in France, Katherine returned to Murry.

Having devoted almost a year to drifting apart and together, Katherine and Murry finally moved into what appeared to be their perfect home in the south of France in January of 1916: a pink house with blue-gray shutters nestled high in the hills, with a flowering almond tree and white stone veranda, called Villa Pauline. In anticipation of Murry's arrival, Katherine went out and bought three dozen roses and six bunches of violets for the house. Everything was perfect. And for a time, they seemed to be finally living out their ideal life, squeezed together at the tiny kitchen table with Murry working on a study of Dostoyevsky, and Katherine writing a long autobiographical story about New Zealand that would become "The Prelude." Both of them would later look back at this as the happiest time in their lives, and perhaps it was. But they nonetheless left abruptly, after only three months. The ostensible reason was that the Lawrences had invited them to stay in a farmhouse in Cornwall. But that in itself does not seem like an adequate explanation for their flight, especially since their last stay with the Lawrences had been so unsettling. Why pack up and surrender this paradise, where they both had been working so well, where Murry said no two human beings were ever happier? One has to imagine there was something in the perfection, the two of them alone with the violet Mediterranean Sea, that threatened them.

In order to avoid conscription Murry found, through Ottoline Morrell's connections, a demanding job in the War Office (though one should note that Murry found all of his jobs demanding, and constantly complained of being dangerously overworked). Katherine lived for a while in a studio in Chelsea, and Murry lived in a ground-floor apartment on Redcliffe Road and the two would meet for dinner and then wander back through the darkened streets to their respective residences. Over the next few years they often lived apart, and their separations took on more and more significance. Ostensibly there were always reasons for them to live apart: she needed a warm climate for her health, which was already failing; he needed to work in London; or they were simply too consumed with work to live together. But the truth is that they had thrown off all practical concerns so many times that there had to be another explanation: their romantic dynamic was now largely structured around parting and being reunited.

Katherine wrote, "I feel our happiness will be simply without end when we are together again." Murry echoed, "I don't exist any longer—I am only a torment of longing to be with you." To read their unfolding correspondence is, in certain ways, an exercise in frustration. It is to read a fat romance novel and never get to the end: one feels the usual impatience, why can't these two characters come together? There are all of the elements—the yearning, the pining, the misunderstandings—but there is not, in the end, the climactic reconciliation;

or rather there are a million climactic reconciliations, one after another, that dissolve like waves in the ocean. But as can happen between writers (take, for instance, the correspondence of Flaubert and Louise Colet), the relationship had become curiously abstract, constructed almost entirely out of words: telegrams, letters, and notes had become the substance of their love, rather than the expression of it. They both seemed at times to revel in the despair of being apart, the lovely sensual anguish of it. Even when they agreed by a flurry of urgent letters and telegrams that they couldn't possibly live apart for another moment, they would somehow manage to remain, quite happily, ensconced on separate continents. In this way their relationship remained perfectly, purely romantic: unmarred by the sight of each other just out of bed or the deep familiarity of a sleeping body under sheets. Later, in a bitter mood, Katherine would call their relation "a nothingness shot through with gleams of what might be."

Murry was also, in his own inimitable way, pursuing other flirtations. In a revealing variation on the love letter, he wrote to their mutual friend Ottoline Morrell on August 31, 1916: "I have at times the queer suspicion that I must be in love with you. I don't know. It's very hard to get at what I feel; so rarely do I feel towards persons any emotion more intimate than amusement or blank terror." Not surprisingly, his overtures never amounted to more than one late-night walk through the garden at Garsington Manor, and a certain amount of excited conversation, but they do indicate that he was not quite living in the state of abject dependence on Katherine that he described so elaborately in his letters.

Katherine, during this same time, had cultivated her own

fairly intricate flirtation with Ottoline's longtime lover, Bertrand Russell, and less seriously, with Solomon Koteliansky, a brilliant Russian émigré whom everyone called "Kot," in addition to several other members of their extended literary circle. She knew how to enchant and bedazzle sensitive literary men, and she didn't hesitate to do so. But for both Murry and Katherine, other people were oddly beside the point: they remained obsessively engaged with each other, picking and prodding at their connection in spite of these theoretical forays into the outside world. There were times when the bond between them would be inscrutable to outside observers, and yet there was a mysterious fierceness to their attachment. They believed that their fluid, modern relationship was more challenging than a traditional marriage: with no legal vows binding them together, they had to wake up every morning and decide that they wanted to be together.

And then Katherine's always fragile health took a turn for the worse. In December of 1917 she came back from Garsington with a fairly bad chill, and later that month she was diagnosed with a spot on her lung that would become tuberculosis. In accordance with conventional wisdom, her doctor urged her to go abroad to seek out a milder climate, and so she moved to the Hotel Beau Rivage in Bandol, while Murry stayed in London to continue his work in the War Office. After a difficult passage, Katherine spent the bulk of her days in bed with fevers and a burning sensation in her lung, and at night she had insomnia and stayed up until dawn reading Dickens. In spite of these unpromising conditions, she was resolved to be productive: "If I am going to languish in foreign parts all alone I must have a great deal of work done—or it will be no use." This would be a constant refrain over the next few years: she was determined to turn her solitude into a blessing, her loneliness into words on the page. Most of the doctors she talked to advised her to go to a sanatorium in the mountains for a complete rest, which was the only treatment for tuberculosis at the time, but she believed that it would kill her to give up work. She needed to write, now more than ever. And she managed, in a heightened, exalted state of mind, to put her ideas down on paper. A few weeks later, she reported to Murry: "There is a great black bird flying over me, and I am so frightened he'll settle— so terrified. I don't know exactly what kind he is." And on February 19 she was shocked by coughing bright blood into her handkerchief. She immediately sent off an upbeat letter to Murry, downplaying the significance of the hemorrhage, and reassuring him that it was "absolutely curable." Her forced cheer is sad: she is clearly worried that her playfellow will wander off if he knows that she is sick.

Meanwhile Ida Baker left the munitions factory where she was working, and followed Katherine to be her nurse. On the surface this appears to be sheer exploitation, even "slavery," as Katherine once termed it, but Ida's loving participation came out of her own peculiar strength of character. In her memoirs, she wrote about caring for Katherine as her art: "Just as Katherine expressed herself in writing, I expressed myself in service." But when Ida arrived, she found a surly and ungrateful patient. Katherine resented Ida's solicitousness, and raged against her, claiming that Ida wanted to "eat" or "murder" her. Violent moods were believed to accompany consumption, but Ida also embodied Katherine's helplessness, was the living manifestation of her need. Even when she was healthy

Katherine kept Ida in a delicate, reeling balance: sometimes repelling her, sometimes pulling her closer. Ida later recalled that Katherine liked her to brush her hair, but if her hand accidentally grazed Katherine's neck or cheek, she would be furious. And then, of course, when she needed to, Katherine could be charming. "You seem so awfully like everyone else in your hat and jacket. Yes I only love you when you are blind to everybody but US. That's the truth." At times, Katherine acknowledged the terrible unfairness of what she demanded: "I take advantage of you—demand perfection of you—crush you" and she also referred to Ida, on more than one occasion, as her "wife."

In her illness, Katherine began to rely not only on Murry's letters to her but on hers to him. In some sense writing to him gave shape to her days: the long hours in bed, the glasses of hot milk, the endless fevers, the overheard snippets of conversation turning themselves into stories. Her letters were wonderful, humorous, perceptive, humming things. The fact that Katherine now spent so much time in bed or on lounge chairs made her focus with a kind of microscopic care on everything around her: a lizard eating an ant, a servant's little habits, the color of the sky. Take this fragment, written when she was quite sick:

Nearly all my days are spent in bed or if not in bed on a little sofa that always feels like lying in a railway carriage—a horrid little sofa. I have seen hardly any people at all since I've been here—*nobody* to talk to. The one great talker is the sea. It never is quiet; one feels sometimes as if one were a shell filled with a hollow sound. God forbid that another should ever live the life I have known here and yet there are *moments* you know, old Boy, when after a dark day there comes a sunset—such a glowing gorgeous marvelous sky that one forgets all in the beauty of it—these are the moments when I am *really writing*. Whatever happens I have had these blissful, perfect moments and they were worth living for.

There may also have been something in Murry's absence that Katherine found fertile. She wrote to him after finishing one of her stories. "All I write or ever ever will write will be the fruit of our love . . . Could I have done it without you? A million times, no." This effusiveness seems strange considering how distant a role he had in writing, how absent he was, at this point in her life, in every sense of the word. But Katherine now had the reassuring idea of Murry, without his sometimes troubling proximity, and the state of constant anticipation seemed to create the secure, yearning space she needed to write. In spite of her enormous struggle with her health, these would be Katherine's most productive years: she sat down and wrote the great stories—"The Man Without a Temperament," "The Garden Party," "Je ne Parle pas Français," "The Stranger"—that would inspire Virginia Woolf's comment that the only writer alive she was jealous of was Katherine Mansfield.

To Murry, not surprisingly, Katherine's illness often appeared to be something she was doing to *him*. He seemed at times to be almost exclusively focused on the poetic potential of his own devastation. He was undergoing what he described as "the most terrible mental struggle a man can undergo, when his love for a woman turns to pity." He wrote of her wasting and frailty to a friend and *Athenaeum* contributor, and in the next paragraph complained that he was suffering from "my own chronic overwork." Many of his letters to his tubercular wife, and hers to him, discuss, at length, his colds; and Murry also did his fair share of complaining to her about what her sickness was doing to him. In one such letter, Katherine circled the number of "I"s, like a schoolgirl studying for an exam, as if to remind herself of his character. She knew, as any clear-eyed expert on human foible would have to know, the extent of Murry's self-involvement, but she could allow herself to apprehend it only in flashes.

2

CHILD LOVE

In the weeks after her marriage, Katherine convalesced in a vast, comfortable hotel room in Looe. She thought her view was like a pretty Dutch painting with milky clouds and fishing boats bobbing on the ocean. Katherine always seemed to inspire protectiveness in hotel staff and maids, and it was no different here. The staff fussed and clucked over her, drawing her warm baths, serving her meals in bed, and stuffing her with puddings—she even managed to put on a little weight—but she still felt luxuriously stranded. She couldn't shake the idea that Murry was trying to get rid of her. From London, he wrote one of his usual extravagant letters about buying roses and musing on the secret of married love, but this time she was not going to allow his flights of romanticism and fired off a cutting response: "An idea . . . Are you really only happy when I am not there? Can you conceive yourself buying crimson roses and smiling at the flower woman if I were within 50 miles . . .

Isn't it true that if I were flourishing you would flourish ever so much more easily and abundantly without the strain of my actual presence?"

At the end of August 1918, the house at 2 Portland Villas, which they called "The Elephant," was finally ready, and the Murrys moved in, with Ida settling into the top-floor maid's quarters as the housekeeper. After all of their wanderings, they finally had a home. Katherine loved her study with its yellow-painted desk and a fur muff underneath for her to warm her feet; she loved the light that she thought suffused the room like the inside of a pale shell. She loved the cats that would arch their backs against her ankles and drink cream from a silver spoon. After migrating from hotels to rented rooms, it was the first time since childhood that Katherine had anything resembling a normal, settled household, with two maids and a cook, and that in itself was blissful. But there were two serious flaws in her new domestic life: one was her health, which was still faltering, still a source of great alarm, and the other was Murry, who was even more absent than usual. That winter he was appointed the editor of the literary journal the *Athenaeum,* which was a relatively stable and prestigious position for him. By this point, he had achieved a certain amount of prominence as a critic, with some, like the Woolfs, thinking him "a swindler" for somehow managing to turn cleverness into the illusion of literary seriousness. T. S. Eliot characterized some of his criticism as "hysterical admirations for great men who have what he lacks." In spite of Murry's comfortable new position, he no longer included Katherine in his intellectual life the way he used to. He forgot to bring home books that might interest her, and even forgot to bring her copies of the magazine;

and in his spare time he played tennis with their mutual friend Brett, who was inordinately fond of him. Katherine wrote, "All this hurts me horribly. But I like to face it and see all round it. He ought not have married. There never was a creature less fitted by nature for life with a woman." In September Katherine had to go to Italy to seek out a warmer climate for her health, and it was Ida, not Murry, who was to accompany her.

A picture of Katherine taken on her departure shows her with her hair untidily pinned up, a black veiled hat perched on her head, dark circles under her eyes, and the sad, transient aura of an ill-treated governess out of a nineteenth-century novel. It's not surprising, then, that when they arrived in San Remo, Katherine and Ida were turned away by a hotel that wouldn't countenance a conspicuously consumptive guest. The other patrons would be terrified of infection. Instead, the two women were offered a primitive villa in Ospedaletti, on a slope covered in olive and fig trees. There were lizards on the garden wall and the sound of cicadas rose through the wild grasses at night. Katherine slept under a mosquito net, and Ida slept on the couch in Katherine's bedroom. Katherine wanted her nearby. She was extremely weak—she found it hard, at times, to walk, or as she put it, creep across a room. She wrote to Virginia Woolf that she wished she could be an alligator, the one creature on earth physically incapable of coughing. But through all of this she was still working. In fact, she was still working at the top of her form. When she finished a story in the middle of the night, she woke Ida up for a "celebration with tea" and the two of them ate sandwiches in their nightgowns like schoolgirls and watched the sun rise through the branches.

Katherine still longed for Murry. She waited impatiently for his arrival. But when he finally came to visit for two weeks in January of 1919, he slept in his own room, and Katherine instructed Ida to slip back into her room discreetly and sleep on the couch as usual. One wonders about this sleeping arrangement. Was he afraid of infection? Did her coughing irritate him? Or had they tacitly separated in a physical sense as she became sicker? At the end of the month, Murry left for London carrying some figs from their garden in his suitcase. He had to get back to the *Athenaeum* offices, and to his house, which he now shared with Katherine's cousin Sydney Waterlow, and which had become something of a social hub, with writers like E. M. Forster dropping in frequently. Katherine did not quite accept the necessity of his departure. Her letters, for the most part, were still full of sweetness and verve, but she was beginning to lash out at him in her fiction. Dashing, weak-willed men bearing a strong resemblance to Murry began to populate her stories. She took up the rich subject of how husbands fail wives and wives fail husbands. Would she have been able to do this quite as spectacularly if she hadn't been angry at Murry? It may be that the cold fury in her life served her well in her art. She also sent Murry a far from oblique poem about a man who leaves his sick wife alone: "Who's your man to leave you be / ill and cold in a far country / Who's the husband, who's the stone, / would leave a child like you alone?"

Murry was bewildered and hurt by her anger and resentment. He felt that it was entirely unfair. He had convinced himself that he was working for their future, that he was living comfortably in London for her sake, that he only wanted to earn money, and enjoy the company of the literary world to gain a better foothold, for *her*. But can he possibly have believed this? They had always kept separate bank accounts, and on one occasion Katherine confided to Ida, he asked her to reimburse him a few pounds for a cab ride to the doctor. For her this was a dark, appalling confession about the nature of her marriage: he had not wanted to pay for his wife's trip to the doctor. One night over dinner he told Leonard and Virginia Woolf that he managed to assuage his conscience with a compartmentalizing philosophy he invented called "Indifferentism," and he did seem to have quite a flair for it. Occasionally, he glimpsed aspects of his moral failure, but for him the interesting subject, as usual, was himself: "I am afraid the evidence is more impressive than I was inclined to allow that I am not quite human."

With all of their violent swings between rage and adoration, one constant feature of the Murrys' correspondence was their enduring fantasy about real estate. They poured a great deal of energy into the shared dream of a house; wherever they were, they would constantly pick out small houses with gardens that could be *their* house. In some sense their relationship took place in these fantastical places: they lived and breakfasted and gardened in them; they were sustaining, brick-and-mortar places for their best intentions, or in their private lingua franca of childhood, "fortresses" and "hiding places." They named their dream house or farm "Heron Farm" or "Herongate," and over the years they would pick out china, or imagine hanging saucepans, or name pets, or sort through the exact shade of jonquil or rose they would plant, with astonishing specificity. In some way, of course, the "Heron" was a code they developed to talk about the almost unspeakable hopes they had for

Katherine's health: it gave them a language to discuss a shared future they both feared would be cut short by her death. Katherine wrote with particular passion about digging and planting, a wishful picture of a physical vigor she no longer possessed. This pleasant mutual imagining was what they were best at, and they plotted the life they would lead, down to touchingly mundane details: "In the evenings we'll sit at the table with the lamp between us and work & then we'll make something hot to drink & have small talk and a smoke." The most banal routines of normal life had become the exotic pinnacle, the impossible culmination of perfect happiness for them. But the fanciful nature of these imaginings crept in as well: Katherine wrote, "I feel we must keep bees, a cow, fowls, 2 turkeys, some indian runner ducks, a *goat*, and perhaps one thoroughly striking beast like a unicorn or a dragon."

But as always, the idealized future was in conflict with the complicated present. And during the long, difficult winter of 1920, Murry made darting romantic approaches to various other women. At this point Katherine was living in Menton, at the Villa Isola Bella, a grand stone house with a stucco roof surrounded by tangerine and palm trees, and a view down to the sea. A picture Ida took of Katherine in the wild grassy garden shows her thinner than she had ever been, with dark half moons under her eyes, leaning on an umbrella, fierce and tired. Katherine was unsure how to respond from her isolated perch to the hints of Murry's liaisons. She and Murry had been together for more than eight years.

For a few weeks in December, he seemed, in fact, to be veering out of control. One night he found himself picking up a prostitute near the Leicester Square tube station; since he had absolutely no desire to sleep with her, he took her out to dinner for a friendly talk, and paid her for her time. He kissed one woman at a dinner party, and another on the walk home; he called Katherine's friend Brett in the middle of the night and went round to her flat and kissed her; and then he kissed the prime minister's beautiful, married daughter, Princess Elizabeth Bibesco, whom he had just met, in a motor car. This frantic flurry of contact was duly represented in a long, honest letter to Katherine, who replied with a telegram: "Stop tormenting me with these false depressing letters be a man or don't write me, Tig."

In his memoirs, Murry claimed to be bewildered that so many people of both sexes succumbed to his "personal charms," but they had all his life. There was something of the orphan left on a doorstep in the way he presented himself to women. He was the kind of man who used crisis, in all of its manifestations—not eating or not sleeping, for instance—as a mode of seduction. His sudden bursts of desperation created a tear in the normal social reserve, which brought women closer to him. He also managed to be both coldly self-involved and extremely needy, which proved to be an irresistible combination to women with strong personalities who did not want to be entirely in control.

That winter Murry had two serious affairs, one with the horsey, adoring Brett, who carried around an ear trumpet because she was hard of hearing. (D. H. Lawrence wrote about her: "She is one of the sisters of this life, her role is always to be a sister.") The other was with the glamorous, somewhat mechanical Princess Elizabeth Bibesco, who wanted to be a writer. Of the two, the princess was the more serious rival. She had black hair, a heart-shaped face, and lips painted bright red. She was married, but she was infatuated with Murry. Ottoline Morrell said of her: "She is like a quick ticker tape machine, ticking out aphorisms and anecdotes which are all neatly ready-made inside her box." Elizabeth couldn't see how Murry should be so enthralled by a woman so near death. For her part, Katherine struggled to be modern about these attachments.

> I was blind not to have understood the Brett affair—but no—that *was* "wrong" as we say. However *do feel free*. I mean that. What happens in your personal life does not affect me. . . . I have of you what I want—a relationship which is not what the world understands by marriage. That is to say I do not in any way depend on you, neither can you shake me . . . I am a writer first.

Unfortunately for Katherine this retreat into her role as artist was mostly wishful thinking. Much as she wanted it to, her unquestionable devotion to her art did not take the place of a steadfast husband. And a rather influential part of her was extremely old-fashioned; in spite of her nom de plume, she had not entirely left behind the Beauchamps of New Zealand. When Murry announced that he would be publishing one of Princess Bibesco's wooden stories in the *Athenaeum,* Katherine announced an end to her own contributions. In some sense all the Murrys' vaunted communication, their relentless, permissive honesty would not be useful to them. In one of her stories, "Bliss," Katherine writes archly: "They were so frank with each other—such good pals. That was the best of being modern."

And of course, it is exactly that "modern" sensibility that fails her. In an excruciating letter about an upcoming visit of his to Garsington Katherine wrote with wincing embarrassment about her jealousy as a kind of weakness, a failure of character: she expressed it tentatively, and then retreated and then expressed it again. Was it fair to ask Murry not to kiss other women? Was it acceptable for him to pursue other affairs? Katherine's tentativeness was unlike her. In some way, she was groping toward a new etiquette. They had always relied on the idea that either one of them was free to wander off at any time. They believed their pioneering love was so enduring that it need not be tethered to the earth by the usual promises. But now Katherine was trapped by her own poetic excesses. In spite of her occasional flashes of bitterness and anger, she and Murry had so idealized their connection that it now seemed almost an insult to admit that it was susceptible to run-of-the-mill jealousies. Was this rare, resplendent love really no better than anyone else's? By spring, Katherine seemed to have resolved at least some of these issues for herself when she sent off a small masterpiece of condescension warning Princess Bibesco not to send love letters to her husband. Privately, she wrote of her, "She made me think of a *gull,* with an absolutely insatiable appetite for bread."

Both Murry and Katherine felt that what was at stake was their entire conception of "child love." Their childlike connection, radiant, romantic, at least in bursts when all was well, was not adequate in a crisis; it couldn't function the way a more pedestrian relationship functions, when one of them fell seriously ill. They had never been ideal helpmates in the best of times. And now the visceral deterioration of a diseased body was too much to bear. They simply couldn't subsist without the fairy dust of enchantment, two pretty children traipsing through the fallen world. As Katherine noted tersely, "I had stopped his play." The ideas of duty or nurturing, or one of them rising to the occasion as a responsible adult, were alien to them, and to the mythology they had created. And even Murry had to admit that they hadn't gained much by being "dream-children."

Katherine's choice of reading material during her months in Switzerland was revealing. In the evenings she sat by the fire and immersed herself in the volumes of Jane Austen she borrowed from the extensive library of her cousin, Elizabeth von Arnim. She reported to Ottoline Morrell: "It's such an exquisite comfort to escape from the modern novels I have been forcibly reading. Wretched affairs! This fascinated pursuit of the sex adventure is beyond words boring! I am so bored by sex quâ sex, by the gay dog sniffing round the prostitutes bedroom or by the ultra modern snigger—worse still—that I could die." In more ways than one, the nineteenth-century grandeur and clarity of Austen's marriage plots were beginning to appeal. Katherine admired Austen's writing enormously. But was she also beginning to wish that she had lived like someone out of an Austen novel?

For Katherine, the trinkets of conventional life—which she had actively been trying to distance herself from since she was a plump serious child in glasses—began to take on an almost exotic allure. She wrote, for instance, of Ottoline's china and cutlery at Garsington: "I think of her breakfast cups now & her spoons with the tenderness of a burglar. I must say I do love civilized ways." All the teacups and saucers she hadn't bothered to accumulate in her countless, vanished residences now signified domestic security, a near mystical protection against hardship. She was also jealous of Virginia Woolf for what little stability Virginia had shored against her own illness: "There is always in her writing a calm freedom of expression as though she were at peace—her roof over her, her possessions round her, and her man somewhere within call." Where was the Katherine Mansfield who answered the door in a kimono and served tea in giant bowls on bamboo mats on the floor? Where was Käthe Beauchamp–Bowden, mysterious, pregnant traveler in Bavarian hotels? Perhaps it is not surprising that she had faded. Sexual boldness or creativity in romantic arrangements requires a sense of immortality: any brush with pain, or physical frailty, puts the preciousness of love in perspective. In sickness, one begins to yearn for the old structures and certainties: a man who loves you in the next room.

For his part, Murry continued to fail her. He also continued to love and revere her. Virginia Woolf wrote about a tête-à-tête they had during this period: "Poor man! He poured himself out. . . . I liked him, felt with him, & I think there can be no doubt that his love for Katherine anyhow is sincere." His infidelities and his inability to stand by Katherine during her illness did not appear to him to reflect on his basic feeling. He seemed to believe, like many of their contemporaries, that honesty itself would exonerate him. One didn't have to behave well, one simply had to tell the *truth* about one's bad behavior. He could not bear her sickness and decline. He could not stand by her: "The last four years have taken what little courage I had—and I never had any. That is a ghastly confession for a man who is well to make to his wife who is ill. I am utterly ashamed.

But what can I do? I fight against it. But when the moment comes I am just petrified with fear. I can't move."

For years, D. H. Lawrence had been telling Murry that he should be a man and join Katherine abroad. And at this point, finally, Murry saw his way to taking his advice. He resigned from the *Athenaeum,* which was failing in any event, and in June of 1921 he joined Katherine in Europe. He was still stewing in frustrated ambition. Virginia Woolf wrote, "In my theory he's all parched for praise—run mad for the lack of it." In search of crisp, restorative air for Katherine's lungs, they settled in a dark wooden chalet in Montana-sur-Sierre in Switzerland. Katherine's short story collection, *Bliss and Other Stories,* had been a huge success, and there was suddenly a great demand for her economical, perfectly crafted stories. She was now considered by hungry editors an expert on the elusive and fashionable subject of Modern Love. But with snow hanging like clean linen on the pine trees, as she put it, Katherine began, cautiously, to enjoy her time with Murry. The rooms were small and fairly dark, but Katherine's had a balcony overlooking the mountains from which she liked to watch the pale sun melt like a peppermint in the sky. Katherine read, and Murry learned skating and skiing. They occasionally saw Katherine's cousin Elizabeth von Arnim, now a bestselling memoirist, who was living at her grand Chalet Soleil nearby. At first Katherine had been skeptical about Elizabeth. She did not see her as a serious writer, and she was inclined to dislike her for her commercial success. She had, in fact, written to Ottoline, "Elizabeth is coming over without her german garden. How tiresome she will be." But after very little time, she had grown extremely fond of her.

By this time, Katherine understood Murry's limitations as thoroughly as one of her own characters; and still, the irrational, floating love for him persisted. He was selfish, childlike, morbidly sensitive, and yet she couldn't help being charmed. There persisted, in spite of her illness, a profoundly physical admiration for him: his lean limbs, his boyish back, his high color when he came back from skiing. In spite of his thinning hair, she thought he still looked young and splendid. But he also managed, in the middle of the Swiss Alps, to be elusive. She wrote in her journal, "It's a long time now since he started going out every evening. I can't stop him. I've tried everything but it's useless. Out he goes. And the horrible thing is I don't know where he goes and who he is with."

At the beginning of 1922, Katherine left Murry in Montana-sur-Sierre to seek out Dr. Manoukhin's expensive new treatment in Paris, which was said to have worked miracles on Russian soldiers and which involved a series of primitive radiation treatments to the spleen, called séances. Katherine was taken in by Dr. Manoukhin's promise, alone among the doctors she had consulted, that she would be cured. In the end, the painful and crippling treatments did more harm than good. The burning pain, she wrote to Brett, was astonishing: "If I were a proper martyr I should begin to have that awful smile that martyrs in the flame put on when they begin to sizzle . . ." Katherine subjected herself to these debilitating, dubious treatments because she still hoped for a normal life: the months with Murry in Switzerland had given her a taste of what their life together could be. The only obstacle now seemed to be her health.

Murry stayed behind and allowed Ida to accompany

Katherine to Paris to meet Dr. Manoukhin. He was mired in another of his lifeless novels, *The Things We Are,* and felt he was writing well in their Swiss chalet. As usual he did not see the need for them to be physically together. "This love, which devoured her so, demanded for its fulfillment that she should never leave me, nor I her. It meant, in the world of cold reality, that I should stand by and simply watch her die." He seemed to be under the impression that remaining with her when she was sick was the most outrageous request that any wife has ever made of her husband.

By March, Katherine had gained a little weight and was feeling better. She was able to return to some semblance of her normal Parisian life: museums, dinners, and James Joyce coming over for tea. Her improvement was marked enough that Ida decided it was safe for her to return to London. She was planning to start a tea shop with a friend. She had finally resolved to have her own life. But after an arduous trip back to Switzerland with Murry, Katherine was already regretting Ida's absence. Murry found any sign of her illness so alarming that Katherine felt pressure to be cheerful and hide her fatigue and weakness, and the effort of dissembling drained all the energy that she needed to write. She wrote a desperate letter to Ida imploring her to abandon the tea shop, and come back, and to write a fake letter begging to come for her own sake, so that Murry would never suspect that Katherine had sent for her. These labyrinthine arrangements were all to spare Murry's feelings; he could not nurture. Katherine was feeling weak again. Instead of a husband, she needed a wife.

As a writer, Katherine was maturing. During the years of her illness, her will was beaten into a kind of iron: "If 'suffering' is not a repairing process, I will make it so. I will learn the lesson it teaches. These are not idle words." She was being pared down into a kind of vibrating strength, and this intense focus would affect her prose. No flaming sky, no casual exchange with a waiter would be lost. Her writing had a leanness and muscle now. As an invalid she stood outside of life, and could look at it more clearly. She felt her illness was part of her calling; it put her in a unique position to *see*. In other words, she was determined to convert suffering into words on the page. She would force her illness to be a gift.

> And then suffering, bodily suffering such as I've known for three years. It has changed forever everything—even the *appearance* of the world is not the same—there is something added. *Everything has its shadow.* Is it right to resist such suffering? DO you know I feel it has been an immense privilege?

Katherine now wrote in great, fevered rushes of inspiration, sometimes staying up for days writing a story and exhausting herself. Did she write better, more lucidly, more originally, because of her tuberculosis? The fever, she sometimes felt, burned through her consciousness and made everything more beautiful. Was this simply the romanticism of the day surrounding tuberculosis, or her own need for consolation? All the petty things that had occupied and distracted her fell away. She was all nerve and art. In February, Katherine's new collection, *The Garden Party and Other Stories,* came out to enormous critical acclaim; even Rebecca West, renowned for her fierceness, praised the book's astonishing economy in the *New Statesman.* Katherine was at the height of her craft. At a time when most writers didn't bother with short stories, the threat of an early ending had profoundly affected Katherine's style. She once complained that her stories were like "birds bred in cages," but that concentrated atmosphere, that claustrophobic hothouse of emotion, was her talent. Her stories were little masterpieces of compression: she succinctly contained whole lifetimes in a few pages, every moment loaded with as much as it could bear.

In August of 1922, the thirty-three-year-old writer left her last will and testament in her banker's safekeeping. She left almost everything to Murry—the rights to her books, her money, her letters and journals; she left her daisy pearl ring to Murry's brother; a book to D. H. Lawrence; her annotated Shakespeare to her cousin Elizabeth von Arnim; and to Ida she left a gold watch on a chain. She instructed Murry to burn as many of her papers as possible, but if she had truly wanted them burned, it seems likely that she would have left that task to the more reliable Ida. She also mentioned that she did not want a tombstone.

That fall, Katherine became preoccupied with something larger than her romantic dissatisfactions. She began to read *Cosmic Anatomy and the Structure of the Ego* and other books about the occult. Her sweeping romantic ideas about love were slowly being replaced by sweeping romantic ideas about spiritualism: she particularly needed to believe in the spirit's merging into the natural world. During this time, she fell under the sway of the magnetic George Ivanovitch Gurdjieff, with his dark, hooded eyes and Persian-lamb hat. In October of 1922, she moved to his Institute for the Harmonious Development of

Man at Fontainebleau in a fourteenth-century monastery, which was essentially an imitation of a Russian peasant village. Gurdjieff subjected his neurasthenic, arty disciples to manual labor, though Katherine was too ill to do much besides peel vegetables. For most of her stay, Katherine was given one of the grand rooms, with antique furnishings, engravings, empire mirrors, and a view down to the formal garden. At one point, following an ancient peasant cure, she was suspended above cow dung, on a wooden platform covered with divans and Persian carpets. She had come to believe that the problem was in her mind not her body, that if she could spiritually cleanse herself she might somehow clear her lungs. She had, by this point, given up most of her possessions—she kept a fur coat for warmth, but that was it. She was, half consciously, preparing herself to die.

Katherine wrote to inform Murry that she had moved beyond their personal love. She said that she didn't want to see him, at least not for a long time. And then, all of a sudden, she changed her mind. In fact, she urgently needed to see him, and it had to be sooner than the visit they had planned that spring. She wanted him to come in January. Her desire to rid herself of the heavy encumbrance of need had failed. She remained connected to life by her faith in the rather faithless and tattered abstraction: Murry. Did it matter that she didn't have him there, a quiet, calming presence at her bedside? She had never had him there. Her love for him had always existed quite independent of his actions. Her idea of him, as in many marriages, was more powerful, more fiercely potent than any mere reality. She told him to pack warm clothes and to bring a suit, because she still cared how he appeared, still had that remnant of vanity: she wanted her husband to appear respectable in her new community.

In her work, Katherine was a connoisseur of loneliness. She wrote about women eating alone in cafés in Paris. She wrote about spinsters with dolls, and old ladies in furs sitting on park benches wanting to feel part of the world. She wrote about invalid wives stretched out on chaise longues in foreign villas and wives watching their husbands kiss other women; in story after story she cut through layers of delusion and consolation to reveal a fundamental human solitude, and at this point in her life she was almost uniquely qualified to see her own. She was also a talented writer, and she was able to write for herself a spectacular dream, all the while knowing it was a dream. In the same spirit perhaps as a sick person takes a morphine drip, she needed love. She wrote, rather remarkably, in her will: "In spite of everything—how happy we have been. I feel no other lovers have walked the earth more joyfully—in spite of all." And as she wrote these words, they were not a lie. Katherine felt, in her extraordinary gossamer connection with Murry, something sustaining; in the end, it was not his love for her that would sustain her, but rather her love for him. In one of her last journal entries, she faces death:

Fear. Fear of what? Doesn't it come down to the fear of losing J.? I believe it does. But, good heavens, face things. What have you of him now? He talks to you—sometimes—and then goes off. You are important to him as a dream. Yet there is a deep, sweet tender flooding of feeling in my heart which is love for him and longing for him.

When Murry arrived at the institute on January 9, 1923, Katherine announced that she had taken what she needed from Gurdjieff. Fairly soon, she told him, she would be able to move back to England and live with him in a simple country cottage, where he could farm the land. Here was the Heron, still beating its wings. It is not surprising then, that later that evening, her last gesture on earth was running up the stairs without holding the banister with Murry behind her, like a healthy girl bounding up to bed with her lover, and then falling into a coughing fit, and hemorrhaging from the mouth. A visibly panicked Murry helped her to her room and ran to get the doctors. With her hand covering her mouth, she managed to get out the words: "I believe I am going to die." She tried to meet Murry's eyes as the doctors crowded around her, but he allowed himself to be herded out of the room.

Her hearse, bearing a plain white coffin, was led through the narrow cobblestoned streets by black-plumed horses. Her gravestone at a cemetery near Fontainebleau reads, *Katherine Mansfield, Wife of John Middleton Murry.*

FRANK RUSSELL

ELIZABETH VON ARNIM

"Perhaps husbands have never altogether agreed with me."

—Elizabeth von Arnim

SEPTEMBER 27, 1918. A little after dusk, Countess Elizabeth Russell was on the deck of the *Adriatic,* en route to New York to meet her daughter Liebet. As she watched the lights of the shoreline vanish into a thin glowing line over the black sea, she thought about her husband, John Francis Stanley Russell, from whom she had fled without a word. When she left, he had been away on a business trip. With the collusion of the servants, who were for their own reasons extremely sympathetic to her cause, Elizabeth had packed her many suitcases and left Telegraph House with all the drama and secrecy of the fugitive she felt herself to be. "I am practically in prison," she had written to her daughter the month before. "Within the limits of the wire fencing I can go and come if I have first asked if I may go for a walk, but to get outside it means almost every time bad blood." With the wet wind on her face, it seemed almost unthinkable that she would have to ask permission to leave her own house. Who could have imagined that one of England's most independent, successful authors would allow herself to be locked up and subjected to her husband's violent moods? She was determined to clear her head. There had been many precipitating events. But the most recent of them had occurred a few weeks earlier, when she had discovered a stash of cocaine in his study. When she confronted him, he had confessed that he was in the habit of inhaling it, and then the next morning in a fury had denied it, had claimed she invented the whole episode out of some special depravity in her character. This was one of Russell's extravagant peculiarities: he had an infinite capacity for righteous indignation, no matter how incriminating the circumstance. He blamed her for the entire incident with the cocaine. He felt deeply wronged, even wounded.

When Countess Russell and her daughter reached the cottage in the Catskills, she would tell Liebet not to let her contact him under any circumstances because she couldn't trust herself not to return to him. In her bags she had packed the hardback school exercise books in which she liked to write her successful, occasionally sentimental novels.

Anyone watching her on deck would have a seen a tiny, sylphlike figure in a large floppy hat. She was five feet tall and very slight. At first glance she looked like a girl, though she was in fact a little over fifty. There is a stunning, ageless photograph of her at around this time: a long string of pearls around her neck, bobbed hair, thin aristocratic mouth, and pale lively eyes. There was so much of the gamine about her that wherever she went people were shocked to find that she had five grown children. When one of her husband's friends came across her driving a car he had to look twice because he thought he was seeing a small child behind the wheel. Part of this, of course, was her diminutive stature. But it also seemed as if age would not dare mark her face: she was someone who did not quite take experience to heart, who was determined at all cost to remain fresh.

In 1898, Elizabeth's captivating first book, *Elizabeth and Her German Garden,* published anonymously, had been an instant sensation, a bestseller, going into printing after printing over the next decade. The publication sparked international public speculation: who *was* Elizabeth of the German garden?

Living in an ivy-covered sixteenth-century estate in Germany, the anonymous hausfrau had written a lighthearted journal of her garden, her husband, whom she referred to only as "The Man of Wrath," and her three small daughters, Evi, Trix, and Liebet, whom she referred to only as "the April, May, and June babies." She wrote about the ephemera of her daily life: "Today I am writing on the veranda with the three babies, more persistent than mosquitoes, raging round me, and already several of the thirty fingers have been in the ink-pot and the owners consoled when duty pointed to rebukes. But who can rebuke such penitent and drooping sunbonnets?" About her husband, she wrote: "One would just as soon be playful with a graven image." Her personality sold books: there was nothing else in them. And yet her story was densely atmospheric, the perfect book for Edwardian times: the perfumed ambience of her country estate was permeated by tensions between the sexes, but these tensions were presented in an entirely non-threatening way. In a time of both intense nostalgia and fermenting change, Elizabeth's gentle, mocking, good-natured questioning of the social order was exactly what the moment called for. Though she had embarked on a serious critique of the institution of marriage, the book had a light, teasing tone; it was a charming birdcall of a protest.

Elizabeth had always deplored the methods of the suffragettes as too crude and obvious: she preferred revolution through charm, and she drew her power from the drawing-room art of conversation. H. G. Wells, with whom she had a long happy affair, wrote: "She mingled adventurousness with extreme conventionality in a very piquant manner." After the enormous success of her first book, Elizabeth went on to write several minor classics of the gentler forms of feminism: *The Caravaners, The Adventures of Elizabeth in Rügen* and *The Enchanted April* urged women to leave their domestic responsibilities and see the world. *The Caravaners* was based on a trip she had taken with her girls and their tutor, the aspiring novelist E. M. Forster, caravanning through the English countryside with vans and horses and tents—a style of travel that was considered extremely gypsyish and eccentric for a person of her social class. On this trip, she had found the time to visit Henry James at his house in Rye. In her high flirtatious mode, she asked him if she could stay on with him, as a kind of female Boswell. He replied, "My dear, that would be a very long squeezing out of a completely dry sponge." After the book appeared, Elizabeth had scores of fans and imitators, and in certain parts of England, one would see small groups of women vacationing together in the spirit of her heroines. Rebecca West, who had been her rival for the attention of H. G. Wells, wickedly mocked her for "her early successes which saw innumerable tiresome women all over England, smirking coyly about their gardens as if they were having a remarkably satisfying affair with their delphiniums."

But it was before she became the famous Elizabeth that the Countess von Arnim first encountered John Francis Russell.

She had been born Mary, or "May," Beauchamp in New Zealand, the first cousin of Kathleen Beauchamp, who later became Katherine Mansfield; she married a German aristocrat named Henning von Arnim in 1891, and became Countess von Arnim. Three years later, May was in London visiting her parents on one of her increasingly frequent flights from domestic life in Germany, when she met John Francis Russell at a performance of Sarah Bernhardt's. Elizabeth was plainer and more matronly then, a plumpish German hausfrau with her hair swept on top of her head in a complicated arrangement with a comb; only her pale blue eyes bespoke restlessness, a lively, charismatic discontent. Earl Russell was a reedy young man, with longish blond curly hair, steel blue eyes, a faint rakish mustache, a tweed suit, a cane, and according to his good friend the American philosopher George Santayana, the general mien of a well-fed tiger. Her conversation was light, mesmerizing. She felt burdened by domestic life, and in the plushness and fantasy of the theater, she felt free. They began attending more of Bernhardt's performances together, and somehow under the spell of the great actress, the married countess and the young earl imagined that they might be in love. They wrote each other artful letters. And in the one mention of her in his memoirs, *My Life and Adventures,* Earl Russell claimed that he left for America to flee the attachment. He found Countess von Arnim enormously attractive, her company exhilarating, feminine, yet sharply intelligent, but he wondered about her morals—why would a married woman entertain so intense a flirtation?—and could not imagine a serious outcome to his infatuation.

2

GREAT LOVE

After the count's death in 1910, Elizabeth, now a celebrated author, built a monument to her new independence: a sprawling, sixteen-bedroom chalet in the Swiss Alps, where she entertained vast numbers of houseguests, including her five children Liebet, Eva, Beatrix, Martin, and Henning Bernd, who was called HB, their friends and admirers, and sundry suitors of her own. The pretty dark wood Chalet Soleil was set in the steep ledge of a mountain, surrounded by beds of irises and cherry trees, with the sweep of the valley below. Elizabeth attributed great powers to the setting, to the altitude, to the brisk mountain air; it was one of her romantic notions that the chalet clarified and exaggerated emotion, that it endowed her guests with intensities of feeling they would not normally experience.

The most remarkable aspect of the chalet's design was a secret door between Elizabeth's bedroom and the one next door. The door was carefully hidden behind a large wardrobe with well-oiled castors so that at night one could slide it aside with relative ease and creep into the next room without any noise in the hallways. Elizabeth had commissioned this highly unusual feature so that her lover, H. G. Wells, could visit her at night without the knowledge of other guests. She and Wells had begun their pleasant, companionable affair in 1910, after her husband's death, and it lasted for almost three years. They took holidays in Amsterdam, Paris, Florence, Ypres, Orta. On one occasion, they visited her friend Earl Russell's Telegraph House, and groped their way down the dark corridors into each other's rooms. When they were staying in the chalet, they would walk and chatter and take siestas on the pine needles, and wolf down giant lunches of bread and ham and beer and fruit. Wells enjoyed her talk. There was an ease to their relations that was not emotionally promising. And their affair ended when "little e" began to needle him about his closeness to his wife. He was protective of his wife, and did not like her to be abused by his mistresses. In one of their conflicts, Elizabeth accused him of being "half of a lover." Shortly thereafter, he took up with the rising young journalist Rebecca West.

In the late fall of 1913, Wells arrived at the chalet with a suitcase. He was seeking to resume his relationship with Elizabeth, though by this time he was aware of the fact that his new mistress, Rebecca, was pregnant with his child. As they stood together on the terrace, the mountain snow silver in the moonlight, he confided to Elizabeth that Rebecca had conceived a child during their second sexual encounter. He knew that it was his fault, of course, as the experienced party, but he wanted Elizabeth to comfort him. He was expecting the kind of capacious sympathy and acceptance his wife routinely offered. He was expecting the female succor that usually came so easily to him. That night, in his usual bedroom, he waited for hours for her to come through their secret door, but it remained shut. He sat up in the dark. When he left a week later, he chastised her for not loving him enough: "It's because I am common, isn't it?" he asked. That he had a pregnant mistress appeared not to have occurred to him as a possible reason for her rejection. By this point, Elizabeth was losing interest in affectionate trysts. The sheer disorder of Wells's life had lost its appeal. For her there was something sad in her conversation with him on the veranda, a twinkling of mortality in these freighted confidences between old friends. Was all of his celebrated libertinism too much? Was there something unhealthy in the easy intimacy she had with him? Were there no more lines to be drawn? The next morning, as she watched Wells leave from her veranda, she had the feeling of a fever breaking. Afterward her housekeeper noted a great deal of weeping. It was against the backdrop of this extravagant romantic failure that the next episode of her life was to occur.

Elizabeth would later claim that she ran into John Francis Russell in London, and casually invited him to visit her because she knew he wouldn't come. The truth of her motives may have been a bit more complicated, as she had, in fact, invited him to spend Christmas with her, without his stout, blue-eyed wife, Mollie, even though she knew this omission would be controversial. She must also have remembered their whispered flirtation in the plush velvet seats of the theater nearly two decades earlier. They had remained friends over the years, with him sending her an eccentric book he had written on religious feeling, and her praising it lavishly. He had never ceased to be interesting to her.

Russell began the visit with a characteristic moment of imperiousness. As he walked in, he told his hostess to put cinders on the snow-covered walkway. This in itself appears to have endeared him to her. She did not like the way the cinders looked on her walkway, but was taken with the way he had immediately inserted himself into her domestic affairs. She felt as if he were taking care of her.

By this time Russell had rather dramatically lost the attractiveness of his youth, but he retained a certain upper-class presence, a belief in his place in the empire. A photograph from this time shows him on his yacht: a pipe in his mouth, wire-rimmed glasses, stomach swelling against his waistcoat, which was strung together by a gold watch chain: he looked fatherly, solid. And his comfortably aged appearance may have accounted for part of Elizabeth's inexplicable impression of him on this visit as "a reliable, kind, simple, restful man."

Elizabeth's enormous chocolate brown dog, Coco, who had an uncanny nose for suitors, pawed and welcomed the earl with unprecedented enthusiasm. Several of the human inhabitants also warmed to him immediately. Elizabeth's daughter Evi would comment that he was "a perfect dear—so large and simple and truly great." He was a very good talker, a charming, intense presence when he wanted to be. George Santayana noted "his quick intelligence turned upon common things, enquiringly, fearlessly, and universally." And gradually Elizabeth began to notice that she herself was not treating him like the rest of her guests. She began to serve the earl's preferred foods at every meal, which was mostly leg of mutton. She made sure he had the chair he liked. "I can't account for my behavior," she wrote. "I had never before felt any desire to serve, to obey, to stand with bowed head, and hands folded, to be, as it were, the handmaid of the lord. But from the first I was weak and pliable, giving in without a struggle, overcome by that strange sensation of God's hands." What she was experiencing in part was an overwhelming physical attraction. The two spent the next few weeks shut off from the other guests, immersed in their private courtship. But after he left she told the maid to eat whatever leftover mutton there was in the kitchen, and to bring her poached eggs for dinner. She'd had enough of red meat.

From his family estate, Russell wrote to her, "I love you, and it's not with the greed and possessive love I've had for women before but as if the feeling one has for lights on crystals and clean water, the feeling of beauty in deep delicate things has become personified and exalted." Elizabeth found herself reciprocating: this seemed to be a purer, more urgent love than any she had experienced before. But she also began to notice certain warning signs. His moods were electric, at times oppressive. He worked himself into excessively angry states about life's million minor frustrations. It was almost as if one could feel the air pressure rearrange itself around him. When his motorcar broke down he ordered her around with a startling new brusqueness as if she were a chauffeur changing the tire. His abrupt storms and shifts bewildered her, and Elizabeth's diary entries from that fall reflect the great fluctuations in her attitude toward him.

> Nov. 15. F. arrived but was so despotic that I didn't like it at all. Had difficulty remembering that I have a separate spirit. . . .
>
> Nov 22. F. came in for half an hour on his way to London and brought me some flowers and was very dear.
>
> Nov. 28. F arrived at 3 for night, very dear and cheerful. Happy and mirthful afternoon and evening, he telling stories of his various resistances to injustice . . .

Given the minutiae of the record, it is hard to see how Elizabeth could overlook the accumulating evidence of his difficulties. She so wanted to believe in the sweet, attentive Russell that she was willing to forget how he had behaved the day, the hour, the week before. But from the beginning, what confounded her were the extremes. She was either rapturously happy with Russell or completely wretched: there was little of that pleasant, nondescript stability that constitutes the bulk of human relationships. On certain days, this unnerving vacillation could be construed as passion.

Later, in his tract *Marriage and Morals,* Bertrand Russell, the earl's younger brother, would write with suspicion of precisely the kind of grand ardor that Elizabeth experienced. "It may be good—I think it is good—that romantic love should form the motive for a marriage, but it should be understood that the kind of love which will enable a marriage to remain happy and to fulfill its social purpose is not romantic, but is something more intimate, affectionate, and realistic." Elizabeth intuited some of this herself, and was concerned about the long-term prospects of the relationship. Her attraction to the earl was too powerful to be trusted; it was precisely the sort of fierce, turbulent attraction that clouded one's judgment. She was not friends with him the way she had been with Wells.

Given both of their positions in the world, they could have carried on an affair comfortably, but they nonetheless began to talk about marriage. Or rather, the earl began to talk about marriage, and Elizabeth began to listen. The earl did not believe in affairs with members of one's own social class. All appearances to the contrary, he had a strong romantic streak. He wanted his new love to come and live with him at Telegraph House as his third wife. Elizabeth toyed with the idea. But Russell was by nature a demanding, engulfing personality, and she sensed that there would be no exquisite solitary flights into the garden if she married him. That spring, she sat down and wrote him that perhaps it would be better to "leave well enough alone." Elizabeth had always felt protective of her solitude. She had reached the point in life where she could finally enjoy herself with impunity. She had, after all, carved a secret door into her bedroom, structuring her life with architectural precision for exactly these sorts of dalliances. "What on earth did I, of all people, want with a lot of husbands?" she asked herself. She had her writing, her children; she had no shortage of men seeking her companionship. In *Elizabeth and Her German Garden* she had quoted Marvell longingly: "Two paradises 'twere in one, to live in paradise alone." And now she was finally in a position to do as she pleased. Why embark on a venture as risky and demanding as marriage?

But Russell persisted. He wrote to her, "Though I am warped and encrusted and blundering, I'm of your stuff." During this time he was mildly distracted by an affair with his housekeeper, a Miss Young, who wrote him detailed letters about his animals and the upkeep of his estate. But this did not appear to him in any way an obstacle to marriage. He believed in affairs with members of a different class, and marriage with members of his own.

Meanwhile, George Santayana, who had known the earl since he was an undergraduate at Harvard, wrote to Russell urging him against yet another marriage. The earl's previous efforts at matrimony had not been successful: first, he had been married to Mabel Scott, the beautiful daughter of an adventuress, who publicly accused him of homosexuality in one of the most scandalous trials of the decade. He ultimately divorced her, and to the great bewilderment of his friends, married the sturdy, common Mollie, who had taken to drinking water with whiskey in between meals to assuage her unhappiness. Because of his overbearing tendencies, both relationships had been unmitigated disasters. Santayana had been a loyal enough friend to offer himself as a witness in Russell's most infamous trial, but even he couldn't condone another foray into marriage. Santayana wrote frankly, "Like Henry the Eighth he desired to *marry* all of his lady loves; but that only made him wish later to cut all their heads off."

There was, nonetheless, an almost gravitational pull drawing Elizabeth and Russell toward marriage. For Elizabeth, there may have been the deep-seated memory of her first engagement, the faintest shadow of her Victorian girlhood. She was twenty-three years old when her parents took her to Europe with the express purpose of marrying her off. They were worried that their bright, sharp-tongued daughter would never marry. Barely out of the nursery, the inexperienced May sensed her parents' rising panic; she sensed that somehow by her very existence she was straining the bounds of acceptability. At a ball in Florence, she met an imposing German officer, Henning von Arnim, who was fifteen years older than she was. He asked her to marry him on the third day of their acquaintance, at the top of the Duomo, saying "All girls like love. It's very agreeable, you will see." She was alarmed by his embraces, but not by the diamond-and-sapphire ring he produced from his pocket. She liked the importance the engagement conferred on her; she liked the cakes her betrothed bought her when she indicated the slightest interest in a bakery. When the engagement dragged on for too long, and made her parents unhappy, the resourceful girl concocted a scheme: she told von Arnim that she was going to stay in a cottage by the Thames and would be lightly chaperoned. He came to her, and she lost her virginity to him, with the sound of the river outside her window. Her father then insisted they be married. And it may be that the rushed, urgent circumstances of her first marriage contributed to a feeling of panicked dependence that remained with her. A tinge of that earlier desperation, that looming spinsterhood her parents feared for her, may have clung to her, even in her forties: a lingering sense of marriage as the ultimate goal, even for a woman as remarkable and accomplished as herself.

There was also the question of her feelings. Singular and blustery, the earl had a kind of grandeur. He was, with all of his little fixations and sweeping injustices, a riveting personality. The smallest details of everyday life were fraught with near-operatic importance, and this appealed to her natural storyteller's desire for drama. There was something in his moods that she found sweetly masculine. They seemed to make him vulnerable in ways in which she could help him. How could someone so sensitive, so prickly with principle, not be hurt and buffeted by the world? But still, Elizabeth was wracked with misgivings for the entire fall. She had not quite honed her nascent objections: she thought largely in terms of marriage in general, and the rational reasons for avoiding it, rather than the difficulties of the earl's particular personality. Bertrand Russell reported to his mistress, Ottoline Morrell, in September of 1915: "I had a long talk with Elizabeth. She is full of doubts and hesitations, which I urged her to overcome."

In spite of her anxieties, Elizabeth finally gave in. She loved Russell and would do what he wanted. She had found freer, less regimented forms of attachment, like her affair with Wells, ultimately sad and unsatisfying. And she had convinced herself that marriage to an educated, decent woman might transform Russell into a calmer presence. She knew herself to be a powerful personality, and she would change him. But a practical part of her may have already been scouting out life rafts. Elizabeth went to a lawyer and safeguarded her considerable earnings from her future husband, who, though titled, was not rich. And on February 11, 1916, with Bertrand Russell as their witness, Countess Elizabeth von Arnim and Earl John Francis Russell, with a flower in his buttonhole, were married at the registrar's office. As they stepped out onto Henrietta Street, the weather was discouraging. They were engulfed in a dense yellow fog, and it immediately started to drizzle.

3

GREAT BETRAYAL

Countess Russell liked to describe the period following her marriage as a period of revelation. After moving into Telegraph House, she began to witness the machinations of her husband's mind at close proximity. For the first time, she saw the elaborate way he bullied his servants: once he dropped a napkin deliberately on the floor and then berated the servants for it. She saw how deeply invested he was in every minute aspect of his environment, how he approached his personal relationships with what he himself referred to as a "violent reforming zeal," somehow managing to combine a controlling dominance with extreme coldness. One afternoon he got angry at Elizabeth for going into his office and touching his things. She noted: "F. suddenly unkind and extraordinarily unreasonable about my touching anything in his office. Felt I never wished to go near his office again. Had touched nothing. Greatly put off F. and marriage by this and greatly surprised. Really life is a beastly thing and I shall skurry out of it very thankfully when I get the chance."

In Elizabeth's carefully recorded version of events, she discovered the extremity of his temper, the erratic nature of his moods, only after she had moved in with him. But can this have been true, given her serious ambivalence about their marriage, and given the evidence of her diary entries before she married him? In fact, one didn't have to be married to Russell to glimpse his unusual rages. In his memoirs, George Santayana recollected boating with him on the Thames. Santayana fell into the water, and somehow managed to pull Russell in after him. Even though it was a warm, sunny day, and they were in only two feet of water: "Russell flew into an indescribable rage . . . that inexhaustible flow of foul words and blasphemous curses was somnambulistic: he didn't know what he was saying or why . . . it was so outrageously abusive, so persistent that I was cut to the quick."

Even as a boy John Francis Russell had been ornery and complicated. One of his early playmates remembered the young Frank tying her to a tree by her hair. And Bertrand Russell, who was, in his own way, extremely fond of his brother, wrote: "Everyone thought he was Satan, and he spent the rest of his life proving them right." In his love-starved childhood there is much that could have fed Francis's sense that life was against him. A bout of diphtheria when he was five had tragic reverberations: his younger sister caught it and died, and shortly afterward his mother followed suit. After the subsequent death of their father, the two Russell boys were shuttled to their grandparents, where they were raised in the chilly, formal environs of Pembroke Lodge. And it was there, the elder Russell wrote in his memoirs, *My Life and Adventures,* the iron entered his soul. He forwarded his own theory for his willfulness: "I have been told that I had a very naughty and passionate temper when I was a small boy, but I don't remember this. I had some kind of brain illness as a result of which the Doctor gave orders that I was not to be overworked or contradicted." That he became an earl when he was eleven years old, with all of the privilege and indulgence the title garnered him, may not have done wonders for his already imperious temperament.

As he grew older shadowy sexual scandal dogged the young earl. He had intimate relations with servants, and their daughters and sisters, sometimes flaunting them to his friends and relatives. When he was sent down from Oxford because of an allegedly salacious letter to an old male friend, he felt he was the subject of a great conspiracy. When his first wife, Mabel, accused him of forsaking his marital duties for this same male friend out of homosexual inclinations, he felt equally slandered. Russell was eventually cleared of the charges, but for the rest of his life he continued to view himself as the target of various pernicious persecutions. With all the slights and wrongs Russell perceived, in his heightened, paranoid state, he seemed almost to inhabit a private, hermetically sealed world. There was definitely something mad about Russell, but in his madness lay his charisma. At one point, he went to America, married Mollie, and brought her back to England, in spite of the fact he was already legally married in England. Even though he had committed the fairly straightforward crime of bigamy, he was able to muster a great deal of outrage that anyone should take him to task. So convinced was he of his fundamental rectitude, his position as one lone crusader against a malign, nonsensical world, that the notion that he had done something flagrantly in violation of the law seemed not to have occurred to him. He had gone to America, established a temporary residence in Nevada, arranged an American marriage with Mollie, and then brought her back to the country in which his legal wife, Mabel Russell, still resided. When two men came and arrested him, he wrote: "The proceedings were a considerable shock to me. First of all one is not in the habit of being arrested, and it appeared almost an impertinence."

As even his friends, not to mention avid newspaper readers on several continents, were aware of the earl's personal idiosyncrasies, it seems unlikely that they would have come as quite as much of a surprise to an accomplished satirist like Elizabeth von Arnim as she would have us believe. Santayana, on hearing of the romance between the earl and countess, ran out and read *Elizabeth and Her German Garden,* later writing in disbelief: "With such a horror of domestic tyranny, this extraordinary woman was going to marry Russell!" But there may have been more logic to the attraction than it appears. It may be that Elizabeth of the German garden was, in fact, looking for another Man of Wrath. Her choice of lovers, from Henning von Arnim to H. G. Wells, indicates a preference for stormy, demanding men. Could it be that something in his volatile, aggressive spirit drew her to Russell? He was filled with the unpredictable energies of her previous husband, magnified a thousand times.

There had been the faintest hint of violence in Elizabeth's

relationship with her first husband, Henning von Arnim. At one point, she describes locking herself in a room in her slip to write. He bangs on the door. She will not let him in. He bursts through the door and throws a pencil at her. The scene is laughingly described, as is everything in Elizabeth's world, but there is an undertone of physical menace: he is large, demanding, hostile to the writing she feels she must do. Over the years, Elizabeth had come to view her husband as a sexual predator. He pressed her to have sexual relations because, after four daughters, he wanted an heir. Elizabeth desperately wanted to escape the grueling cycle of pregnancy and breeding. When Liebet had her first child, Elizabeth wrote to her: "No wonder you say the next one shall be adopted—as you have a proper decent husband who won't force you, as I was forced instantly before I had even bodily recovered, let alone spiritually, to have another."

And yet, certain scenes from *Elizabeth and Her German Garden* suggest that for Elizabeth there was a powerful frisson surrounding male domination. Take this highly charged argument between her and the Man of Wrath about Russian men beating their wives.

"Do you suppose," he went on, flicking a twig off a tree with his whip as we passed, "that the intellectual husband, wrestling intellectually with the chaotic yearnings of his intellectual wife, ever achieves the result aimed at? He may and does go on wrestling till he is tired, but never does he in the very least convince her of her folly; while his brother in the ragged coat has got through the whole business in less time than it takes me to speak about it."

"Pray my dear man," I said pointing with my whip, "look at the baby moon, so innocently peeping at us over the edge of the mist just behind that silver birch, and don't talk so much about women and things you don't understand. What is the use of your bothering about fists and whips and all of the dreadful things invented for the confusion of obstreperous wives? You know you are a civilized husband, and a civilized husband is a creature who has ceased to be a man."

"And a civilized wife?" he asked, bringing his horse close up beside me and putting his arm round my waist, "has she ceased to be a woman?"

"I should think so indeed—she is a goddess, and can never be worshiped and adored enough."

"It seems to me," he said, "that the conversation is growing personal."

One gathers from this passage that on some level brutishness, even the faint specter of physical violence attracted her. There is in the Man of Wrath's condescension, in the sheer male assertion of power something that intrigues her.

The chasm between the spirited, bantering Elizabeth of the German garden, and the muted, submissive Elizabeth of Telegraph House is hard to ignore. But she may, on some level, have been playing out a fantasy, following through on a rogue, erotic imperative. Russell was, after all, almost a parody of male dominance. At one time, in an uncharacteristic moment of indiscretion, Elizabeth referred to Earl Russell's sexual style as "sadistic," but the attraction was visceral, unthinking. The sexual side of their marriage was strong. She was drawn to his aggression, to the slightly perverse rock of his character. She had written that when she was with him she felt a stirring desire to be "handmaid to the lord." She who was so powerful a personality wanted a man who was more so. In fact, even with her swaths of admirers, it had been tremendously difficult for her to find a man who could hold his own with her. The young novelist Frank Swinnerton observed, "Elizabeth who was small, drawling and relentless, frightened large numbers of people. She, in repose, was demure; but in reality she was a born and courageous adventurer, whose perception and speech could be so destructive that she could mock slower-witted persons into fury." And at a party at Somerset Maugham's villa on the Riviera, the journalist Arthur Marshall noted that her wit easily "topped" all the great men in the room. Much to her embarrassment, Elizabeth would often be compared to Jane Austen; but she was less like Jane Austen herself than a Jane Austen *character*—strong, witty, clever, luminous—and like Jane Austen's characters she overpowered many men. It took one of the great talkers of the time, H. G. Wells, to command her attention. Elizabeth wanted to feel fragile and feminine, she wanted to feel protected and cared for, she may even have wanted, in a perverse way, to feel only equal to a man, and for this she needed someone larger than life.

It is also possible that the issue of temper was her blind spot: Elizabeth was used to men's tempers being comic, something to be got around, an amusing obstacle to life's daily routines. Her father had raged in her childhood home, and she explicitly admired her mother's ability to manipulate, soothe, and maneuver him into a better humor: to Elizabeth this was the height of the feminine arts. It is clear from her books that Elizabeth was used to a sort of spirited debate in response to male bluster, to conflict and sparring as a prelude to reconciliation. She had not experienced anyone like Earl Russell.

In *Vera,* the dark, comic novel Elizabeth would eventually write about her marriage to Russell, the husband, Everard Wemyss, is tyrannical with servants. He is intrusive, even smothering, with his young wife, whom he calls "my sweet upety dumpety little girl." The crueler he is the more convinced he is of his rectitude, his injured status. He is a tour de force of comic creepiness, perhaps the most appalling domestic villain ever written. But when Elizabeth's friends remarked that the real Russell couldn't have been quite that bad, Elizabeth replied only "He was worse!" The heroine in *Vera* is practically a child, a young, sheltered girl who knew no better than to get involved with him. This was not, of course, Elizabeth's situation, as a widow in her late forties with five children. But her choice of heroine may reveal a deeper truth of how she felt: innocent, in love.

After only three months of marriage, Elizabeth recorded a dire new strategy in her diary: "Have made up my mind not to take anything to heart but sedulously cultivate not caring. It means letting great love for F. go and has been a terrible decision to arrive at." She had decided that she was not going to allow her happiness to depend on his moods. She would stand back and let her marriage "wash over her," as she put it in *Vera.* Her husband would be a tornado passing through her dining room, a piece of weather to be watched and waited out. In this way, Elizabeth hoped to regain her usual twinkling, ironic perspective. But this proved harder than it seemed, and by June of 1916 things were very bad. Bertrand Russell reported to

Ottoline: "Found Elizabeth who is desperate, and *begged* me to come to Telegraph House for a few days."

Further distressing to Elizabeth was Russell's stream of affairs. She was humiliated when she walked into a room and found him in the arms of his secretary. She wrote in her diary: "Shall I ever forget these T.H. days later in life? I hope someday to see them from their humorous side." Elizabeth was, after all, accustomed to taking her tribulations lightly. Her defense was essentially comic, transmuting difficulties and yearnings into frothy anecdote. She had somehow not allowed the Man of Wrath to touch her innermost self, had escaped spritelike into her garden, into her hard-back composition books. But by August she was writing to Liebet, "I would rather die than go on living as I am."

4

ALL THE DOGS OF MY LIFE

Russell arrived in Santa Barbara in early January of 1919, fairly certain of a warm welcome. In the beginning of November, Elizabeth had slipped away from Liebet and cabled him her whereabouts. Earlier in the trip, she had taken to calling Liebet her "frying pan" because her daughter was supposed to keep her out of the fire. There was in all this a quality of addiction: a sweet, irrational longing that hovered over her as she traveled across the country by train, past orchards filled with orange trees and houses smothered in white flowers.

When she cabled Russell, she and Liebet were staying in an isolated cottage hotel called San Ysidro in the hills of the Pacific coast. Elizabeth had fallen in love with the Southern Californian climate: the "beautiful, great, bland light;" and the air, which was "brilliant, windless, orange scented." Every morning they would play tennis. Afterward, Elizabeth would retire through the lush gardens with their acacia and hummingbirds, to her private Stone Cottage to work on converting one of her novels *The Benefactress* into a play. Together she and Liebet would break for a lavish, sociable lunch in the hotel's main building. Everywhere she went, Elizabeth made swarms of friends, and they were soon bombarded with invitations. But when Russell arrived, their pleasant, lazy rhythms changed. Once he came, Liebet wrote, in a biography of her mother written under the pseudonym Leslie De Charms: "All their comings and goings were now strictly ordered by a heavy hand, and there was instant retribution in the form of prolonged ill humor at the slightest, even accidental deviation." Elizabeth, her daughter incredulously observed, "bowed to it all, was ever anxious to assuage, to pour balm, to agree to the most outrageous demands." By the time they left, it seemed futile to protest her mother's return to England. Elizabeth had become once again the handmaid to the lord.

Nearly everyone who knew Elizabeth marveled that she went back to Russell. She seemed to require proof after proof of her husband's malfeasance to believe what was already plain to the most casual observer. But why should it be so hard for Elizabeth to absorb her husband's character, even with all of the evidence at her disposal? In *Elizabeth and Her German Garden* she had written cleverly about women in general: "It is useless to tell her that she is man's victim, that she is his plaything, that she is cheated, downtrodden, kept under, laughed at, shabbily treated in every way—that is not a true statement of the case. She is simply the victim of her own vanity, and against that, against the belief in her own fascinations, against the very part of herself that gives all the color to her life, who shall expect a woman to take up arms?"

Elizabeth also tended naturally toward optimism. As the tide began to turn toward modernism, Elizabeth's popular novels were increasingly criticized for their fluffiness. Quite in opposition to literary fashion, she was writing fantasies. After living in her estate in Germany for four months as a tutor to her girls, E. M. Forster wrote: "I couldn't find the famous garden, the house appeared to be surrounded solely by paddocks and shrubberies." He could easily have been making this up for effect, and he probably was. But it is not impossible that the world-famous garden she so lovingly describes was largely a product of her own inner resources.

At some point in their private negotiations, Elizabeth told Russell in no uncertain terms that their reconciliation was dependent on his absolute fidelity. He agreed immediately. For the first few weeks, Elizabeth reported in slightly sheepish bulletins to Liebet that their reunion was happy: "I haven't seen anybody yet because Dad envelops me to the exclusion of the world," and "I am so rushed off my feet by overwhelming Dad as you can well picture to yourself, and never have time to do anything real to my poor book." But she nonetheless felt bathed in love; the earl had mustered all of his considerable charm and was behaving beautifully.

At the time, Elizabeth was feeling the cumulative effect of the deaths of several loved ones. During the war, she had mourned so many people that she felt shaken, and her perspective on relationships, however flawed, changed: First her daughter Martin died of pneumonia; then her nephew, Jack; and finally one of her longtime admirers and oldest friends, Charles Stuart, whom she called "Cousin William," died of gunshot wounds. The latest brush with mortality pushed her closer to Russell. After hearing of Stuart's death, she couldn't tolerate being alone. And she wrote to Liebet, "Lieb, darling, death is a most dreadful thing—it behooves one to live in the utmost peace and love with each other while we've got each other—however tiresome and difficult we are sometimes we're still alive—that awful, cold, endless death, that wiping out forever of love and dearness is intolerable to think of. . . ." She seemed, finally, to be feeling her age, and her love for Russell tethered her to the earth. She seemed to need his possessive, overbearing affection.

Within a few months Russell had secretly rented an office outside the house in order to conduct an affair with a new secretary, Miss Otter, with greater impunity. He had also been having an affair with a different secretary in his study inside the house, but this had proved inconvenient. It continued to bewilder Elizabeth that Russell needed so many other women when he was so evidently still fond of her; the fact that most perplexed her was that their sexual life was still vibrant. He had also begun gambling for high stakes and concealing the magnitude of his losses from her. Elizabeth wrote about all of these developments in letters to her daughter. "He has engaged a girl for carrying on purposes and has taken an office—he has one already in this house, but I inevitably see more than he wants me to, so he has taken secretly another." This, however, was not enough to make her leave him. There appears to have been something else that unsettled her, something more dire than an affair with another woman, though it is unclear what the precise nature of the transgression was. She wrote cryptically that she "discovered behavior of a secret nature that made it impossible for a decent woman to stay." This time, Elizabeth was resolute. She would not look back.

In March of 1919, she escaped, again by stealth, to her brother Sydney Beauchamp's house. She had always been close to him. He was a doctor who lived in Berkhamsted. She kept her whereabouts a secret from Russell. All of her dramatic, secretive flights confirmed her image of herself as a princess imprisoned by ogrish tyrant; she only half believed in her ability to walk away. Could Russell have stopped her if he knew where she was? She seemed to believe, even at this point, that he could have, which may indicate a lingering distrust in her own resolve. She knew that she would have to remove her books, linens, family portraits, and possessions from Telegraph House, and their London town house, at 57 Gordon Square, when he was away, like a thief, as he would not accept the permanence of her departure.

And indeed after she left Russell was devastated. In the strange internal landscape of relationships, Francis felt abandoned even though he had been the one carrying on affairs. It made no sense to him that his wife would leave him because of these insignificant dalliances. He loved her, after all, and that seemed to him to be all that mattered. There was in all of this no possibility of Russell taking responsibility for his actions. His unshakable conviction of his innocence effectively insulated him from any feelings of guilt. Meanwhile, Elizabeth surreptitiously moved her possessions out of Telegraph House while he was away. In early July he brought a suit against the removal company, Shoolbred & Shoolbred. A testament to the emotional tenor of the suit is that among the items of his he claimed she had stolen were tennis balls.

Along with most of the earl's friends, Bertrand Russell strongly discouraged his brother from bringing the lawsuit. He said that he was not acting solely out of affection for Elizabeth. He did not believe the suit was in his brother's best interest. Even though the earl's previous brushes with courtroom justice had been victorious, they had splashed embarrassing details about his private life across the front pages of newspapers across the world. His first wife had accused him of everything from forcing her to act as his valet, threatening her with a gun, to brutally throwing a cat at the ceiling. (The earl claimed in his testimony that he had only been playfully tossing the cat into the air.) And in his case against Elizabeth and the removal company, he seemed to be opening himself up to lurid charges of prolific adultery. He himself had written that the earlier cases had made him feel "skinned alive." But he may, on some level, have thrived on his court cases, if only because they dramatically demonstrated how spectacularly ill-treated he had been. He liked a great stage for his wrongful persecutions.

He certainly must have been expecting a public vindication through gavels and editorials. He saw Elizabeth's flight as one more example of his hideous maltreatment, and he had no doubt that everyone else would see it that way too. But this time around the public lawsuit was an unmitigated disaster for him. Russell was flushed and blundering on the stand, and Elizabeth, who was so tiny that a box had to be brought for her to stand on so that she could see above the podium, was so likeable and composed that there was from the outset no ambiguity over who would win. And sheer absurdity of the testimony brought out the bloodthirsty glee of the newspapers. Elizabeth was grilled by his lawyer and her own.

> Q: Now with regard to the hammock. Do you say you did not give that to Lord Russell?
>
> A: Certainly not. It was entirely for me. It would not have held him.
>
> Q: The hammock, I take it, was to be for general use at Telegraph House?
>
> A: No, it was solely for me. I used to allow small guests to sit in it.
>
> Q: Now about the hammock. You bought the hammock on the 17th of April 1916.
>
> A: Yes.
>
> Q: Is it a suitable hammock for Lord Russell?
>
> A: No.
>
> Q: Did you ever give it to him?
>
> A: Never.
>
> Q: You have more regard for life.
>
> A: And for the hammock.

Before the trial, Elizabeth had carefully gathered together invoices and receipts proving that almost all of the possessions she had allegedly stolen were purchased by her. The earl, of course, was aware of this, and was aware of the money she had given him to improve his homes. None of his friends could understand his motivations—why bring a suit against her for removing her own possessions?

On some level he felt robbed. According to some deep, emotional logic, he felt Elizabeth herself had been stolen from him.

After the trial ended in an expensive, exhausting victory, Elizabeth moved back to her chalet in Switzerland, and after a while began to recover her spirits. She filled the house with guests, took long, brisk walks through the mountains, played endless games of chess on the terrace, put fresh flowers on the tables, and resumed her usual frivolity. She wrote to a friend from the chalet, clearly back to her normal self: "I'm so glad I didn't die on the various occasions I have earnestly wished I might, for if I had I would have missed a lot of lovely weather, wouldn't I?"

Stewing over the separation at Telegraph House, Russell remained deeply embittered. He raged at his brother for taking Elizabeth's side. And it was true that Bertrand remained quite close to Elizabeth, dining with her once a week when she was in London. As he reported to Ottoline Morrell: "I am very fond of her, but embarrassed by the necessity of not rousing my brother's jealousy, which is quite oriental." In fact, there were rumors that Elizabeth and Bertrand had begun an affair, which the earl most likely never heard. But he nonetheless nursed his sense of being wronged, firing off angry diatribes to Elizabeth, circulating a parody of her plotless, atmospheric new novel, *In the Mountains,* which had developed a cultish following, to her friends; and sending her a copy of the Bible with every mention of faithless wives underlined. (It is a symptom of his disease that he would not recognize the irony of *him* having been the unfaithful party.) Though he began to focus more productively on his political career, he never recovered from her departure.

And toward the end of his life he confessed in a letter to George Santayana, "When Elizabeth left me, I went completely dead and have never come alive again. She never realized how I worshipped and loved her."

Elizabeth began to work on *Vera,* which she said was extracted from her by torment. According to many critics this would be her finest book. Elizabeth's cousin, Katherine Mansfield, who was now quite sick with tuberculosis, and her husband, John Middleton Murry, were staying near the Chalet Soleil at their own small mountain lodge. Elizabeth would often visit Katherine and bring her great armfuls of flowers and apricots, and the two very different cousins developed a fondness for one another. Elizabeth envied Katherine the seriousness of her writing. And Katherine envied Elizabeth what she saw as the ease and lightness of her life—Elizabeth had somehow managed to live a full domestic life with children and husbands, *and* achieve literary success—but in spite of these jealousies the two nonetheless remained close, and Katherine signed her last letter to Elizabeth "your sister, Katherine."

When *Vera* appeared Earl Russell was enraged, and briefly contemplated another lawsuit. The reviews, and more importantly their friends, treated the novel as the clever roman à clef it essentially was. Russell confronted H. G. Wells at the Reform Club, and demanded Wells admit that chunks of it were entirely fabricated. He asked, did he or did he not hang enlarged photographs of his ancestors in Telegraph House? Wells admitted that Elizabeth may have exaggerated on that one point. He politely reminded Russell it was a novel, and changed the subject.

For her part, Elizabeth was maddened by Russell's frenzied

efforts to undermine her with all of her friends. Yet some strain of wistfulness remained between them, a connection that however angry retained some elements of love. Elizabeth continued to sit in the gallery in the House of Lords and watch Russell debate. And in 1922, Elizabeth published a novel called *The Enchanted April,* a sentimental fiction in which estranged spouses are reunited at a vine-covered castle in Portofino. Even though she had already taken up quite seriously with another man at the time she wrote it, one detects in the pages of this novel a faint yearning for Russell, in spite of all. In this fantasy that a place will change the deep-seated pattern of a relationship lay a wish: That brusque, moody husbands are literally transformed into tender devoted lovers; that they return to their true selves. What, she was asking herself, would have happened if Russell had changed? In this implausible, lovely, silly romantic universe, one sees much of Elizabeth: a sense of adventure so unusual, a sensitivity to nature so resplendent that it can alter the course of a marriage. There is a beautiful place, a house and garden in the world that can affect its magic on human relations: a vista out to the sea so inspiring that it opens the heart.

Later Elizabeth bought a honeysuckle-yellow house in the south of France, called Mas de Roses, with a spectacular view down the hill to the sea. The simple, cube-shaped house was surrounded by olive groves and long-stalked pink and white daisies, and Elizabeth loved to climb up to the roof and survey her kingdom. She and Wells lunched as old friends at the rambling house he had built nearby with his latest mistress, Odette Kuehn. Elizabeth found she was finally able to enjoy him. In her domestic affairs, Elizabeth was finished being dominated. Her next substantive relationships were with a devoted and handsome young Cambridge student some thirty years younger than she was, named Alexander Stuart Frere-Reeves, and a series of large dogs—Pincher, Chunkie, Woosie, Winkie and Knobbie—whose adventures she chronicled in her slyly evasive memoir, *All the Dogs of My Life.*

A week after Frank died, in 1931, Bertrand Russell wrote to Elizabeth informing her that his brother had left every single one of her letters to his secretary, Miss Otter, the mistress who had been, at least overtly, the final cause of their break. Elizabeth wrote back to Bertrand:

> Dearest Bertie.
> How characteristic of Frank.
> I shall make no effort to get my letters back. May Miss Otter read them to her heart's content. They are the record of a great love and a great betrayal.
>
> > Bless you, Elizabeth.

Ever the piquant mixture of adventurous and conventional, Elizabeth had never bothered to seek a divorce.

DUNCAN GRANT

VANESSA BELL

CLIVE BELL

"I find it odd the way in which the minds of the rising generation seem to be perpetually and wholly engrossed in love . . ."

—Vanessa Bell to Virginia Woolf, 1910

WINTER 1918. In an old farmhouse with a tile roof four old friends sat at a table. There was the painter Vanessa Bell, her husband, Clive Bell, her old flame the art critic Roger Fry, and the man she was currently living with, the painter Duncan Grant. Duncan's lover, David Garnett, whom they all called Bunny, would have been there too but he had gone to London for the evening. This unlikely convergence of dinner companions was not unusual in this house. The emotional arrangements at Charleston were so complicated, at times, that one needed a chart like the one at the beginning of a Russian novel to keep them all straight. On this particular winter night, the four close friends were talking about love. There was a chill in the room because coal was still scarce. Vanessa brought in a pot of her potent, acidic coffee. The dinner dishes were scattered across the round gray table which had been elaborately painted by Vanessa herself. They were deep in one of their favorite kinds of analysis—a rigorous moral inquiry of their personal lives. They were talking about whether a person should sleep with someone who does not return their love. Clive said that he would rather not because it would be too humiliating. For a moment no one spoke. There was no electricity, so the room was lit with paraffin lamps and candles. Duncan glanced anxiously over at Vanessa, and saw that she was wrapped in her own thoughts. She sipped her black coffee and said very little for the rest of the evening. Vanessa's beauty was still elemental. She had a darker, earthier version of her sister Virginia Woolf's looks—the same hooded eyes, the same drama of cheekbones and lips. She had an innate elegance that would not be obscured by the fringed shawls she threw over her shoulders, or the scarves she tied around her head like a gypsy, but on nights like this she could look worn. In fact, it could be said that she looked older than she was. After dinner, Duncan ducked into her bedroom and found her brooding and upset. The conversation had veered too close: Vanessa slept with Duncan sometimes, even though he did not fundamentally view her romantically. How much had she lost by her involvement with him? Was she, as Clive said, humiliating herself? Clive, in his voluble, bumbling way, had struck a nerve. The critics talked their way into the hushed and sacred parts of life. The painters preferred things half enchanted: certain facts were so delicate they could not endure the exposure of words. As Vanessa allowed herself to sink into a voluptuous unhappiness, Duncan felt his usual sense of guilty responsibility, but part of him was distracted wondering where Bunny was. He had said that he would come back that night.

The house itself reflected the unusual, frenetic aspirations of its inhabitants. Every surface was painted with nudes, swimmers, nymphs, flowers in vases, still lifes of fruits, paisleys: tables, door panels, fireplaces, mantels, screens, lamps, and vases were decorated, doodled over, drawn on. Chairs and couches were draped in patched, vibrant fabrics, in great mélanges of stripes and flowers: the gestalt was artful shabbiness, a highly thought-out disorder. It was as if the paintings had spilled out of their canvases all over the house and everything in it. The visual effect was abundant, beautiful, bursting, chaotic: there was no place for the eye to rest. In these trompe l'oeils lay their philosophy of everything: a table was not a table; a door was not a door; a husband was not a husband; everything under the sun was an opportunity for self-expression, a uniquely crafted venture with no known rules.

This, however, was one of those rare, painful evenings that threw Vanessa's life into relief, accentuating what she called the oddness of it. She sat at the round table bound to all three men, and to none. She had embarked on her marriage with all of the usual expectations. She had furniture from Paris, silver, and unbleached linens folded in her closets. She had been as devoted and exhausted and thrilled as any new mother, had given up precious painting time for her infant sons. She had been a wife and mother like any wife and mother. But after the sea change in her marriage, her life had never settled down into the usual Noah's ark–like pairing. She had love, perhaps in more abundance than most, but she did not have the ordinary, requited, conjugal variety.

Since they had separated, a gradual process that began in 1911, relations between Vanessa and Clive had become a masterpiece of tact. They remained deeply enmeshed in each other's lives, remained truly friends. The gulf that often opens between estranged spouses simply did not exist. Somehow she,

Clive, Duncan, and Roger all remained capable of living under the same roof for extended stretches of time. That they were ideologically committed to maintaining friendship, in all of its glorious, quixotic variety, helped in this endeavor. Nor did it hurt that they were so invested in the *idea* of friendship, and that they were all so invested in being rational. But ultimately it was a unique quality of Vanessa's character that kept them in her orbit. Vanessa managed to make each of her male friends feel admired and appreciated, without feeling slighted by the existence of the others. And they all remained curiously entangled in her life. Together, Vanessa and Duncan designed Clive's library in London with the same decorated door panels and bright, ornate fireplaces as Charleston. And Clive's mistresses were accepted into the fold, if slightly mocked. Vanessa would say of the fashionable Mary Huchinson: "Mary I think is made for salons. Her exquisiteness is not lost upon us, but it ought really to be seen by the polite world." At one point, Clive considered leaving Fitzroy Square, where Vanessa and Duncan and their close friend, John Maynard Keynes, lived. Clive was thinking of moving to Chelsea with Mary, but in the end, he decided against such a radical gesture of independence. According to his son Quentin, Clive was prone to "desperate womanizing, an impulse to catch hold of and make love to any young woman who came within reach." This diffuse romantic energy emerged from the slow estrangement from his wife. Clive never again loved anyone as wholly as Vanessa, and he would often become bored after a few weeks alone with his assorted paramours. Roger, who had been heartbroken when his own affair with Vanessa ended, remained among Vanessa's most intimate friends. He wrote of her elaborate, shifting ménage:

"It really is an almost ideal family based as it is on adultery and mutual forbearance with Clive the deceived husband and me the abandoned lover. It really is rather a triumph of reasonableness over the conventions."

2

DANGEROUS LIAISONS

When she was in her late twenties, the serious, ravishing Vanessa Stephen told her brother Thoby's best friend, Clive Bell, that she would never marry him. With his longish sandy hair, Clive already cultivated a solid middle-aged air of hunting parties and pipe smoke. He was amusing and urbane, possibly the most worldly and presentable of Thoby's Cambridge circle. He was certainly the most straightforwardly heterosexual. But he was less brilliant than the others. Virginia had nicknamed him "paraqueet," because of his vanity and plumage and chatter. Like Vanessa, Clive was interested in painting and art criticism, and he helped her run the "Friday Club," which met weekly to talk about new ideas in the art world. The young Stephens were the center of a nascent group of young writers, intellectuals, and artists who would later be grouped together under the name "Bloomsbury." The circle of friends included the eccentric social critic Lytton Strachey and the emerging economist John Maynard Keynes. They would later be known, not only for their substantial intellectual and artistic contributions, but for their innovative personal lives and flamboyant domestic arrangements. At this point in their careers, however, their daring acts of bohemianism were largely confined to staying up late talking in mixed company.

After Vanessa refused him Clive continued to press his suit. Lytton Strachey wrote, "He's fallen into a sort of distraction—it seems at times to be almost a mania. When he is alone I'm convinced he's haunted, desperately haunted, by visions of Vanessa; his frightened pathetic face shows it, and his small lascivious body oozes with disappointed lust." But Vanessa was adamant in opposing his advances. She wrote in a letter to a friend: "I could no more marry him than I could a fly—so there is an end of it . . ." But her certainty was eroded by external events. Two days after Thoby died suddenly of typhoid, she agreed to marry Clive. The decision was clearly made under duress. There had been so much death in the past decade—first her mother in 1895, then her sister Stella two years later, then her father, and then Thoby—that she no longer felt able to be alone: it was a decision made out of vulnerability, out of a moment of blind weakness, but it nonetheless appeared, at the outset, to have been a good one.

After an extended honeymoon in France, Vanessa and Clive set up house at 46 Gordon Square. The front door was painted vermillion, in contrast to the black and gray doors of the surrounding houses, and the interior was decorated according to the most up-to-date, modern principles: bare white walls hung with a few paintings. The young were tired of the sentimental clutter and velvety darkness of the Victorian interior, and they defined their own homes against it: they wanted light, air. They wanted the physical spaces they inhabited to unambiguously reflect their aspirations to create new kinds of homes.

Vanessa's domestic skill and organizational brio have been extolled by nearly everyone she knew. As Roger Fry put it: "You give me a sense of security, of something solid and real in a shifting world." With all of the theatrically helpless and artistically fragile people around her, Vanessa was sturdy and magnificent. As a nineteen-year-old, she had run her family's household after her mother and older sister died, and she carried this precocious competence into her various homes. In spite of her fierce ambitions as a painter, she seemed oddly suited to domesticity: "God made her for marriage," Virginia wrote, "and she basks there like an old seal on a rock."

In spite of her lush appearance, Vanessa had not yet had much experience with men, and marriage provided a great awakening of the senses. After her wedding, Virginia wrote, Vanessa was suddenly "tawny and jubilant and lusty as a young god." Lytton Strachey, who had until very recently been "Mr. Strachey" to Vanessa, recalls one visit to 46 Gordon Square in which the young couple entertained him lying side by side on their double bed. This was part of a sudden, liberating break from the last remnants of Victorian propriety that had clung to Vanessa's various households: Vanessa and Clive were consciously creating their own etiquette, based on ease and rationality. One should follow one's feelings, one's natural inclinations. In the beginning the various forms this project took were fairly superficial, like dispensing with napkins or elaborate wallpaper, but later they became more significant and encompassing. Vanessa and Clive were determined to live freely and rationally, unlike their parents and grandparents.

In the months after her marriage, Vanessa basked in her newfound contentment. She was amazed to find that she was never bored with Clive, that they could babble to each other about nothing for days without exhausting the conversation. Her painting gained momentum and confidence. Their old

friends were constantly dropping by. In spite of all of her trepidation about marrying Clive, Vanessa was flourishing.

But after their son Julian was born in February of 1908, the
household at Gordon Square shifted perceptibly. Vanessa remained in bed for a month, as was customary. She was trans-
fixed by the new arrival, wholly absorbed. Clive was not. The
screams of the baby overwhelmed him. The tableau of nursing
mother alienated him. He felt excluded from Vanessa's affection, and he was squeamish about holding the baby, finding him
too fragile and helpless. Within a few weeks, the baby had become Vanessa's project, and Clive had moved out of Vanessa's
bedroom.

Virginia, meanwhile, was nursing a similar strain of jealousy. She had always had a wildly possessive, almost amorous
love for her sister, and Vanessa's marriage had deeply unsettled
her. She wrote a playful, strangely revealing letter on the eve of
Vanessa's wedding that began: "We the undersigned three Apes
and a Wombat wish to make known to you our great grief and
joy at the news that you intend to marry. We have wooed you
and sung many songs of winter and summer and autumn in the
hope that thus enchanted you would condescend one day to
marry us. But as we no longer expect this honor we entreat
that you keep us still for your lovers . . ." As Vanessa commented, with something bordering on pride, anyone reading
her sister's letters would think that they were love letters. The
sisters had always been unusually close, and the multiple deaths
in their family had brought them even closer. Because of
Virginia's fragile mental health, Vanessa had assumed an intimate, controlling, maternal role, and the possibility of losing
her attention was devastating to Virginia. Virginia could not en-

tirely accept the idea of sharing her sister with a husband, let alone a squalling infant. Having children was somehow more of a betrayal, as Virginia had already divined the fierceness of maternal love and the displacing power of its obsessive hold. Over the years, Vanessa would try to downplay her love for her children to Virginia, often referring to them as "the brats" in her letters, but Virginia knew the intensity of her feeling. One day she would write rather vividly tc Vanessa that she knew Vanessa would just as soon have all of her friends burned to cinders for a single day of her daughter's happiness.

With the arrival of Vanessa's first child, the sisters entered a new era in which they couldn't be everything to each other, and Virginia was, in her own peculiar way, struggling to adjust to the new circumstances. On her side, Vanessa felt an overwhelming guilt for abandoning their childish union, for leaving her delicate, destructive sister alone, for having children and a full sexual life, when it seemed that her sister most likely would not. And it was into this emotionally rich and dangerous territory that Clive began to insinuate himself.

That April Clive and Vanessa and the baby joined Virginia, who was on holiday at their family home in Cornwall, which would later become the memorable setting of Virginia's novel *To the Lighthouse.* Clive and Virginia took long walks together in the dunes at St. Ives, while Vanessa attended to the baby. They had endless winding talks about Virginia's novel-in-progress, *Voyage Out,* and pleasant, abstract discussions about the nature of art, while Vanessa remained tied to the intensely physical world of babies. Both Clive and Virginia felt safe and buoyed in the world of intellect. It was still cold on the beach, and they were bundled in sweaters. As they walked by the ocean, their feelings of anger and exclusion slowly transmuted into a dangerous affection for each other. Virginia resembled Vanessa, but a paler, more ethereal Vanessa, who would somehow never be connected to the earthy, female realm of childbirth and nursing. Clive wrote that her presence was "vivid and strange and bewildering." Without either of them entirely apprehending what was happening, a powerful seduction had taken place. They apparently never kissed throughout the entire interlude they both referred to as an "affair," although Virginia told him that she wanted to; but they both agreed that they had "achieved the heights."

After they returned from St. Ives, Clive and Vanessa's estrangement continued. "I see nothing of Nessa," Clive complained to Virginia in December. "I do not even sleep with her; the baby takes up all her time." That fall, he had rekindled an affair with Mrs. Raven-Hill, his mistress from before he married Vanessa, whom he viewed as "delicious and flashy." And Vanessa would echo the complaint of estrangement in her own letters to Virginia: "I hardly see Clive alone, and besides I feel that we are both oppressed by the family weight."

At times Clive and Virginia seemed almost to be using each other as a conduit to Vanessa. In their letters one often has an unsettling, almost visceral sense of Vanessa's long, graceful body stretched out between them. Virginia wrote frequent variations on this sentiment to Clive: "Kiss her, most passionately, in all my private places—neck—and arm, and eye, and eyeball, and tell—what new thing is there to tell her? how fond I am of her husband?" It was as if her ardent, eccentric love for her sister had cracked open to include Clive. And somehow through all of this Virginia's relation to Vanessa remained, at least on the surface, unruffled. Interspersed with her heated letters to Clive were affectionate, quasi-erotic letters to Vanessa. For a time, it must almost have seemed that her affair with Clive was performing the magic she, on some level, must have wished it would: namely, bringing her closer to her married sister. Virginia's fantasy was in some sense to merge with Vanessa, to be carried into her stronger, sturdier life. Years later, when the sisters had achieved some degree of separation, Virginia would write: "Nessa came again. How painful these meetings are! Let me try to analyze. Perhaps it is that we both feel that we can exist independently of the other." What Virginia craved, especially in this raw period after Vanessa's marriage, was absolute fusion and dependence.

How could the three of them have tolerated for so long what seems like an intolerable situation? As part of the emerging philosophy that would later be slapped with the crude name "Bloomsbury," they all valued the idea of breaking down the normal barriers between people; they valued anarchic intellectual connections and rogue sparks and passions that transcended mere physical attraction. They tended their friendships like gardens, unlike most adults. But there was, nonetheless, a brazenness to Clive and Virginia's romantic fixation, a blatant disregard for Vanessa's feelings that seemed to mask a simmering resentment on both of their parts. Their affair, however ethereal, was a terrible violation, and yet they adamantly refused to view it in moral terms. They acted as though the miraculous affection they had discovered was, somehow, beyond all worldly consideration. Lytton Strachey guessed at the currents beneath the surface, and grilled Virginia about them. Virginia wrote back: "So you've noticed it then?

How clever you are, and how unkind!" When pressed in this way, she admitted that the situation might be "a little uncomfortable" for Vanessa, but she would not go farther than that.

Through the winter and spring, Virginia and Clive continued to correspond like lovers. Though their affair did not enter the physical realm in any of the more obvious ways, Clive seemed to have awakened nascent sensual stirrings in his virginal sister-in-law. Virginia wrote to Clive: "I am really shy of expressing my affection for you. Why? Do you know women? I had a walk yesterday after tea, between the downs, that almost crazed me with desire to express it; I gave up at last, and lay with tremulous wings. I wish for nothing better—unless it were a kiss to crown all." Virginia and Clive also met to discuss her writing—he would later characterize himself as her "literary confidante" during this period—and she showed him the short imaginative sketches she was working on.

During this period Vanessa remained curiously silent. Although she was hurt by their mutual fascination, and later admitted to Duncan that she had been more painfully jealous of Virginia during this period than of anyone in her entire life, at the time, her response was inertia. Vanessa suggested only that perhaps Virginia was wasting too much of her aesthetic energy on her letters to Clive, that perhaps he would be satisfied with the functional communications traditionally dashed off to one's family. She also complained under the protective cover of a letter-writing game their group had embarked on in which they all used fake names that she often heard about her sister only indirectly through her husband. But Virginia had suffered another breakdown during this period, and Vanessa's sense of guilt and obligation may have been so vast and consuming that she felt she owed her sister something as precious as her own husband. In any event, she did not confront her.

In April of 1909, the three of them planned a trip to Florence and the surrounding countryside. Virginia wrote flirtatiously to Clive on the eve of the trip: "Why should I excite you? Why should you be so glad to hear that I and my bundle of tempers come with you to Italy? Ah how pleasant a world where such facts do exist!" On the trip, Vanessa was reading *Les Liaisons Dangereuses* while Virginia and Clive continued their flagrant absorption in each other. In Florence, they stayed in a *pensione* with palatial rooms and a veranda. And at night the three strolled by the river. Clive and Virginia quarreled in the narrow streets of Siena, and she later gave him a postcard with an inked X, saying "Here Clive quarreled with his sister-in-law." Finally the entire situation proved to be untenable, and another quarrel in Bargello forced Virginia to cut short her trip and return home. En route she stopped at the Hotel Manin in Milan, and stayed up with a party of nuns, who seemed to her extremely contented and aloof.

With characteristic quietness, Vanessa absorbed the conflict. Virginia had once observed that there were "volcanoes underneath her sedate manner," but Vanessa did not create scenes. She needed to keep both her sister and her husband close to her. She was too steeped in loss to voluntarily let anyone go. But after his flirtation with her sister, Clive would never again be her husband in quite the same way. There was no perceivable rift between the sisters: neither of them would allow it. Though both would later admit the shattering pain of the episode, which went on for years, the affectionate surface was maintained. Virginia would write that the "affair with Clive and

Nessa" turned the knife in her like nothing else in her life. She wrote about it as if it were something that had happened to her, rather than something she had done; and it may have been that was how it felt. Within two weeks after leaving Italy, Virginia was ending her letters to Vanessa, "Beloved, I adore you, more than I can say."

For several years, Clive and Virginia continued a frank, flirtatious discussion of their attraction. As late as 1911, Clive was writing seductively to his sister-in-law: "In your black velvet coat and hat and red pink carnations, you looked so lovely that I utterly lost my nerve and head for a time, and could only stumble through the end of the conversation and tumble silent into a taxi-cab." Relations between the three eased only when Virginia became engaged to Leonard Woolf. And for the rest of her life, Virginia would sense an irritability between her and Clive, a personal grievance behind his constant needling and teasing.

In August of 1910, Vanessa gave birth to another son, Claudian, who would eventually be renamed Quentin. When the baby was two months old she was worried because he didn't seem to be gaining weight, and it wasn't clear why he was so frail. She felt alone, wrapped in her worries. One night during this stressful period, Roger Fry came to dinner. He was infamous for organizing, earlier that year, the first Post-Impressionist Exhibition at Grafton which had scandalized established art circles with the works of Matisse, Cézanne, Gauguin, and Picasso. Roger had small wire-rimmed glasses, irrepressible graying hair, pointy, elfin features, and disheveled professorial attire. When Clive ducked down to the basement to get another bottle of wine Roger asked after the baby, and he seemed so authentically interested in her concerns that a vista of sympathy and engagement opened up for Vanessa. With all of the vaunted openness of her friends, Vanessa couldn't talk frankly to anyone she knew about her passion for her children.

In spring of 1911, Vanessa left on a trip for Turkey with Clive, Roger, and their friend Harry Norton, who was an appealing but somewhat unattractive Cambridge mathematician harboring a secret infatuation with Vanessa. Vanessa had to delay her departure because of a fainting spell, perhaps suffering from some mild shadow of Virginia's nervous ailment. The strain of the past few years, of Clive's involvement with Virginia, and her sick baby, had taken a toll. Clive had wanted to turn back when the boat was delayed and the passage too rough, but Vanessa insisted that they persevere: she felt she needed to leave England. Roger, meanwhile, had departed the country after a confusing night with Ottoline Morrell, thinking he might be in love with her. As Vanessa reported in a letter to her sister: "We are all extremely amicable & polite to each other. Roger seems to be business-like and capable—haggles with the waiters and officials and tried to write Turkish in his spare moments. Clive looks after me like an old Granny." Everywhere they went Vanessa and Roger sketched and painted mountains and people. Roger was like a little boy with bottle openers and scissors and India rubbers in his pockets. He had a Turkish phrase book, which he used, along with elaborate hand gestures to navigate through Istanbul. They took a boat tour on the Marmara Sea, floating past white mosques and red Byzantine walls set against the brilliant azure sky. They wound their way through street bazaars and bought richly colored djellabahs and silk capes, which would later be used by the children in elaborate dress-up games and plays at Charleston. Vanessa was exhilarated by the change of scene, the cacophony of foreign languages: "It is delicious to get out of England," she wrote to Virginia. "Nothing gives me the same sense of complete irresponsibility and freedom."

And then one afternoon, in the small town of Brusa, Vanessa fainted after lunch. Afterward she had what was most likely a miscarriage, and suffered a complete mental and physical breakdown. The shabby Turkish inn where they were staying was not well-equipped for illness, and there was no doctor residing in the town. In the makeshift sickroom Clive was rattled and anxious, so it was left to Roger to nurse her to health. Roger was experienced in nursing because his former wife had suffered from severe mental illness. He stayed up at night with Vanessa and brought her trinkets like printed handkerchiefs, and shawls, and rugs from the bazaars, when she was well enough for him to leave her bedside. He made little drawings and paintings of the scenery and brought them to her. At one point, Roger wrote to Ottoline, in the strictest confidence, that he was worried about Vanessa's sanity. But Vanessa recalled: "He told me then he possessed some tremendous power, some queer force which gave him complete self confidence." And in the course of her slow recovery her affection for Roger became richer and more vivid. They would not become lovers until they were back in England. But when Vanessa lost the pretty French engagement ring Clive had given her, in a well in a Turkish garden, she wrote: "I was more distressed than I could quite understand. It seemed to me as if something obscure but terrible had happened."

3

THE DUNCAN YEARS

The curious stage of Vanessa's relationship with Duncan Grant began with a bath she took in his presence. It was November of 1911, and her marriage had evolved into a cordial friendship. Roger was not just her lover but a vital critic and muse. "I believe you do have an extraordinary effect on other people's work," she told Roger. "I always feel it when I am with you." Under his encouraging influence, her painting had spread from the confines of canvas onto pottery, furniture, and handblocked fabrics and wallpapers. She was working on the new decorative designs for his group enterprise, the Omega Workshop. One of the missions of Omega was to allow whimsical human art to animate the surfaces of everyday things; to bring bold colors, like the salmons and emerald greens and lemon yellows Vanessa adored, into the home. The *Morning Post* had referred to a set of their scarlet chairs as "immoral furniture." Their radical ideas would literally furnish a new world. And it was during this happy, fruitful period, that Vanessa's good friend Duncan Grant stood shaving at the mirror as she stepped naked into her bath. This was one of those moments where the self-conscious laxity of Vanessa's household, the deliberate shaking off of the Victorian proprieties could be palpably felt. She was very aware that she was Bathing With a Male Friend. She wrote to Roger at the time: "You see he wanted to shave and I wanted to have my bath and he stayed to dinner and he didn't see why he should move and I didn't see why I should remain dirty, and Clive was there and didn't object—and so! But I am afraid he remained quite unmoved and I was really very decent. I felt no embarrassment and I think perhaps it was a useful precedent!"

Duncan was gay, but he had a careless, childish, affectionate nature that left room for a certain amount of versatility. He occasionally found himself attracted to a woman and did not shy away from acting on that attraction. He was also exceedingly handsome. His dark, side-parted hair was always bed-rumpled, and he wore borrowed clothes and hand-me-downs that didn't quite fit. He blinked a little when he talked. Both Vanessa and Duncan were a little outside the high intellectual talk that often went on around them, and this strengthened their connection; they were the artists among the chatterers. With both men and women, Duncan was an enchanter. He threw champagne parties with other people's champagne. He was selfish and hedonistic but in a refreshingly simple and straightforward way. One legend of his charm has it that after irresponsibly ramming his car into a fancy Daimler he befriended the owner and ended up with a commission for a painting. While most of his complicated cohort inspired rivalries and suspicion in those outside of their circle, there were very few people who didn't love Duncan.

Over time, Vanessa's attraction to him deepened. Slowly, she began to turn away from Roger and devote more time to her ambiguous, charged friendship with Duncan. She had a great admiration for his paintings, writing once to a friend that "he will do finer things, far, than any of us." By this time his shimmering, layered paintings *Dancers* and *The Queen of Sheba* had already garnered a great deal of critical attention for their innovations in post-impressionist style. He had solo exhibitions, and both he and Vanessa had paintings in Roger Fry's second Post-Impressionist exhibition.

One night in 1914, Vanessa went to visit Virginia, and confessed that she had fallen in love with Duncan, then collapsed into tears. Virginia was flummoxed. Why would her sister leave the devoted and fascinating Roger Fry for a man whom everybody knew loved men? Virginia found Roger so fascinating she would write an entire biography of him after he died. She most likely sensed the powerful sexual attraction between Vanessa and Roger. But a dam had broken in Vanessa, and it was impossible for her not to follow the inexplicable current of her feelings. Her life had entered a new, complicated phase, but it was some time before Duncan understood the nature of her affection. He was one of those people who do not perceive things that are not convenient for them to perceive. One night, Vanessa was waiting for him to leave one of Ottoline's dress-up parties, and she saw him kissing a female violinist named Jelly D'Arani in the stairway. She swept up her things and ran out onto the dark street without him, and he couldn't avoid seeing where she stood.

Their close friendship had a depth he had not yet defined for himself. Duncan was devoted to Vanessa in his own inimitable way. Over the ensuing months, the two became companions, who both were and weren't together, and both were and weren't lovers. Their amorphous, surprisingly enduring affection resembled marriage in that they lived together and were the most intimate of friends, though Duncan continued to have affairs and flirtations with men and Vanessa continued, at least in name, to be married to Clive.

One late afternoon in October of 1916, Vanessa, Julian, Quentin, a nurse, a housemaid, a cook, Duncan Grant, Bunny Garnett, and a dog arrived at Charleston by taxi. The house was covered in Virginia creeper, with a beautiful old willow tree overlooking a large duck pond, and a sweeping view of the downs. Charleston was by no means luxurious—there was no telephone, no heat, no radio, no electricity; but, nearby, Duncan and Bunny could do the farming they needed to do in order to avoid conscription, and Vanessa would have an appropriately pastoral setting in which to do her painting. There was a walled garden that would yield cornflowers, opium poppies, roses, lilies, pink geraniums, and apple trees. At night, they would sometimes hear the zeppelins overhead. Vanessa and Duncan painted and smoked under the vaulted ceiling of their shared studio. Their paintings were going in similar directions. At the same time, both of them were working on designs of printed fabrics, and tiled vases, and furniture for Roger's Omega Workshop and continuing their development of a mutual aesthetic vision. It is unusual for artists to work together the way the two of them did, in the same space, but that was how they chose to work. They were, for distinctive, ambitious artists, strangely conjoined. Virginia would write of the two painters in wartime: "How I envy them! There they sit, looking at pinks and yellows, and when Europe blazes all they do is screw their eyes up and complain of a temporary glare in the foreground."

They ate vegetables from the nearby farm and hunted game in the neighboring woods, so the rationing did not affect them terribly. Vanessa's mesmerizing black-and-white photographs from this period show the long-haired boys running naked and marble-limbed through the garden, like the classical nudes that she was painting, and in the background of other photographs is Clive in a hat, head bent over a newspaper. Sometimes Vanessa would slip into Duncan's bedroom or he into hers, but mostly their attachment was one of intense romantic friendship. They both felt that the precise nature of their bond was best left unplumbed. Definitions always seemed damaging; the prospect of putting into words what was between them always perilous. They were both extremely sensitive to labels: Duncan was once terribly offended when Vanessa described his feelings for her as "brotherly." He explained in his diary: "I suppose the only thing lacking in my feelings for her is passion. What of that there might be seems to be crushed out of me by a bewildering suffering expectation of it (hardly conscious) by her. I think I felt that if I showed her any, it would be met by such an avalanche that I should be crushed. All I feel I can do in this case is to build slowly for her a completely strong affection on which she can lean her weary self."

On the whole, Vanessa found it easier to subsume Duncan's lovers into her world, rather than risk losing him to theirs. This often meant that she had to watch the man she loved enthralled with another man under her own roof. She found herself having long conversations with Duncan about his flights of jealousy over the twenty-four-year-old Bunny, who was blond and handsome and restless and only partly homosexual, but she rarely discussed how she felt in these electric, unstable, domestic triangles. She wrote to Roger, who had, in many ways, evolved into her closest confidante, "I don't think I can write about my relationship with him . . . it's too difficult."

The sexual energy between the three of them was not wholly centered around Duncan. Since Bunny was also interested in women, he was inevitably drawn to Vanessa. One afternoon when Duncan was out, Bunny propositioned her, and she diplomatically turned him down. Her main concern, as always, was Duncan. How would Duncan feel if she succumbed? During this period, she made a haunting painting of a woman standing naked next to a bath, with a vase with three flowers in the window. Later she tinkered with the painting and changed it to two flowers.

Once, after a particularly anguishing few weeks, Vanessa admitted to Roger: "I think perhaps it was a rather difficult situation. I can't pretend I was always happy for it's impossible not to mind some things some times . . . But it is an odd disease we all suffer from, and I see one can't expect always to be rational." In Vanessa's thinking, rationality and reasonableness were elevated to the highest virtues: they allowed her to tolerate high degrees of suffering, and were cornerstones of the unlikely domestic tranquility she was able to create.

The makeshift family lived increasingly in their private idyll, but every now and then the opinions of the outside world intruded. At one point, Vanessa's old friend Madge Vaughan wrote asking her to clarify her living situation and morality, before she would consider renting Charleston for a few months while Vanessa was traveling. "I am absolutely indifferent to anything the world would say about me, my husband or my children," Vanessa shot back angrily. "My relations to other people are no concern of yours, nor could you possibly understand them." The fierceness of her tone implies that she is not quite as indifferent as all that: she could have brushed the whole thing off as a joke if she had not been truly unsettled. In some sense, her removal to the countryside was a removal from the world and its prying: as her choices would reveal she was not *entirely* comfortable flouting the conventions she grew up with.

In the meantime, all of her friends agreed that Vanessa managed her unusual ménage beautifully. It may have helped that, unlike her sister, she did not feel the need to put everything into words. "Unluckily for myself, I'm probably a very inexpressive person," she once wrote to Roger. And much in her life remained concealed, unroiled. She never, for instance, alluded to her half-brother George Duckworth's inappropriate fondling of her and Virginia when they were young, except on two occasions: once to Sir George Savage, the psychologist treating Virginia during a serious breakdown, and another time in a letter to a cousin. In spite of her overt pleasure in bawdy talk, ever since the days when Lytton Strachey read aloud his dirty poems to the Stephen sisters in their sitting room in Fitzroy Square, her response to the secret sexual currents beneath the surface of life had always been silence. And paradoxically, it seemed there was an element of Victorian tact required to maintain the thoroughly bohemian household, with all of its perversities. The hard-won peace she had hammered out with Duncan was preserved through mystery and obfuscation, through wordlessness. There was amidst the flowers and generous lunches of cold mutton eaten in the garden and the joyously, wildly, anarchically painted rooms of Charleston, an inviolable privacy between its inhabitants, as rigid as that of the most upright home in London.

Vanessa presided over her unusual household as a kind of sexualized mother figure, and her sons would later say Duncan's presence was that of a sort of ambiguous, older brother figure. They sensed the rich maternal warmth Vanessa lavished on him, certainly. They sensed an intimate connection of an amorphous sort. In spite of the photographs of the boys running naked through the garden like characters from *A*

Midsummer Night's Dream, well into their adolescence the ambience of complete and utter openness between the generations was deceptive. The two boys lacked certain crucial pieces of information. Vanessa's son Quentin recalls walking down a dark hallway with a candle and stumbling on Vanessa and Duncan kissing in the doorway to Duncan's room. He dropped his candle, which diffused the awkwardness, but he remembers being extremely startled. He had no idea that his mother and Duncan were romantically involved. Through all of this, Vanessa managed to create an impression of naturalness, converting volatile, subterranean emotions into an atmosphere of freedom and domestic calm. This was one of her gifts.

On Christmas of 1918, Vanessa's daughter, Angelica, was born. Duncan was her father. Vanessa had very much wanted to have a baby with Duncan, and Duncan had agreed. But Clive consented to pretend to the world, including to Angelica herself, that he was the father. In some sense the choice to deceive Angelica and the rest of the world was puzzling given Vanessa's stated defiance about "anything the world would say." In fact the ruse smacked of precisely the Victorian hypocrisy that she had spent her life breaking down in both her art and her household. The timing of her decision made it doubly incongruous. This was the same year that Lytton Strachey's *Eminent Victorians* was published to enormous critical acclaim and astonishing sales. Katherine Mansfield had written to Virginia Woolf: "I love to hear of Lytton's success . . . I put my head out of my window at night and expect to find his name pricked upon the heavens in real stars." The book was a series of frank biographies of Victorian figures, like Florence Nightingale, that exploded the remaining myths that clung to that genteel era. Strachey's ambitious project involved debunking the Victorians, exposing their self-righteousness and morality for the naked ambition and selfishness he believed it was; and the spirit of this project had been refracted in myriad tiny ways in the personal lives of his friends. The warm reception of *Eminent Victorians* was a sign of the widespread acceptance of a more tolerant and modern approach to morality, but in her own particular situation, Vanessa did not feel that the truth would benefit anyone. She consoled herself that Angelica would really have two fathers watching over her; though her daughter would in fact come to feel as though she had none. Vanessa's real motivation is somewhat hard to decipher. Was she protecting Angelica from a world not quite ready for her birthright? Or was she protecting Duncan, who would never have the temperament to be a father? She would later say that she felt Duncan was too young to take on paternal responsibilities, but he was, at the time of Angelica's birth, either thirty-three or thirty-four. His immaturity was more or less a permanent condition.

Vanessa did not tell Angelica the truth until she was seventeen years old, at which point the knowledge was extremely shattering. Given her striking resemblance to Duncan, the sheer visual evidence that she belonged to him, it is telling that she had never considered the possibility that he was her father. Julian and Quentin had long suspected the truth, but these suspicions were not articulated. In the family tradition of concealment, Angelica did not immediately reveal to her mother her distress on finding out the news, but it took a toll on her nonetheless. She could not discuss the issue with either Clive or Duncan, and instead would seek out a much less appropriate, far more damaging father figure.

In fact, the question of her paternity was not the only curiously Victorian aspect of Angelica's bohemian childhood. While sexual matters were discussed freely, and joked about among the adults, they were never explained in a matter-of-fact way to the children. Before Angelica went off to drama school, Vanessa felt unable to have the necessary conversation about adulthood herself, and instead sent Angelica to a distinguished specialist, Dr. Joan Malleson, to teach her about sex. Dr. Malleson was astonished at the breadth of Angelica's innocence. She lacked the basic information that most girls of the time, raised in far more conventional circumstances, possessed. With all of the unorthodox attachments in the house, there was also the iron knowledge that nothing could be probed. Even in adulthood, after extensive exposure to psychoanalysis, Angelica's childhood seems to have left her dazed and inarticulate. In both her and her brother Quentin's descriptions of their youth there is a thick honeyed air of enchantment, as if they were drugged. The secrecy created a fundamental insecurity, a loaded emotional environment that was extremely puzzling. "I see now," Angelica wrote, "my childhood was a precarious paradise, like a cradle slung over a cloud."

4

LOSS

In 1936, Julian Bell went off to Spain to join the fight against fascism as an ambulance driver. Vanessa was terrified that something would happen to him. At twenty-eight, he was still coddled and unformed, and Vanessa could barely bring herself to let him go.

Shortly after he left, news arrived that Julian had volunteered to carry stretchers in one of the most dangerous areas of the front. "It's a better life than most I've led," he wrote to his mother, and in spite of unprecedented discomfort and peril, he felt that it was. Before the war, Julian had been drifting through China with vague artistic aspirations, writing poetry and trying his hand at painting, and immersing himself in a doomed and compelling entanglement with a married woman. He had spent hours writing long, confiding letters to Vanessa in his dark blue silk robe on his veranda in China. He expressed bursts of affection for her frequently and easily: "I love you more than anyone else, and always have done so, ever since I can remember." Of her children, Julian was the closest to her, or the one with whom she had the least complex closeness. He was handsome, with straw-colored hair and a softness in his face that kept him from being too perfect looking. He was prey to all sorts of romantic notions and sensitivities, about women, about war, about landscapes. A photograph of him at this time shows him in a white linen shirt, loosely unbuttoned at the collar, gazing at the world: secure, boyish, yearning.

At around the same time, Bunny Garnett had descended on them to flirt with the eighteen-year-old Angelica. She had grown up to be extraordinarily beautiful, a dark-haired pixie with a mischievous face that so resembled Duncan's it is hard to imagine that she did not guess her parentage. On the day she was born, Bunny had written to Lytton: "Its beauty is the remarkable thing about it. I think of marrying it," an intention he announced to everyone, but of course no one had taken him seriously. In the years since Bunny had lived with Duncan and Vanessa in his twenties, he had written the bestsellers

Pocahontas and *Lady into Fox,* among many other novels, and become a respected editor. He had also married and had a family, but his wife, Ray, was sick with cancer. Given the family constellation she had grown up with, Angelica was flattered rather than surprised or scandalized by his attention. She did not understand why Duncan and Vanessa seemed so shaken by the prospect of her involvement with their old friend. Because of the opacity thrown up around the past, she did not quite know that Duncan and Bunny had been lovers. She did not quite apprehend that Duncan had sexual relationships with men. "I should of course have asked questions; but I had been told the 'truth' so many times I thought I must know it," Angelica wrote bitterly in her memoir, *Deceived with Kindness.* "I had been brainwashed until I had no mind of my own."

During this tense period, Vanessa continued to receive letters from Julian. He believed that driving the ambulance was a meaningful contribution to the fight against fascism. The cosseted, dilettante son had finally found a purpose. But in February of 1937 he wrote: "Dearest Nessa, I may as well confess I'm suffering from fits of homesickness, particularly for Charleston." And then in July, while painting at her studio on Fitzroy Street, Vanessa received the news that Julian had been killed by shrapnel. She immediately collapsed, howling like an animal, unable to speak. (In a characteristic moment, she would later apologize to Quentin for losing control of herself so completely in her grief.) She was not well enough to move to Charleston for several days. At first Virginia was the only person whose company she could even begin to tolerate. She took the sleeping pills that she had been prescribed, and gradually she recovered enough to begin to eat. She spent her days on a daybed in the studio, near the door that opened onto the garden, patches of sun pouring through the window. Vanessa later recollected Virginia's presence: "I remember all those days after I heard about Julian lying in an unreal state & hearing her voice going on & on keeping life going as it seemed when otherwise it would have stopped."

The loss was all the more crippling because her children were the great passion of her life. Clive wrote frankly: "My life is so full of things—mostly vanities—that the hole will fill up . . . but I doubt whether the hole in Vanessa's life will ever fill up." In better times, Vanessa's absolute devotion to her children freed her to live more experimentally than she might have otherwise. If Vanessa remained reasonably content with her lopsided relationship with Duncan, for instance, it was partly because her love for her children was so fierce, so consuming. She said once that she never envied Virginia's genius because Virginia had not known the pleasure of having children, and there is no reason to doubt that is how she felt. While her art mattered deeply to her, it was not, and never had been, the center of her existence. Her real creation was her family. Virginia once elaborated this fantasy in her diary: "Nessa is at Charleston. They will have the windows open: perhaps even sit by the pond. She will think 'This is what I have made by years of unknown work—my sons, my daughter.' She will be perfectly content . . ." Vanessa's love for her children was absolute, and at times they felt overwhelmed by its force. Quentin would write, "For us the reassuring comfort of being so well loved had also to be set against the pains of being so fearfully adored."

After his wife died, Bunny persisted in his perverse courtship of the emotionally fragile Angelica. She finally lost her virginity to him, an event that suitably enough took place in H. G. Wells's spare bedroom. Bunny began to talk about marriage. Vanessa and Duncan felt strongly that it was too early for her to contemplate settling down; they wanted her to feel free to pursue a career in theater or painting. Duncan confronted Bunny and asked him not to involve Angelica in anything too serious at this delicate juncture in her life. The conversation did not go well. Duncan found himself extremely disturbed by the confrontation, but he lacked the language to analyze his feelings. He wrote in his notebook: "I was very much agitated by the whole affair because all sorts of unnecessary emotions had suddenly welled up inside me, which I do not rightly understand even now." And Bunny, for his part, did not respond well. He accused Duncan of assuming the absurd role of Victorian Father. What right had Duncan, who had not even acknowledged his paternity, to act as a father to her, especially one out of the last century?

When Vanessa tried to discuss the relationship with Angelica, according to her daughter, she became hysterical. Once again Vanessa found it difficult to express herself. Angelica wrote: "In the drawing room at Charleston there was a scene between Vanessa and myself. She may have tried to tell me what her feelings really were, but became hysterical—an unnerving experience, which I could not face the risk of repeating." Vanessa was so unused to open conflict that she could not conduct a rational conversation about something so loaded and personal: here was the "volcano" beneath the sedate surface that Virginia had written about. This difficulty may have prevented her from giving Angelica the necessary information for her life choices. In the course of the imbroglio, Vanessa became so desperate that at one point she stooped to intercepting and reading letters sent from Bunny and Angelica to Quentin.

In the spring of 1942, Bunny and Angelica were finally married, with a champagne lunch at the Ivy Club. Angelica, in a pink dress and a straw hat with a rose pinned to it, had a fleeting fantasy of saying "no" at the crucial moment in the ceremony. Neither Vanessa nor Duncan had been invited.

Presented with a fait accompli, and desperate not to lose another of her children, Vanessa repaired her frayed relationship with Angelica as well as she could. She wrote her long, newsy letters from Charleston. When her granddaughters arrived one after another, she enjoyed them tremendously, making clothes for their dolls, and playing elaborate dress-up games with the little girls, including one in which they dressed up as brides and pretended to marry Duncan or Clive.

In spite of a few harrowing close calls, one notable one in which Duncan nearly left her for the painter George Bergen, Vanessa and Duncan remained together at Charleston, in what Virginia called their "left-handed marriage," for forty-five years. For the most part, Vanessa felt that she had reaped the reward of her boldness, that Duncan, whatever portion of him was hers, was worth any compromises she had made. She had not wanted contentment, but the richness and splendor of strong feeling. Transposed against the risk and pain she lived with, what happiness she found was that much more vivid. When Julian had been entangled with a dubious woman in Rome, Vanessa advised him against marriage, with a rather telling piece of advice: "I do terribly want you to be yourself—to have freedom to grow and be whatever you have it in you to be. The one terrible thing seems to me not so much unhappiness—which is inevitable—as being thwarted, stunted, to miss opportunities and not live fully and completely as far as one can." This was the distillation of her credo—to accept the unhappiness that accompanies the deepest loves, as the price of feeling fully alive.

One of the mysteries, and almost aesthetic achievements of Vanessa's life was how effectively she managed her closeness with everyone she had ever loved. She was able to create a vividness and ease in relationships that are usually faded and fraught with tension. She made space for intimacy outside of the normal framework of romantic relationships: this required a constant act of imagination, an energetic reinvigoration of the old structures. In her letters, one can feel her working at it, a constant effort at evolving definition, a seductive, continuing claim for intimacy that adapted eternally to new circumstances. She wrote to Roger: "I believe one gets to think being 'in love' less and less important, but loving people never gets less important and you are one of the people I love most, as you know well, and however much either you or I may happen to be in love with other people my real feeling for you doesn't change." Often she delighted in the sheer unconventionality of her life, in the fact that she had somehow pulled off such an improbable arrangement. Over Christmas of 1923, when she found herself celebrating at Charleston with Clive and the children, she joked in a letter that they should take out an advertisement in *The Times* to announce how conventionally domestic their holiday was. Her close romantic friendships with Roger, Clive, Virginia, and Duncan all remained crucial to her well-being. It was through these different loves, pieced together into a kind of jigsaw of emotional fulfillment, that she was able to create a life.

Virginia had always harbored a heightened romantic notion of Vanessa's domestic skills: she wrote once in an effusion of admiration that flower blossoms would open when Vanessa walked by. And she often portrayed her sister as a sort of walking fertility goddess. Some of this was excessive, as Vanessa well knew. Virginia liked to invent a caricature of her sister. She liked to write her like a piece of fiction. But there was something remarkable about Vanessa's ability to make so many people feel loved. Like Mrs. Ramsay in *To the Lighthouse,* Vanessa possessed an exceptional, poised warmth that made everyone feel like the center of the universe. Roger once called her a "bird of prey" because she continued to keep so many men in her power at the same time. If each person who drifts out of one's life is a small death, Vanessa had accomplished the impossible thing she most wanted: not one of her admirers was lost. Everyone who loved her remained close, beguiled; each moment with someone she cherished was caught in the amber of a peaceable affection. That was her rather improbable creative act.

And yet, in the months after Julian died, Vanessa questioned her choices. She had once expressed her worry to Virginia that she had split herself among "too many stools." This odd phrase is revealing. The problem was not only that she didn't have enough support from her many men, but that she had split *herself:* she was not whole enough to meet tragedy. Would it have been easier to emerge from the crises of her later life if she had had a solid, traditional relationship? If she had lived her life as one woman in relation to one man? The delicate constellation she had created required work and nurturing and maintenance, and when she didn't have the energy it did not entirely hold together. There was no one for whom she was the center, and she suffered a little because of it.

In March of 1961, Vanessa and Duncan took turns reading *Mansfield Park* aloud at Charleston. In spite of her ardent interest in modern art, and her fondness for her own sister's innovative modernist fiction, Vanessa's favorite author had always been Jane Austen. One can easily imagine her admiring Austen's cleverness, which had in its sharpness some resemblance to her own. But was there also something in Austen's sweet, clear happy endings that she missed in her own life? Did the fantasy of elusive neatness, of a full, perfect love, persist? Did she sit with Duncan in the low, angled wooden chairs in the garden at Charleston and wonder what it would be like to drink strong black coffee with a man who shared her bed? In April she suddenly became ill with bronchitis, and a few days later, at the age of eighty-one, she died. Duncan fell to pieces, believing that he had failed to love her as she should have been loved. Angelica, now separated from Bunny, was devastated that she had missed being at her bedside. Quentin brought his young son, Julian, to the funeral. And it is testimony to the grace and endurance of her extraordinary attachments that after Vanessa's death, Clive and Duncan stayed on together at Charleston.

OTTOLINE MORRELL

PHILIP MORRELL

"Conventionality is deadness."

—LADY OTTOLINE MORRELL

MARCH 1917. Several of Lady Ottoline Morrell's weekend guests at her country estate, Garsington, noted that she was distracted. That was the only manner in which she telegraphed that the entire foundation of her life had shifted. A few days earlier, her husband, Philip, had revealed the sort of roiling, melodramatic secret that threatens a marriage. Ottoline now knew her entire view of him and the past ten years they had shared had been skewed, but she managed to maintain her poise; it would be inhospitable to do anything else, and the generous, insecure Ottoline was never inhospitable. "It does not do to show that one is unhappy," she wrote in her journal. "People feel it and it makes them uncomfortable."

With her copper hair, turquoise eyes, prominent nose, and gargantuan height, Ottoline was a true *jolie laide:* a woman who could look stunning or grotesque depending on the angle. Her penchant for outlandish, fairy-tale clothes, from giant feathered hats to Turkish harem pants to flowing satin tunics, only intensified the natural drama of her appearance. She dressed as if she were about to be painted, and she often was.

By this time Ottoline was known in London as a consummate literary hostess. She was known for the "Thursdays" she held at her house on Bedford Square, and her gorgeous, eccentric country estate, Garsington Manor, was a second home to many of London's literati, intellectuals, and artists.

Ottoline had high aspirations for Garsington: she wanted life there to be lived on the same plane as music and poetry, and she ensured that the physical environs lent themselves to high drama. She had an exquisite and startling sense of design, with brilliantly painted wall panels in scarlet and emerald, and gilt moldings. She had several pieces from the Omega Workshop. One of her hallways was painted pearl gray with a hint of pink to simulate the precise color of a winter sunrise. Candles and incense and potpourri scented the air, along with the oranges stuck with cloves that sat on the mantles. Some of her guests found the environment overdone or contrived, like Virginia Woolf who noted dryly: "Even the sky was done up in yellow silk." But nearly everyone found the gardens lovely, with lavender hedges and yew trees and an oblong reflecting pond surrounded by Italian statues and peacocks. Among those who passed through Garsington were Vanessa and Clive Bell, W. B. Yeats, Katherine Mansfield, John Middleton Murry, Lytton Strachey, Winston Churchill, Charlie Chaplin, H. G. Wells, Bertrand Russell, T. S. Eliot, Duncan Grant, Mark Gertler, Lady Dorothy Brett, Aldous Huxley, Roger Fry, and D. H. Lawrence. Most of them mocked her, some of them fell in love with her, many of them wrote about her or painted her, and all of them appreciated her. As D. H. Lawrence put it: "There is only one Ottoline. And she has moved one's imagination."

Philip delivered his wild revelation on the evening of

March 7. He rushed into the nursing home in Chelsea where Ottoline was recovering from a minor ailment. There were no curtains on the window, and her bed was bathed in moonlight, as if in parody of the romantic lighting Ottoline ordinarily adored. Without preamble, Philip launched into a wild confession that he had not one but two pregnant mistresses. One was a former maid of Ottoline's, Eva Merrifield, who had puzzled Ottoline because, unlike any of her other servants, she seemed to dislike her. The other was his secretary, Alice Jones, a demure, responsible girl who had often come to stay with them at Garsington. It is a measure of the distance between them that Ottoline was entirely taken by surprise. She had absolutely no inkling that Philip had ever been unfaithful to her. She asked him to stay and discuss the situation calmly, but he was in too nervous a state to remain with her. He hurried back to the House of Commons, but he appeared so agitated that he was immediately sent home. A doctor was called. Afterward, he tried to return to the nursing home but he was not allowed in because of the lateness of the hour. He left a note saying: "Darling O, I love you and *only* you. Forgive me, oh forgive me. I am dying of grief. Your P."

One might wonder why, after more than a decade of casual infidelities, Philip felt a sudden urgency to unburden himself. He may, in part, have been spurred by the fact that Ottoline's friends Dora Carrington and Aldous Huxley had seen him and the conspicuously pregnant Eva together at a show a few evenings earlier, and that he had noticed that Carrington was sketching members of the audience in a notepad.

In response to his revelations, Ottoline wrote him a letter that he would not find the courage to open for several years. It began: "Don't, don't, oh don't ever again deceive me." She was undone with the fresh wound. In the course of his confession, Philip had begged her to help him. He hardly needed to point out that the scandal, if unchecked, would do enormous harm to the pacifist movement that they were both so invested in. Within Parliament he had been one of the most prominent and outspoken critics of the war. His career had gained gravitas over this central, divisive issue, and it was the subject of his greatest eloquence. The conservatives and warmongers would love nothing more than to smear the name of a well-known pacifist member of Parliament with tangible evidence of wanderlust. Ottoline, if anything, was even more passionate than he was about the war; she had, as always, provided the animus and spirit behind his politics.

But even if it hadn't been for the political ramifications, Ottoline was extremely loyal, and she would have summoned her considerable powers to protect Philip no matter what. Over the ensuing days, she tamped down the scandal and arranged for one of the pregnant mistresses (Eva) to receive compensation without any direct contact with Philip; the other (Alice) had stated her intention to raise her child on her own. In all of this, Ottoline assumed her accustomed role. She soothed, fussed, forgave.

At Garsington a few days later, Philip was still in a highly disturbed state of mind. Because the Morrells were the Morrells, there were guests lingering in the house. Philip summoned two of them up to his bedroom and harangued them with a diatribe about how *he* was really the intelligent one, how *he* was responsible for Ottoline's cleverness. He informed them that this piece of wisdom was so important they should write it down for posterity. He was in such an alarming, altered state that a doctor was called, and the possibility of moving him to a mental asylum was discussed. One of the guests, Gerald Shove, reported the scene to Clive Bell, who managed to spread the news, which then entered the nastier netherworlds of higher London gossip. Lytton Strachey wrote: "Clive came to tea on Saturday, and *immediately,* before he sat down, began the story of Philip—that the poor man took leave of his senses, sat in his bed gibbering, moping, mowing, and babbling of green fields, until at last he returned to sanity—or to such sanity as he usually possesses. I never knew before that one could go mad for a week-end—like catching a cold, but so it was." In the meantime, Ottoline was determined to keep Philip home and avoid any public action that would ruin his career. She sent a letter, in the greatest confidence, to her friend Bertrand Russell, who sent her a book on insanity and advised her to seek professional help.

In the midst of all of this, Ottoline allowed herself a few moments of self-pity as she strolled miserably through her gardens under the stars. She read Shelley. She wrote great, poetic flights of what D. H. Lawrence's wife, Frieda, called her "soulmush." As her many talented satirists noted, Ottoline had a tremulous romantic temperament. She was filled with yearning for intimate conversation, for love, for nature. And if this quality subjected her to her more acute friends' cruel parody, it was also this same earnestness that disarmed them. Virginia Woolf remembered one afternoon at Garsington. "Halfway up a hill in the sun, she stopped, leant on her parasol, looked vaguely across the landscape and began a discourse on love: 'Isn't it sad that no one *really* falls in love nowadays?' . . . Here, chiefly in order to get us home, I said that love meant a great many different things . . . Unluckily this remark led Ott. to lean on her parasol once more, & look longingly at a wheatfield. 'Yes. I love that—just for itself—the curve of that wheatfield seems to me as divine as any person. . . .' "

It was certainly fair to say that the sensitive aestheticism Ottoline cultivated was often absurd; she aspired to living her life as poetry, with all of the excesses and pretensions that entailed. When D. H. Lawrence parodied her in *Women in Love*, he wrote: "There was a terrible void, a lack, a deficiency of being within her. And she wanted someone to close up this deficiency. To close it up forever." Ottoline idealized everyone she knew. Her world was all scented candles and moonlight. It must have seemed shocking to her, then, that her marriage should devolve into the stuff of a penny novelette, not the lofty business of soul searching out soul, but sheer physical lust.

A tense period followed. Ottoline did not feel that Philip should see her struggling with her moods. She had to reassure him that everything was fine for the sake of his mental health. She had to protect *him*. She wrote: "I have now to manage him and hide my inner solitude from him. It can't be helped." In this instance, it is hard to determine which of the two had more of a theatrical flair: the famously dull Philip seemed, for once, quite skilled at drawing attention and sympathy to himself, in what should, by rights, have been Ottoline's tempest. He had quite successfully hijacked the position of victim, and for her part, Ottoline felt she had to nurse and cajole him back to health and stability. It is interesting to note that at no time during this crisis did Ottoline seriously think of leaving him. She had never seriously thought of leaving him. In fact, the raw need he displayed now was precisely what bound her to him.

To outside observers of the Morrells' marriage, it seemed peculiar that Ottoline should be so devastated when she herself had been unfaithful to Philip, most notably and publicly with Bertrand Russell. In part what shattered her was the enormous deception. Philip had known about her lovers; she had not known about his. In addition, Ottoline had half-convinced herself that any physical indiscretion on her part was in the service of Knowledge and Art, one of the minor, unspeakable duties of a muse. But it is also likely that the primary cause of her distress was wounded pride. Ottoline had allowed herself to believe that Philip was not attracted to her because he lacked a healthy feeling for women in general. She wrote in her journals at one point: "Any deep stirrings of passion rather bore him." This was one of those convenient fictions, those intricately crafted private myths, which had risen up in her mind to protect herself from the inherent rejection of a cold spouse. She felt betrayed, also, because of the pregnancies. The Morrells' own son had died after three days, and these prospective children were an assault: they brought to life all she could not give Philip, all that lay barren and unfruitful between them.

When the babies, both boys, were born later that summer, Ottoline sent them christening presents of books, but beneath the mannerly, magnanimous gesture were stores of pain: "I must occupy my intellect so as to have other ideas and images," she resolved, "for if not they will kill me." During this time, guests continued to flow into Garsington. The invitations, hand-written in sepia ink on rose-colored stationery, continued to go out. But for the rest of the year, Philip suffered from what Ottoline called "violent nerve-attacks." And their eleven-year-old daughter, Julian, filled the pages of her diary with small drawings and sketches of ominous men in black masks.

2

CLEOPATRA

Philip Morrell's first glimpse of Ottoline Cavendish-Bentinick was on a bicycle: a striking six-foot-tall girl in a white dress, with copper hair and brilliant blue eyes. As she navigated the cobblestoned Oxford street, her long, distinctive face was set in an expression of intense concentration. Philip immediately wanted to know who she was. He wanted to know how he could see her again. Perhaps in retrospect it is not surprising that this image of Ottoline in motion, whirring by, should be what captivated him, inert, depressed, as he was.

At that moment, Philip was walking home from his disappointing job as a solicitor at his father's law firm, Philpott and Morrell. If Ottoline had noticed him at all she would have seen a tall, pleasant-looking man with a high forehead, dark wavy hair, and blue eyes, but there was something nervous and correct in his bearing that made him blend into a crowd. In fact, the outward orderliness of his existence concealed the violent upheavals of his recent past. Philip had been delicate and often ill throughout his childhood and had suffered a full-scale nervous breakdown after three unhappy years at Oxford. Shortly after he regained his equilibrium and joined his father's law firm, his handsome younger brother, Hugh, the family favorite, committed suicide. Philip was the stunned recipient of the package of his brother's bloodied clothes from the army. Hugh had been sent abroad after an unhappy affair with a commanding officer's wife, and had shot himself in the first days of his new post. Two years later, Philip was still reeling from the aftereffects of his brother's death. He felt himself sleepwalking through a life he had not chosen.

The appearance of a woman like Ottoline in Oxford did not go unnoticed, and Philip heard from his mother that she was the sister of the Duke of Portland. The aristocratic family was extremely wealthy, with a sprawling, magnificent estate called Welbek, and extensive properties throughout England. Ottoline was at Oxford taking classes on Roman history and political economy to fill in the lacunae of the paltry girl's education she had received.

When Ottoline inevitably appeared in a black satin dress studded with pearls at the Morrells' home for a dinner party— it was a small town—she did not single out Philip from the throng of admirers. But two years later, in October of 1901, he contrived to drop her home in a hansom cab after another dinner party, and as she climbed out, Ottoline invited him to come visit her one afternoon at her house at Grosvenor Square. Over a series of teas in her sitting room, they began to recognize each other as outsiders in their upper-class families. They both felt themselves unsuited to the dull comfortable life they had been raised for, and they were both searching for a different way of life they could not yet put into words.

Ever since early adolescence Ottoline had felt alienated from conventional aristocratic life, with its ample luxuries and casual exploitation. She spent years nursing a demanding, invalid mother, and in the interim had grown into an extremely serious, isolated young woman. Ottoline first turned her romantic nature to religious fervor, organizing prayer meetings for her mother's footmen, and later to traveling through Italy, visiting relatives and soaking in the frescoes and paintings. Along with a female companion, Hilda Douglas-Pennant, Ottoline toured Florence and visited Vernon Lee, a colorful artist and lesbian who had hangers-on who wore men's clothes and smoked cigars, and it was here that Ottoline had her first thrilling taste of bohemianism. She also managed to elude Hilda to have a brief, consuming affair with a charming older doctor and writer, Axel Munthe, in his villa on the Amalfi coast. This was her first, and possibly most exhilarating, sexual relationship.

When Ottoline arrived home at twenty-eight, newly confident and worldly, she considered the question of where she would live. She did not want to remain in the comfortable care of her brother, the duke, because she felt superfluous and unwanted in his house. Hilda Douglas-Pennant, who it seemed was half in love with her, urged Ottoline to set up house with her in Bloomsbury, but Ottoline demurred. She was beginning to think that she might want to get married. What she had in mind was a modern husband who would not curtail her freedom. She wrote: "In many women there is such a strange intuitive feeling of pride in their solitary life that when marriage really comes it is, to a certain extent, a humiliation." She may have had the model of a malleable, modern man in mind when she began having her teas with Philip Morrell. Ottoline was taken in, perhaps, by Philip's mildness and by the faint, clinging atmosphere of tragedy that lent his conventionality an aura of majesty, at least to someone with Ottoline's romantic leanings.

One sensed it was a struggle for Philip to maintain his plodding existence, that superficial orderliness was, to him, a supreme effort. Ottoline felt instinctively that she could take care of him, that she could be of use to him. One can easily imagine the eager missionary to her mother's footmen taking on the sad, aimless Philip as a project.

Over the next few months Ottoline did, however, entertain serious doubts about their burgeoning romance. She knew that she did not feel as ardently about Philip as she had about her first love, Dr. Axel Munthe. In her unfortunate phrase, she did not feel the same "smoldering furnace" of desire. She felt a calmer, she thought, steadier affection for Philip. "I do love you very deeply," she wrote him frankly, "but I am not sure if that is enough."

In a gesture of seriousness, Philip invited her to visit his family estate at Black Hall. This gave Ottoline her first inklings of his intentions, and she responded with a mild panic: "I sat up all night in my bedroom by my fire trying to push away the feeling of pressure that was closing in on me. I felt his personality almost physically elbowing in on me." In fact, the pressure may not have been coming from him, but from something within herself. Philip claimed that he did nothing so aggressive as "pressing his suit." In the margins of her journals from this period he actually felt called upon to pen a correction: "In fact I was filled with doubt as to whether I could ever make her happy, in consequence of the great differences between us in respect of upbringing and way of life. So I was determined not to be persuasive and pressing and must often have seemed, as my letters clearly show, a hesitating, backwards lover." He nonetheless mustered the energy to meet her at King's Cross station after her Christmas holiday with an impressive bouquet of lilies, and they were married on February 8, 1902, at St. Peter's on Eaton Place. Ottoline wore a billowing, long-sleeved dress, and her family was extremely relieved to see its most eccentric member attach herself to someone remotely acceptable. One of her brothers joked that he could not imagine anyone daring to marry Ottoline. Her other brother, the duke, gave Ottoline a batch of new magazines to read on the trip. The couple looked appropriately radiant as they waved to the gathered guests and boarded their train. But Ottoline recalls: "A voice told me that if I started this new life, it would mean difficulties that I must bear alone."

The Morrells set off for a two-month honeymoon in Italy. Ottoline recorded the trip in a white vellum-covered journal. It was here that she began to write floridly about the union of husband and wife as that of "brother and sister." Her choice of language covered a disturbing truth: she had discovered that Philip was not terribly attracted to her in a physical sense. She was, however, relieved to find no other grave incompatibilities. Her early, almost comically unsuitable, nickname for Philip was "my little king."

When they returned Ottoline devoted her considerable wifely energies to Philip's professional malaise. He hated working in his father's law firm and Ottoline felt that she could help him find a happier occupation. Like Ottoline, Philip was a clandestine liberal from a staunchly Tory family. He harbored vague political aspirations. He also thought of becoming an architect. Through her connections and energy, Ottoline transformed Philip from a disgruntled thirty-year-old solicitor to a liberal member of Parliament. She entreated her lofty political friends to endorse him, and helped him find funding from the Liberal League. She campaigned by his side, often leaving London after dusk for the three-hour ride into the countryside. She was tireless and supportive at campaign stops that could be quite arduous. Sometimes they would be pelted with eggs, and once they had their cart turned over by angry Tories. The difficulties were compounded by the fact that Philip was not a natural public speaker, and his talents did not lend themselves to campaigning. Ottoline noted in her journal after one appearance: "My darling Philip so disappointed that he was not better, but he will improve and must learn." Ottoline was clearly the motor behind his candidacy, and he was eventually elected to the seat from South Oxfordshire in 1906. Later Ottoline wondered if she had done the right thing: "If one could have seen more clearly and judged his capacities more accurately, I think it would have been better and more natural to him if he had devoted himself to literature and history and had not entered politics."

In spite of his rocky start, Philip made a name for himself as an ardent pacifist during the war. He was the member of Parliament who gave a speech against entering the war in the August 4, 1914 debate on the subject, and throughout the war he maintained his steadfast position despite the open hostility of many of his colleagues. But in spite of his rather distinguished record, and his general likeability, he never rose to the cabinet. Hints of his mental instability may have marred his chances of ascending higher in the liberal government. Ottoline recollected that he came home one day saying that he had rambled incoherently on the Parliament floor on the subject of Persia, without knowing what he was saying for quite some time, in a strange, excited state. The doctors said it was nervous exhaustion.

On their quiet evenings at home, Philip read aloud to Ottoline from *Antony and Cleopatra*. And Ottoline continued to hold her famous "Thursdays" in their house at 44 Bedford Square, inviting artists and intellectuals, along with liberal politicians and socialites. These lively and useful gatherings were Ottoline's contribution to the artistic world she admired. As she wrote in her memoirs, she believed quite fervently that "the only thing that really matters is to create something." But she had enough humility to know that she was not an artist. She came to view herself as someone with the painful sensitivities of an artist but without the talent, and she devoted herself to making the world more hospitable to artists, introducing starving painters to rich collectors, buying expensive gifts of jewels and rugs for the writers and thinkers she took under her wing, and opening her homes to interesting people. Her aristocratic background brought a particular frisson to her friends in the arts, and their creativity gave her a passport to worlds she might otherwise only imagine. Virginia Woolf described the charged dynamic this way: "They are always conscious that she comes from a distance, with strange colours upon her; and she that these humbler creatures have yet a vision of the divine."

The atmosphere of Ottoline's Thursdays became notably wilder during the war. The gathered company would play elaborate dress-up games with Turkish and Persian costumes, with both men and women bedecking themselves in brilliantly colored djellabahs and silks. Philip gamely showed up in a brown velvet waistcoat and played Brahms's *Hungarian Dances* on the pianola, as the guests began their frenzied dancing. But Ottoline's friends continued to view her husband as dull and conventional. Vanessa Bell and her cohort referred to Philip as "Pipsey," and Lytton Strachey and Virginia Woolf mocked his pompous habit of reading aloud the political articles he wrote for newspapers. Consequently, at his own glamorous gatherings, he often found himself alone, in the corner of a room, ignored.

During the war, however, many of Ottoline's friends needed Philip's assistance as conscientious objectors. He helped with their petitions, lending his weight as a member of Parliament, as well as taking them in as farmers at the Morrells' country estate, so that they could avoid conscription by doing work of national consequence. Once they arrived at Garsington, their farming was lackadaisical at best. But they did not appear to Philip to be at all grateful, and he did not feel accepted or comfortable in their midst. Philip may in fact have been the model for Katherine Mansfield's brutal story, "Marriage à la Mode," about a sweet, plodding man mocked and exploited by his wife's interesting and artistic weekend guests. Toward the end of his life, Philip wrote a sad, extraordinary letter to Virginia Woolf thanking her for inviting him to come stay on his own, "as if you really liked me for my own sake, and not merely as O's husband, being the only person for these last 36 years who has ever made so brave an experiment."

3

DAY OF JUDGMENT

On the evening of May 18, 1906, Ottoline gave birth to twins. Ottoline, who was so warmly maternal to so many, had mixed feelings about the literal state of motherhood, referring to her pregnancy as an "invasion" of the Morrells' life together, but Philip was thrilled at the prospect of parenthood. When the twins arrived, the girl, Julian, was only three pounds and the doctors were not sure she would survive, but the boy, Hugh, was robust and healthy. Philip was particularly pleased that a new Hugh would redeem his brother's death, that nature seemed to be replenishing his family. Now that he had embarked on a new career in Parliament, he felt that he was finally coming into his own. But when Hugh was two days old Ottoline recorded in her diary that he seemed unwell. The next day, his condition grew worse, and by night he had died of a brain hemorrhage. Philip was deeply distraught, especially when it became clear that Ottoline could have no more children. The Morrells did not speak of their grief to their friends, and a great, silent rift opened between the two of them. Ottoline mourned both her son and the new chill she felt from Philip. She wrote wildly in her journals that if she could only give him another son, it would bring them closer, but she also knew her speculation was futile. That phase of their life together was over.

Over the next few years, Ottoline hurled herself with greater dedication into her varied and demanding social life. This was partially a response to her husband's increasing distance, and partially an answer to her own ambition. Given the value Ottoline placed on creativity, and the slightly self-conscious atmosphere of decadence that surrounded her, it was perhaps inevitable that she would strike up romantic alliances with the artists and writers in her circle. And in the fall of 1909, she began an affair with the temperamental blond painter Henry Lamb, who drifted moodily in and out of her life for nearly two years.

In some sense, Ottoline's dense romantic history represents the collision of an old-fashioned romantic sensibility with a modish modern world. She had enormous distaste for promiscuity, but she managed to bring to her flirtations a musky, moonlit ambience. She somehow incorporated the modern fashion for love affairs with an older, more euphemistic tradition of courtship. Where some of her Bloomsbury visitors wryly noted middle-of-the-night door slamming in the hallways at Garsington, Ottoline wrote prettily that life there was lived on the level of music. She did not like to see the heady, ethereal bonds between her guests reduced to what she saw as the baser impulses. She preferred to think of a sonata enacted, a stanza written, a great love expressed.

In spite of her old-fashioned ideas, Lady Ottoline managed to project a commanding sensuality. Vanessa Bell's son Quentin would later observe Ottoline's tremendous sexual presence, but her attraction was, at least in part, a talent and hunger for intimacy: in fact, Ottoline was never wholly comfortable with physical expressions of affection. She found even giving her friend Lytton Strachey a consoling hug in a moment of despair required a demonstration of physicality that she was simply not capable of. Her sexual adventures were therefore masked by the vague language of souls connecting, rather than that of frank, physical love. She was not as comfortable as her friends Vanessa Bell, H. G. Wells, and Lytton Strachey with the crasser, modern view of sexual congress. Instead, she chose to view her affairs as giving herself to intellectuals and artists in order to help them. In a certain sense, her love was something else she gave, an extension of her hospitality, her small gifts, and offerings to the inspired. She wrote, for instance, of her involvement with Henry Lamb: "I was much older than him, and I had the instinct that I had something in me which would supply what he needed, some ingredient in which he was lacking." In fact, her affairs often took on an overlay of almost religious sacrifice. As she wrote, rather peculiarly, about another lover: "It seemed that I could not refuse to take upon me the burden of this very fine and valuable life." Love, then, was a burden she was taking on, a service. This somewhat unorthodox perspective may go part of the way toward explaining the ultimate rebellion of some of her lovers, and of Philip himself: the convert does not always love the missionary.

The affair that overshadowed all the rest was Ottoline's long entanglement with Bertrand Russell. At first, the possibility of intimacy between the abstract mathematician and the arty, shallow hostess would have seemed highly unlikely. When Ottoline became acquainted with Russell in Oxford in September of 1909, she wrote: "His notice flattered me very much and though I trembled at the feeling that in half an hour he would see how silly I was and despise me, his great wit and humor gave me courage to talk." He did indeed seem to notice how silly she was, as he wrote later of this first encounter that her use of scent and powder offended his puritanical sensibilities. He further expounded, in a description that wounded her enormously, that her face was long and thin, "and something like a horse." And yet as he came to know her better, Russell was impressed by her tireless work on her husband's campaign for Parliament. The truth was that while her vibrant, theatrical manner may have offended his puritan spirit, it also attracted him.

After a period of distant friendship, Russell wrote to ask her if he could stop for a night at her house en route to Paris in the middle of March of 1911. Philip was out of town, and Ottoline had invited several other guests, including her friend Ethel Sands, over to dine. After the company went home, Russell stayed up late talking to Ottoline by the fire. Over the course of the evening, the pleasant environs of Bedford Square had begun to work their charm, and Russell felt cared for and comfortable, for the first time in a long time. Ottoline had already observed how much tension Russell seemed to hold in his body, how his posture revealed a great, repressed unhappiness. She tried to draw him out and persuade him to talk to her. This was all of the encouragement he needed. Russell began to confess his unhappiness in his marriage, and as he talked, it began to occur to him that Ottoline might be receptive to his advances. He began to wonder, could he make love to her? Was he, in fact, in love with her? He later wrote to her: "I did not know I loved you until I heard myself telling you so—for one instant I thought, 'Good God, what have I said?'" It is interesting that Russell felt this unlikely, sudden bolt of love, as many men would offer Ottoline instant romantic declarations in precisely that vein. She seemed to evoke these sudden bursts of enchantment, these incongruous declarations; something in her character, extravagant, inviting, warm, seemed to draw them out of men.

A few weeks later, on the night of March 30, Roger Fry made a similar declaration of his own. Ottoline had been helping him as he curated the first Post-Impressionist Exhibition.

She was on the Post-Impressionist Exhibition committee, and had written to her friends in support of the controversial venture. Fry had told her that he wished she could come to Paris and help him with the process of choosing the paintings, and that no one's opinion was more difficult for him to go against than hers. They were sufficiently close that he invited her to accompany him on his upcoming trip to Turkey with the Bells, and though Ottoline was tempted, she declined. She did not feel that she could leave Philip for such a long stretch of time. On this particular night, Roger had come over to her house after an evening party they had both attended. And in a sudden rush of emotion, it appears that they slept together. Later that night, he sent around a note, scribbled in pencil: "still all amazed and wondering and can't begin to think—I only know how beautiful it was of you, how splendid . . . it's made me feel absolutely humble before you." He then left for Turkey with some ambiguous sense that the two of them might run off together. He seems to have placed the matter in her hands, telling her; "I know you will decide right for us." He was apparently unaware of her burgeoning relationship with Russell.

In the meantime, Ottoline was grappling with Russell's astonishing urgency: on the one hand, she had the uncomfortable feeling that they were virtually strangers, that he was using her as a way out of an unhappy marriage; and on the other, she found herself extremely flattered by his attention and drawn to his brilliance. In a state of great confusion, Ottoline reported Russell's confession of love to Philip. Here is her account of what ensued: "When Philip returned, I told him all that had happened and I was terribly hurt by his saying to me, 'Do you want to go? You must if you want to.' I felt hurt that he could ever imagine such a thing. How could he suppose that I should wish to part from him with whom my life is entwined, to whom my love and confidence had been given? The thought made me utterly wretched." Philip reported the exact same scenario, though in his recollection it occurred some weeks later. He remembered saying the words "Do you want to go? You must if you want to," but he remembers hurling them out "in a moment of anger." In this central moment, an inflection meant worlds of difference: Ottoline believed Philip to be cool and indifferent; Philip recalled being bitter and furious. The gulf in communication between them was that great.

From the beginning, Ottoline's attraction to Russell was not primarily physical. He somehow lacked the physical grace she found desirable. She described her developing interest in somewhat uncomplimentary terms: "The beauty of his mind, the pure fire of his soul began to affect and attract me, and magnetize me with an attraction almost physical, carrying me up into ecstasies such as Donne expresses; his unattractive body seemed to disappear . . ." Though they did sleep together on and off over the years, for Ottoline, the attraction never moved beyond the somewhat unpromising plane of "almost physical." Often, as a pattern in their relationship, Ottoline would try to put their affair on more platonic grounds. She wanted love, and she wanted the brush with divinity she felt love with such a brilliant man entailed, but she was less enthralled with the actual mechanics of a sexual affair with him. She was never wholly in love with him. She wrote to him at one point: "Is there such a thing as mutual attraction without *volupté* that makes it possible for two creatures to help each other and yet keep their separate lives sane and uninebriated?"

Russell was distressed by what he saw as the "solidity" of Ottoline's life: namely, her absorption in things other than him. Unlike him, she was not ready to leap together into a void. Her family and friends and houses meant something to her. Slowly, he began to understand that she was not going to leave Philip, that she had never had any intention of leaving Philip, and he was driven mad by the fact that he cared for her more than she cared for him. Her journals confirm this impression. She wrote: "The very intensity of his demands seemed to crush me." That summer, she went to stay at the Morrells' summer cottage in Peppard, and Russell took rooms nearby, visiting her by bicycle every day. His wife's brother, Logan Pearsall Smith, imposed on them the condition that they never spend a night together, and they had agreed, both eager to avoid a divorce scandal that named Ottoline, and ruined her husband's career. So, at midnight every night, Russell bicycled back to his rooms.

On some level, Ottoline's appeal was to the sensual side of Russell, to his latent desire for normal pleasures. She devoted herself to the worldly comforts, whereas he had long been immersed in a joyless relationship with his wife, Alys, and had focused all of his passion on the tortured production of his opus, *Principia Mathematica*. He had begun to view himself as a disembodied brain, and easily got carried away with his misanthropy. He himself said one of Ottoline's main contributions was to get him to laugh at himself. In her journals, Ottoline wrote a very revealing description of Russell dancing: "Bertrand Russell would be dragged in by one of the Aranyis. It was very comic to see him—a stiff little figure, jumping up and down like a child, with an expression of surprised delight on his face at finding himself doing such an ordinary human thing as dancing." This image could easily stand in for all that Ottoline gave Russell: the ordinary human things.

Some of Russell's intimates had taken to calling him "Day of Judgment," and Ottoline received the full heat of his reforming zeal. Bertrand Russell was brilliant, cranky, demanding. She wrote of their compelling, difficult relationship: "He has battered and scourged me, shaking off the dead leaves of sentimentality." This may have been overly modest. In the end, her sentimentality would prove a match for his philosophical rigor, but they were, for many years, emotionally and intellectually entwined. It often seemed with Russell that Ottoline absorbed abuse. He would harangue her with her limitations, and she would accept his harangue. In this way she was extremely maternal—her love steady, unconditional, the smallest bit elusive.

When Roger Fry returned from Turkey, now fully in love with Vanessa Bell, he went to visit Ottoline. She settled comfortably into an armchair across from him thinking he was going to launch into a report of his exotic travels, but instead he began berating her for supposedly telling people he had been in love with her. She denied that she had told anyone any such thing, but the conversation was sufficiently acrimonious that the friendship between the two was severed. Possibly at Vanessa's instigation, he turned violently against Ottoline and viciously maligned her character to all of their mutual friends. In an attitude characteristic of her milieu, he still expected her to buy the furniture and fabrics made by his Omega Workshop, and to hold meetings for the Contemporary Arts Society in her house at Bedford Square.

For the next few years, Ottoline kept Russell in a delicate balance: feeling the pressure of his desire, his need for more of her, and resisting because of the demands of Philip and Garsington. From these years, she remembered the sinking feeling of seeing him watch for her out the window, his face anxious, wild with need. She felt desperate at not being able to give him what he wanted. She loved him, nonetheless, and had no desire to lose her hold over him. Possibly because of the sexual inequity between them, and possibly because Russell needed more sheer attention than Ottoline was able to give, he gradually began to engage in other flirtations. Ottoline reported in her journal on Russell's interest in Katherine Mansfield: "Bertie and Katherine had long talks together, so late into the night in the red room, which was under my bed room, that the sound of their voices kept me awake most of the night. I made them look uncomfortable the next day by telling them that I had heard all their conversation, which of course wasn't true."

What is surprising is how many brilliant men felt that Ottoline was like them. They would deny it to their friends, would write cruelly about her later, and gossip viciously behind her back, but they would feel, in private conversation with her, that their deepest ideas had found acceptance. Russell wrote to her: "Often I can hardly know whether it is your thoughts or mine that I am expressing, they seem so much the same." One imagines that this cannot be literally true of the brilliant philosopher and the airy socialite. It's far more likely that this is one of the sweet illusions of love, but so many of her brilliant consorts felt this about Ottoline that there may have been something else at work. Garish, silly, vapid as she sometimes seemed, she was, in essence, a singularly effective muse. Like Russell, Roger Fry at one time took her intellectual contributions seriously, writing to her after the first Post-Impressionist Exhibition: "I can't tell you how it helped me to have you at such a difficult time, to help and advise. I don't think I could have done it without you." Ottoline had a singular ability to draw out a man's thoughts, to foster and cultivate his creations. D. H. Lawrence wrote to her: "There is a bond between us, in spirit, deep to the bottom." Ottoline's infinite, wide-eyed belief in art, her almost fawning appreciation of the artist, made her the ideal companion, soothing the myriad and paralyzing insecurities of the artistic temperament. Her unswerving, good-natured, unenvious faith gave the writer or painter something rare and precious in the brilliant, sniping social world they inhabited. At their better moments, the artists she befriended recognized this.

Ottoline's marriage involved a dependence she felt extremely comfortable with, though it didn't quite satisfy her. She wrote at one point of Philip: "I would love to help him more if he would let me. I wish this so much." But this was not a feeling Russell could understand; he had left his wife, Alys, destroyed by his departure. The idea of leaving rubble in his wake came naturally to him, and he would eventually leave another wife, in equally painful circumstances. But for Ottoline, the feeling of being needed was central to her conception of life. Her late teenage years nurturing her mother provided this model of consuming love: "There was not a moment of the day or night that I was not at her service—all my love, all my devotion were poured out upon her." Ottoline based her experience of passion on this paradigm of service. Over and over, Ottoline framed her love affairs in terms of what she could give, and she couldn't resist the feeling that someone needed her; in fact, she built her whole dangerous social life on the idea of helping people who were ambivalent, and sometimes vicious, about that need. She lavished jewels and expensive gifts on the men she loved and admired. She wanted to take people into her home and take care of them. Many of the writers she loved most dearly would be scathing about her: D. H. Lawrence parodied her as Hermione in *Women in Love;* Aldous Huxley satirized her in *Chrome Yellow;* and Lytton Strachey, to whom she was enormously devoted, and who passed many months at Garsington was unbelievably cruel about her in his letters. Ottoline was wounded by the sheer number of her intimates who appeared to have turned against her. She could not understand how they had enjoyed her hospitality, had opened themselves so completely to her, and still appeared, in their writing to hate her. In the end, her generosity itself was dangerous: it engendered an inflammatory, vivid resentment in both her friends and her lovers.

By the spring of 1917, Russell had drifted farther from Ottoline than ever before. That summer, in answer to a direct question, he wrote baldly: "It is true that I am not in love with you now." By this time, Russell had begun to involve himself wholeheartedly with other women, including a young actress named Lady Constance Malleson. On a visit to Garsington in April, Russell and Ottoline were walking through the woods and he told her that he had been having an affair with Constance Malleson for nearly a year. Ottoline was surprised that he hadn't told her and was jealous, as always, at the prospect of being replaced, but she made heroic efforts to be magnanimous. It is possible that her very magnanimity irked him. He said as they climbed the stiles on the way back to the manor house: "What a pity your hair is going gray." Ottoline was able to see the absurdity of this piece of nastiness, even as it cut her.

In the winter of 1918, Russell was jailed for his political views. He was placed in the comparatively comfortable Brixton prison where his brother, Earl Russell, had been famously jailed for bigamy. Ottoline diligently came to visit him, and brought him warm, effusive letters concealed in flower branches, and slipped surreptitiously inside the uncut pages of new books. She brought him *Eminent Victorians,* which made him laugh out loud. She had again become his confidante, and when he was released from prison the following fall he wanted to go on holiday with her to the beach. After a day in her company, he wrote: "It's a great joy to find things so imperishable." Philip vetoed their trip alone to the beach, but Russell came to stay at the cottage at Garsington for months, taking all of his meals at the manor house.

Even after all her painful disillusionments, Ottoline could not help hoping for the perfect, symbiotic friendship. She devoted herself to the beautiful young war poet Siegfried Sassoon among others, and was disappointed that he was not as devoted to her. And in August of 1917, John Middleton Murry came to stay at Garsington on his own, without Katherine Mansfield. He and Ottoline bicycled through town, happily chatting about Chaucer, and French literature. Before heading up to bed, he stood by the fire in the red room and asked Ottoline if he could "come into her heart." Ottoline wrote: "My answer, as far as I remember, was rather vague, as

I was quite unprepared for any emotional intimacy with him." But later that night she felt, as she often did, that she simply had to see her flowers by moonlight. When she looked up at the house and saw that the light was still burning in Murry's room, she called up to him: "You must come down, Murry. It is wicked to miss this lovely night." In inviting him down in the middle of the night, she could hardly have intended the purely friendly stroll through the grounds she reported wanting in her journals, but nor, most likely, was she hoping for some sort of physical interlude. In truth, this sort of emotionally charged evening was heaven for Ottoline—the romantic declaration, the drama of checked affection, the lawn of her beautiful house bathed in moonlight. It is most likely that Ottoline simply could not let the delicious moment go—the unconsummated flirtation held brimming at the surface for a few more hours. Ottoline wanted to be loved, more than she wanted to act on that love.

The next time Ottoline saw Katherine Mansfield, the short-story writer was extremely cold to her. Katherine canceled plans for the Murrys to stay at a cottage near Garsington. As Ottoline discovered, the reason was that Murry had told her Ottoline was madly in love with him. Ottoline was appalled by his flagrant distortion. But her journal entry about their midnight walk reveals her interest to be a little less innocent than she pretends: "It was heavenly but don't run off and think it is a love affair. All his love is Katherine's. It is only an affectionate friendship."

On one visit in the summer of 1919, Philip propositioned Virginia Woolf for the first time. She appeared to take a polite interest in him, and appeared to him the least threatening and friendliest of Ottoline's friends. She had come to see him as a rather poignantly outdated Victorian figure. After she rebuffed him, he asked her to burn his letters, but he continued his pursuit over the years. Woolf would write dryly to her friend Ethel Sands: "How nice at my age to have a little love."

4

LADY CHATTERLEY

By 1920, the Morrells' marriage had reached a new plane of remoteness. Ottoline now slept alone, on a narrow bed with a white bedspread, which seemed incongruous in the riotous glory of Garsington. On some level, she may have been returning to the religious years of her adolescence in creating for herself a perfect replica of a nun's bed. For Ottoline there was poetry and theater even in physical isolation. She still mourned the lack of warmth in her marriage, but she was resigned to the sacrifice it demanded.

Yet as her hope for intimacy began to recede, everything changed. In June of 1920, a young man named Lionel Gomme came to work as a gardener at Garsington. He was tall and beautiful, with a sensitive, intelligent face, and Ottoline's first, irrational thought was that he was her son come to life. In the beginning she did not talk to him as he was laying the terrace on the east side of the house. Instead, she contrived reasons to be outside, busying herself painting a lawn chair blue green. Slowly, she struck up a friendship with him. She took him on a tour of Oxford, and invited him for tea, and, at some point over the summer, an affair was struck up. The physical side was a revelation to her. This was the first time that Ottoline felt a greedy pleasure in an affair; it may have been the first time she felt true sexual abandon. Lionel, or Tiger, as she called him in her journals, talked mostly about football and cars instead of books or art. He was not sensitive or brooding. Ottoline nonetheless wrote about him as her "ideal companion, the one perhaps on earth who could love me."

As always in Ottoline's treacherous circles, secrets were not sacrosanct, and news of the relationship made its way out through Mark Gertler and Dorothy Brett, and it is not unlikely that it influenced D. H. Lawrence's *Lady Chatterley's Lover,* and informed its plot of a rich woman's affair with her gamekeeper, while her strangely incapacitated husband remains at home. Ottoline sounds eerily like Lady Chatterley when she wrote: "It is not an easy thing to have met across the great gulf of the world, conventions and positions, etc. But—I jumped, and he jumped." It seemed to her that for once, after all of her giving, she was finally allowed to receive. Her love, for the first time, could not be described as a burden or a sacrifice.

In the spring of 1921, Ottoline went off on a six-month tour of Europe with Julian. She had some qualms about leaving Tiger for such a long stretch of time, but the trip had already been planned. As she and Julian stopped in on Picasso, André Gide, and Katherine Mansfield, who had warmed toward her since their rift over Murry, she secretly pored over her letters from Lionel.

During this same period, Russell and Ottoline remained extremely close friends, and her hold over him remained powerful. He and Ottoline were in almost daily communication as he traveled through China with his soon-to-be-wife, Dora Black. While he was away, his letters suddenly stopped, and

Ottoline grew concerned. He was, in fact, extremely ill with pneumonia. When she arrived back in London, his brother, Earl Russell, asked if she had any news of his death. Rumors had circulated that he had died of double pneumonia, and a rather snide obituary ran in one of the papers. Ottoline was devastated. The rumors turned out to be false, and Ottoline realized how important Russell still was to her. While he was lost in delirium, Russell repeatedly tried to write letters to Ottoline: "I want to tell you how profoundly you have been in my thoughts all this strange time."

That summer, Ottoline was in London undergoing a minor operation when a telegram arrived from Tiger's foster mother saying that he was gravely ill. Ottoline immediately telephoned the local doctor to go attend to him. She rushed back to Garsington. When she arrived, she found him lying in the stable yard, after a brain hemorrhage. She sat down on the ground and held him and he died in her arms. Shortly after Tiger's death, at the advice of W. B. Yeats, she began to visit clairvoyants, and instead of gossiping or playing games after dinner at Garsington, the guests began to consult tarot cards. In her loneliness, she wanted Tiger to be her "spirit companion."

In 1928, the Morrells were forced to sell Garsington, and its contents were auctioned off on the grounds that summer. They had long been experiencing financial difficulties. Out of a mysterious, malicious impulse, Ottoline's mother had effectively disinherited her, though Ottoline had nursed her through her declining years; and Philip had run the farm into the ground. Though all of her artistic friends had assumed the Morrells were bottomlessly wealthy, this was not in fact the case. Ottoline's generosity, her well-stocked table, especially during the war, was more the trick of a clever hostess than the bounty of a rich woman. After it was sold, Ottoline mourned the dismantling of her beloved Garsington: "I don't really see what was wrong. Why it aroused so much venom in others, and why so many people turned against us." In order to economize further, the Morrells moved to a smaller, more modest brown-stone on Gower Street, and certain of Ottoline's former guests, like Lytton Strachey, felt her comedown too depressing to bear and refused to visit unless lured by a movie star like Charlie Chaplin. Bertrand Russell continued to come to lunch at Gower Street nearly every week. His second marriage broke up when he fell in love with his children's nanny, and he contin-ued to find sustenance in Ottoline's companionship.

In 1937, Ottoline's health deteriorated. She suffered from bone cancer and a series of small strokes. As Ottoline lay dying, many of her estranged friends flocked to visit her, including Roger Fry. Duncan Grant wrote her a letter that she kept by her bed. Philip made one last effort to seduce Virginia Woolf, who by this time had begun to view Ottoline as a true friend. She wrote him a letter of sympathy at Ottoline's final sickness, and he wrote a six-page letter back, chronicling their insubstantial meetings over the years and asking her to meet him, perhaps at the National Gallery. Woolf did not reply.

For all of his last-minute philandering, Philip seemed to have loved Ottoline. As his sixty-four-year-old wife lay in her upstairs room on Gower Street, he must have thought back on the decades of their marriage. Was it so incongruous that they had read *Antony and Cleopatra* aloud together by the fire in the early years of their married life? That chronicle of passionate romantic love? The larger-than-life attraction, the pain and devotion that ended in tragedy. It is not unlikely that Ottoline would have been attracted to the legendary, theatrical Cleopatra. Was the Morrells' dogged connection its own form of transcendent romanticism? They had endured. There is a photograph of them taken a little before this, before she was very ill, in the garden at Gower Street: still impeccably turned out, Ottoline is wearing a geometric-patterned dress and ropes and ropes of pearls, her hand idly flicking a cigarette. Philip is turned toward her, white haired, distinguished, rapt. There are flowers set out in a vase on the table. Her bony hand is wrapped possessively around his, and she looks at the camera, amused, as if interrupted in the middle of a story. Ottoline was still writing in her journals about how much she wished that she could be close to Philip. Philip wrote in the margins, after she died, that he wished she could have known how much he longed to talk more intimately with her but had been put off by a coldness in her expression: one last, sad misunderstanding among many.

UNA TROUBRIDGE AND RADCLYFFE HALL

> *"To find oneself lonely with the creature one loves is to plumb the full depths of desolation . . ."*
>
> —RADCLYFFE HALL

1934. The exemplary union of Radclyffe Hall and Lady Una Troubridge might have continued unperturbed if Una had not eaten something rich in Paris that disagreed with her, and if she had not then suffered serious stomach troubles on their first day of vacation in Bagnoles, and if they had not then called the American Hospital in Paris for a nurse. The nurse who arrived in a crisp white uniform was a dark-haired Russian émigré in her early thirties named Evguenia Souline. She had milk-white skin, high cheekbones, and distinctive slanting eyes that were only partially obscured by thick black plastic glasses. Evguenia lived in their hotel rooms for two weeks, along with their canary and dogs. She proved to be a competent nurse with a faint, unsettling air of tragedy, and Radclyffe Hall, whom everyone called "John," was besotted.

Some months later, Una reported in her daybook: "John gave my ex-nurse lunch at La Perousse. I am sorry for the poor child who is lonely and unhappy." At La Perousse that afternoon Evguenia was so nervous she ate nothing. And at some point later, in Hall's dauntingly lavish suite at the Hotel Pont Royal,

Evguenia apparently said in her not-quite-perfect English: "Do you want to kiss my mouth?" But what ensued was a child's kiss. Evguenia was either so innocent she did not know how to kiss, or she was so clever she knew to feign innocence.

John, at fifty-two, had closely cropped dark blond hair, blue eyes, and a strong, aquiline nose. She could not have been pretty, but she somehow managed to be handsome, successfully cultivating a mannish appearance: wearing a man's poplin shirt, one of her collection of ninety-four neckties, and a suit made by the finest Bond Street tailors. She was so deeply invested in her masculinity that she had altered a portrait done of her as a five-year-old girl by a society painter: the soft shoulder-length curls above the frilly white muslin dress were repainted to show a boy's short hair cut above her ears. Crucial to her private mythology was the idea that, even while growing up, she had always been more boy than girl. She had been born Marguerite, but she renamed herself "Radclyffe" after her father Radclyffe Radclyffe-Hall, whose nickname "Rat" hinted at the exorbitant debauchery which would be the most substantial achievement of his life. At the precise moment of her birth, he could have been found cavorting in the bed of a maid. Like her father, Radclyffe Hall was extremely rich, and unlike her father, who had dabbled in various art forms with no success, she was famous. She had written what her publishers happily advertised as the "most controversial book of the century": *The Well of Loneliness*. It was the first serious chronicle of a lesbian's life to appear in print, and it had been a runaway bestseller in several countries, and a cause célèbre in her own.

Una had done everything in her power to prevent John from seeing Evguenia. At forty-seven, Una herself was still striking with her monocle, her blond bob, her leopard-print coat. She evoked all that they had been through in their eighteen-year union: the public trials over morality and obscenity, her own illnesses, her tireless support of Hall's career. She even appealed to Hall's standing as a public homosexual, arguing that Hall stood for fidelity in inverted unions, that she had a responsibility to the public on behalf of homosexuals everywhere to uphold her respectability. But John's restlessness and misery finally persuaded Una. She had convinced Una that she simply could not live without Evguenia. Una gave in, allowing John to see Evguenia provided she would give her word of honor not to be unfaithful "in the fullest sense of the word."

In one of her earlier novels, *Adam's Breed,* John had mused on what she called "the infinite sadness of fulfilled desire," and that was the peculiar malaise she was now suffering from. She loved Una but she was no longer in love with her. The first flush of illicitness had been subsumed in their long-standing domestic tranquility. Their relationship worked, but in working it was no longer interesting to John. For Radclyffe Hall, ardor always had to do with a state of difficulty. The obstacles to love were the true focus of her work, and of her mental energy.

As always, John's power over her ambivalent new paramour was at least partly financial. She sent the impoverished Evguenia gifts of money. Evguenia wrote frankly: "I resented it at first but really who could resent it for long when one is in dire need of everything, starting with a pair of pajamas." In fact, John was enraged when Evguenia showed any signs of pursuing economic independence. When Evguenia embarked on another nursing job for a wealthy old woman named Mrs. Baker,

Hall wrote to her angrily: "If you are anyone's slave, you are going to be mine."

The eccentricity of the financial underpinnings of the arrangement lay in how explicit they were. John, it appeared, did not delude herself that her personal attractions would be enough to hold Evguenia's interest. She was not confident that Evguenia was truly a lesbian, as she was attracted to both sexes. She also knew that Una's unshakable presence severely compromised her own desirability as a lover, and so she often evoked all she would do for Evguenia and the grand inheritance she would eventually settle on her. John's intense possessiveness of Evguenia was tangled up with the rather ugly notion that she had somehow bought and purchased the younger woman. She wrote to her, in one of their more bitter moments: "If I left you for twenty years you'd have to starve. No one but me has the right to touch you." As their relationship developed, John would become more and more explicit about the allowance she gave her, and exactly what it purchased: the amount was docked when Evguenia did something to displease her.

Arriving back in England in the fall of 1934, John wore a little Russian cross that Evguenia had given her around her neck, and placed Evguenia's photograph in a place of honor on her writing desk. She devoted herself to her letters to Evguenia, for whom she had dreamed up the unflattering, affectionate nicknames, "My Royal Chinkie Pig," and "and my darling most chinky faced tartar." The letters themselves were abject, artful, and the smallest bit cruel. They dwelled on a voracious sexual future that would eventually come to pass. "Sweetheart," John wrote, "were I in very truth your lover in the ultimate sense of the word—I might not always be very gentle. I might try to be so but I might not succeed, because the sex impulse is a violent impulse—I can't explain this to you very well because you know so little about the subject."

John's physical seduction of Evguenia stretched out over a very long time. This may or may not have been intentional on Evguenia's part. She held John in a powerful state of unconsummated longing, wondering aloud if it was entirely "right" for them to become involved. John brought all of her rhetorical force to bear in convincing Evguenia that inverts had a place in God's universe, that the divine attraction they felt for each other could not possibly be wrong. When they finally consummated their relationship, John wrote that taking Evguenia's virginity was the most perfect experience of her life. Afterward, she fed Evguenia from her plate as she sat hunched at the table, and comforted her as if she were a baby. These powerful images of Evguenia's helplessness would recur in Hall's private mythology; she would write to her, at one time: "Never learn to speak English quite properly, will you?" John also fretted about Evguenia's health and whether she was warmly enough dressed. And she felt an almost tyrannical need to control every small aspect of Evguenia's life: she was not to wear red lipstick, or clothing that was green or gray, and once when Evguenia ate a green plum John had warned her against, John slammed her fist on the table and demanded that she leave the dining room at once.

Naturally, Una was deeply hurt by the emerging affair, but she was also stubborn. She was simply not going to allow herself to be supplanted. She would fight passively with the only weapon she had—her presence. As insulted as she felt, she wrote: "Everything else shrivels away in comparison to the fear of separation." Other people in her situation might have withdrawn, might not have insisted on inflicting their presence on the two lovers; other people might not have been able to bear the sheer awkwardness of their proximity, but that was not Una's strategy. Una was very interested in occupying the official position of Wife, even though technically, there was no such position. She was determined to claim the rights of the married spouse, and grant no space or ease to the subterranean affair. Insofar as possible, she would be there for every minute of it. On the surface, she sometimes tried to pretend a certain amount of affection or solicitude for Evguenia, giving her linen handkerchiefs once as a gift. But she secretly despised her and wrote that "it was like sharing one's life with a rather underdeveloped child."

When John found herself alone with Una in the English countryside, she grew restless and depressed. The peace and sociability of their cottage in Rye vanished into a torment of boredom. John was desperate to see Evguenia and could think of nothing else. Una's perfect domesticity, the fires blazing in every hearth, the flowers tumbling from vases, furniture polished and glowing, only reminded John that she wanted to share it all with Evguenia. She wrote to Evguenia in Paris: "You have made me a stranger to what was once my life."

In the summer of 1935, the uneasy threesome traveled together through the south of France and the Italian Riviera. They took three separate rooms in grand hotels, and in the daytime they bathed naked in the turquoise sea. At night John disappeared in her best silk pajamas on the pretext that she was going to rub a product called petrol hahn into Evguenia's coarse black hair. Una wrote in her daybook: "I hate this camouflage, these transparent devices which are so unworthy of us both. I said suddenly, Why call it that darling? You're going to sleep with her every night."

In the meantime Evguenia chafed at having to spend so much time *à trois*. She had become fond of John, and it seems, somewhat sexually enthralled, but she was stifled by their mutual obligation to Una. It didn't seem fair. She pointed out to John that rarely did the mistress have to spend so much time in the company of the wife. At one point she began packing her clothes into her suitcase, and John locked her into her room. Meanwhile the three watched the political developments in Italy with interest: John bought all three of them black shirts, and they wore fascist ribbons in their lapels. They admired the aesthetic of Mussolini, the uniforms, the magnificent orderliness. Toward the end of the trip John hired a large, flamboyant pink bus to fit the three of them and all of their luggage and their dogs, as they drove conspicuously through Italy.

It may, in part, have been Evguenia's spirit, her resistance, that drew John's attention. She was used to the fawning self-abnegating attention of Una and the quasi-maternal doting of her first love, Mabel Batten, and this fiery, resistant energy was something different. Evguenia did not respect or desire to serve her genius. She was not overly impressed with her writing—in fact Una later claimed, with great outrage, that she could not even name the characters in Hall's books. At one point John scolded her: "Now listen Soulina—do you know who I am? I am really a very well-known author whose career is watched by a very large public." In fact Evguenia's youth, her patina of indifference, her bisexual tendencies, and strong urge toward independence gave her power. No matter how many gifts John showered on her, no matter how fierce their sexual attachment, she somehow retained her separateness. She also maintained a geographical distance between them, remaining in Paris while Una and John were based in England. Meanwhile, John's obsession began to devour the routines of her normal existence. To Una's enormous chagrin, John had lost all interest in her writing. She no longer wanted to write novels. "You are quite right," she told Una. "I really don't want to do anything in the world but play around with that girl."

Through all of this, John did her best to appease Una. One night after staying out late with Evguenia, she left Una an azalea tree in her room, which made Una cry; and another night after coming home late, she whispered to Una that she was only truly happy with her. John intuited that she needed Una and she would never leave her. She wanted the solid security of a traditional marriage, or she wanted to come as close as she could to it as a lesbian, but she also wanted the thrill of an affair: she had never resigned herself to the comforts of being settled, in part, perhaps, because they had seemed so out of reach. She wrote in *The Well of Loneliness* about what she called the "terrible freedom" of homosexuality, of being removed from the forms and obligations of heterosexual love, and it was this terrible freedom, with its dubious, exhilarating privileges, that she was now enjoying.

Of course, if she had wanted to, John could have prevented the constant collision and perpetual friction of her two loves. John could have chosen to keep her mistress and her "wife" more separate; she could have used her money and resources to create two discrete households, in the manner of H. G.

Wells, but she elected not to. She wanted a harem, and she wanted that harem around her as much as possible. She seemed, at times, almost to revel in the tension in her ménage, even as she insisted that it didn't exist. At one point she bought two bullfinches, one for Una and one for Evguenia. She named them Caterina and Bambino, and she put them in the same cage. When they nearly pecked each other to death, she separated them.

On Evguenia's birthday, June 9, 1936, the three of them went out to a celebratory dinner in Paris. John ordered caviar, duck with pineapple, and pancakes. Una irritated John by not eating. Afterward, they went on a tour of clubs, the Monte Cristo, the Melody, and Le Monocle, and drank brandy cocktails until five in the morning, with Una grumbling the entire time. It cannot have been a very festive birthday for Evguenia.

A few weeks later, John dropped by unannounced at the large, sunny flat that she had rented for Evguenia. Evguenia did not seem happy enough to see her, and John went into a violent frenzy, destroying things, shattering picture frames, and cutting up a crocodile purse she had given Evguenia as a gift. She had somehow managed to convince herself that there was someone else. With each of these messy and dramatic scenes, Una was hopeful that a more permanent rift would establish itself. But jealousy and torment only seemed to stoke John's hunger for Evguenia's attention. What was Evguenia thinking? Was there another lover? John involved Una in endless analyses of the intricacies of Evguenia's state of mind. In John's mind, the mix of rage and desire she constantly felt was passion in its purest form. She wrote to Evguenia: "This placid, contented and painless love is not love at all as you & I know love—it's something that has a certain beauty, of course, but it isn't love, it's affection." In the meantime, John's newly published novel, *The Sixth Beatitude,* floundered, but she was too distracted by the vicissitudes of her personal life to take much notice. The gossip columns in Paris newspapers were by this time peppered with references to the "trio lesbienne."

In the course of this spectacular trial, Una had grown thinner; she seemed now to be all nerve and bone. John registered this physical protest and tried to reassure Una that her position was secure. She told Una explicitly that she could get fat because she wasn't going to leave. Through everything, Una remained fairly clear-eyed about where she stood: "I am always coming across things that hurt, the door I must not open, the letter I must not read, the thing I must not say, the caresses that are given elsewhere and not to me. *She* is the holiday the excitement and the pleasure and I am the tired old routine who offers nothing new." Released from the pressures and distraction of constant companionship, Una suddenly had time to think in her beautiful, empty hotel rooms, and the situation must have seemed eerily familiar: she herself had once been the holiday, the excitement, the pleasure.

2

TRIANGLES

One sticky August day in 1915, Una went to an elaborate tea party at her cousin Lady Clarendon's house in London. Among the guests was Radclyffe Hall, who was expensively dressed all in white, her dark gold hair in braids pinned tightly against her head, and a hat with feathers that fanned back from her face.

She was holding a tiny fox terrier. Una thought she had the face of a beautiful young man, and her androgynous energy, her absolute confidence in what she was, whatever that might be, was fascinating.

At the time, Una was unhappily married to a much older man, Admiral Ernest Troubridge, who had given her syphilis, and she was living with him, her three stepchildren, and a small daughter, Andrea. When Una was younger she had ambitions to be a sculptor, but due to some failure of imagination or courage, she had ended up as a conventional officer's wife. She found herself, or the last remnants of what she had thought of as herself, thoroughly consumed by the taxing demands of her household. But now that she was back in England after their posting abroad, she had begun to worry that so much of her identity had been eclipsed. She still wanted to be an artist. She still wanted some intangible pleasure out of life she had not yet found. Though her complicated domestic life had made her dreamy and passive, she was, in a way that she had not yet discovered, an extremely driven person.

John was living with Mabel Batten, who was also one of Una's first cousins. John called Mabel "Ladye," which was a nod to the feminine magnificence she cultivated. The two had been living together for eight years. Mabel was twenty-three years older than John. She was fifty when they met, but still an unmistakably Irish beauty, with dark hair and dark blue eyes. She was a singer, with a rich vibrant voice, and she was also intellectually accomplished. She had lived a great part of her youth in India, where her good-natured older husband had been posted, and she had had affairs with various men. Her husband died after she ran off with John, but he had not much minded the union while he was alive, as he was older and concerned for her happiness.

Under Mabel's influence, John felt drawn to the life of the artist. She began to write poems, and rather florid stories that showed signs of emerging talent. Mabel encouraged John's writing, introducing her to the prominent publisher William Heinemann. After he read one of her stories, the three of them met for lunch. John was too shy to eat anything, or to talk much. The publisher told her to write a novel. He told her, in fact, that the story she had given him was one of the most promising stories he had read. In the face of this rather substantive praise from an experienced editor, John seemed to falter. True she liked the idea of writing, but she could not quite find the discipline to follow through. As she saw it, she was too consumed in life, in life with Mabel, to write about it.

In the weeks following Lady Clarendon's tea, Una and John struck up an intense, romantic friendship, with Una often coming to tea with Mabel and John and losing track of time and staying through dinner. She had become such a fixture in their household that Ladye had begun, without quite admitting it, to feel slighted. Una seemed to have insinuated herself into their most intimate domestic patterns. In September of 1915, the three women went away on holiday together in Cornwall. And because Mabel was not in the best of health, the two younger women were thrown together. They went on brisk walks together on the cliffs and the beach, while Mabel stayed in her room. John and Una increasingly excluded her, and Mabel became increasingly distressed. One night, she had a nightmare that her eyes were on fire, and woke up drenched with sweat.

On November 29, John and Una went alone to John's country house in Malvern, which they called the White Cottage, to inventory the furniture before the tenants arrived. It was a damp day with a luminous white sky, the windows were blurred with mist, and the house was empty of servants. John made an impromptu, festive lunch, and it was then, in the quiet, unlived-in house, that the two embarked on a full sexual relationship. This was an anniversary they would mark into calendars and celebrate for the rest of their lives with bouquets of yellow roses—the beginning of what Una would call coyly, in her memoirs, their "conviviality."

But still the parameters of the fling remained unclear. John was enthralled, but unsure. Her main loyalty lay with Mabel. She would not even contemplate leaving her. She wrote frankly to Una: "How do I know if I shall still care for you in six months' time?" She nonetheless felt seriously enough to give Una a platinum ring inscribed with their names, and the two began to spend more time together.

On the afternoon of May 14, John and Una went to a breeder to pick out a new bulldog for Una. When they walked into Una's flat, still elated from their outing, from the newness of their intimacy, which was thrown in pleasant relief by the expedition out of their normal environs, the phone was ringing: it was Mabel calling, annoyed with John for being so late for dinner. John returned home sulkily, and over dinner they argued, yet again, about Una. Mabel launched into what was by now becoming a familiar diatribe: she was willing to tolerate Una's presence in their lives, but she did not think John should be spending so much time with her. To Mabel this appeared to be a reasonable, even modest request. But John raged at Mabel for possessiveness, for trying to control her movements. She intended to stay with Mabel, but she intended to stay on her own terms. She was not the sort of person who responded well to being controlled. The dinner proceeded frostily. Mabel nonetheless ate well and drank a glass of red wine. And then something happened: Mabel felt unnaturally cold, and then she felt pins and needles running down her side and a sharp pain in her chest. What she was experiencing was a seizure, and she crumpled to the ground. She was rushed to the hospital, where she lay on the narrow hospital bed, paralyzed and speechless. John did not leave her side. The doctors explained that Mabel had suffered a cerebral hemorrhage. On several occasions she appeared to recognize John, and attempted to speak to her, but she was never able to get the words out. Ten days later, she died. John wrote: "The thing that hurt me when she died was the terrible idea that any peevish words of mine had caused the attack . . . I shall never forgive myself that I allowed her to be annoyed over Una's constant presence."

In the days following Mabel's death, John was undone. She could no longer bear to be in the flat she had shared with Mabel, and camped out at the house of a cousin. For a while, John refused to see Una. When she did see her, there was no physical intimacy between them. John couldn't bear the idea of touching her. On some level, it felt as if they were complicit in a murder. Una developed heart palpitations and a racing pulse. She destroyed her diaries from that year with the alacrity of a criminal destroying evidence. And then, to assuage John's guilt, they began to see a medium to contact Mabel's spirit. They went to a blond woman with lots of face powder named Gladys Leonard who lived in a basement apartment with a red lightbulb in the window. She told them that they could only hope to reach Mabel when there was clear, dry weather. The three contacted Mabel in the afterlife, and she appeared to forgive John, and discussed their earthly love. Sometimes Una and John would go for sittings as many as five times a week, and by the end they felt the need to employ a full-time secretary to manage the paperwork generated from the séances. Una endured endless sittings with her erstwhile rival, and jotted down the notes herself. Here is a sample of the transcript:

> Una: Tell my Ladye she's got to help me to take care of Twonnie [Mabel's name for John].
>
> Medium: She says yes, she wants that, she puts you in her charge.
>
> Una: Tell her I am honoured and will do my best.
>
> Medium: She says she is afraid you hardly appreciate the magnitude of your task, it will be perfectly awful sometimes, terrible.
>
> Una: Tell her I'll stick to it all right.

The two became so deeply immersed in contacting Mabel that they delivered a two-hundred-page joint research paper, "On a Series of Sittings with Mrs. Osbourne Leonard," to the Society for Psychical Research. At night, they read Ladye's diaries aloud. John kept all of Mabel's clothes. In all of the houses they would live in, they set up a shrine to her, with paintings and burning incense, and a candlelit Madonna; she somehow became a shared goddess benignly overlooking their love. Una, it seems, was willing to tolerate this ghostly visitation in order to get her wish: the possession of Radclyffe Hall.

Over the next few months, the two were virtually living together in Una's small house in Chelsea. But by the end of February of 1917, Una was thrown out of the house by the landlady, who didn't approve of their relationship. Sometime later, they took another house, near Windsor, largely paid for by John, where Andrea, Una's daughter, whom they called "the cub," was boarded out to a local dog breeder.

Una's husband came back from his tour abroad, but she refused to see him without John. In his view, his wife was nearly mad, but he was helpless to do anything about it. Because of their Catholicism divorce was impossible. Meanwhile, a slow controversy began boiling at the Society for Psychical Research. John had been nominated as a member of the Council. One of the members, John Lane Fox-Pitt, objected to the dubious domestic portrait that emerged from their research paper: though not explicit, he picked up on the controversial love triangle that took shape in its pages. One evening, he ran into Admiral Troubridge in London, who confirmed Fox-Pitt's view of the immorality of the arrangement. He then accused John of "gross immorality." He wanted her to be thrown out of the organization. Hall had the sense of entitlement of any member of the landed gentry. She demanded that he apologize and rescind his accusation, and when he didn't she struck back by accusing him of libel. She claimed that she and Una were respectable women, that he didn't have a shred of proof for his scandalous accusations.

The trial began at noon on November 18, 1920. Una wore a huge hat with a bow. Hall wore a fashionable cloche and a ruched skirt. Naturally, a trial about aristocrats, lesbianism, and séances garnered a great deal of gleeful publicity, and they arrived to a packed gallery and a full representation of the press corps. It would be very hard to prove that anything immoral had transpired. Lesbian relations were not against the law, because they were not acknowledged by the law. Faced with the magnitude of the scandal, Admiral Troubridge backed down, and did not testify. He could not bring himself to make his accusations in the open court—instead Fox-Pitt floundered alone, trying to claim that he had never made any accusation of immorality at all—and the jury awarded Hall five hundred pounds. On the surface, this was a clear victory for Una and John, but John became ill from the strain of the trial. There was something galling in the lie that they were forced to uphold: why should she and Una have to hide what they were? There was a subterranean shift occurring in her attitude toward her place in the world.

After all the drama died down, Una and John tried to return to their domestic routine. In 1919 they had bought a crenulated castle north of London that they called Chip Chase. The furniture was polished every day. They had four maids, who were expected to wear aprons and caps, a gardener, a full-time secretary, and a chauffeur. Una often read aloud to John in the evenings, and one of their favorite books during this period was *Elizabeth and Her German Garden,* by Elizabeth von Arnim. Something in von Arnim's light domestic chatter entranced them. Una was rapidly taking on the position of housewife, devoting herself to what she referred to as the "raptures of home-making."

But in December, after the trial, they put their perfect home, Chip Chase, on the market. This marked the beginning of a telling pattern: John would settle into a house, establish an elaborate household, revel in its perfection, and then leave. Her wealth enabled her to bring her most ornate fantasies of British domesticity to life. But in the end, the manor of her dreams, the traditional Victorian estate, could never quite contain her. Each time they moved, according to Una, they were "completely convinced that here at last we had discovered the perfect home for all the years to come and for our old age. And each in its turn seemed ideal and in none of them did we remain longer than four years." John had written about what she called the "melancholy of the invert," and this primal restlessness was part of it: she would never feel like she fit into these ideal, old-fashioned households because she was an invert, none of these residences could grant her the respectability she craved, none would transform her into the married gentleman she longed to be, and yet she continued to create them, one after another, nonetheless.

3

THE WELL OF LONELINESS

By 1925, John and Una had drifted in the slight, natural way that people sometimes do after a decade of shared life. The incendiary sexual energy had dissipated into the comfortable affection of a more conventional marriage. John now stayed up late at her oak rolltop desk, smoking endless cigarettes and working. She wrote her novels longhand in her elegant handwriting, with appalling spelling mistakes, because she had never learned to type. Her work sustained her with the same passionate intensity as love had. She and Una no longer stayed up late, curled up in one of their beds, talking. She no longer liked to have Una in the room with her while she worked.

Radclyffe Hall had achieved critical acclaim with her first novel, *The Unlit Lamp,* and even more with her second book, *Adam's Breed,* which won several prestigious literary awards, including the Prix Femina. She had finally garnered a reputation as a serious writer with respectable sales. She was beginning to be featured in the pages of women's magazines. She was not interested in high literary experimentation like that of Virginia Woolf or James Joyce; instead she was resolutely middlebrow. She wanted to tell stories, and she told them in the overwrought, purple tones of popular Victorian fiction. At home, she now made an effort to entertain prominent literary figures, like Rebecca West, May Sinclair, and Violet Hunt, in addition to the usual coterie of glamorous lesbians.

For her part, Una was now galvanized by a new sense of purpose in her life: to serve Hall's genius. She sent publicity postcards out to friends, and cut out reviews and pasted them into a scrapbook. She was John's first reader and critic, and she often dictated her scrawled pages to the typist, or typed them herself. She also came up with the titles for nearly all of John's books—that was her particular talent. As she would later say: Hall was not just her beloved but her occupation.

During this time the two were extremely social. They went to lesbian bars in Soho where they could dance together, like the Orange Tree and the Cave of Harmony. And their set was particularly fond of elaborate masquerade parties, where they would sometimes stay out until 4:30 in the morning. At one such party, John was an American Indian. Their friends were a mix of artists and heiresses and wealthy expatriates, all of whom seemed to float above the confines of normal life: they had affairs and tired of them, they had salons in Paris in which handfuls of rose petals were known to fall through the skylight onto the guests. As their friend Romaine Brooks put it, their ethic was: "One should be slave to nothing except one's toothbrush." In contrast, Una and John were rather staid in their committed domesticity, but they nonetheless enjoyed the vicarious excitement of the group's gossip.

John was trying to feel her way to her next book. There were lesbian novelists, but they didn't write lesbian novels. Instead they wrote deeply coded fiction, in which they used the pronoun "he" to cloak their true subject. Their stories were ostensibly heterosexual. But at this point in her career, John wanted to write directly and openly about her subject. She wanted to air the grievances and abject self-contempt of the inverted. "There are so many of us," she wrote, "thousands of miserable, unwanted people, who have no right to love, no right to compassion because they're maimed, hideously maimed and ugly." She wanted to bring the vivid shame she had felt coming of age onto the page. For the first time she would write openly about "her strangely ardent yet sterile body." It was an ambitious, daring, and grandiose project. She viewed herself as the spokesperson for her kind. She referred to them as a persecuted class, though of course, the lesbians she knew, like Natalie Barney or Romaine Brooks, were moneyed, titled, or artistic, with magnificent villas in the south of Italy, and famed salons in Paris: it would be hard, even for someone as eloquent as Hall, to argue that they lived arduous or persecuted lives.

Before embarking on her most famous work, John approached Una and asked her permission to proceed. She knew that a frank treatment of inversion could cost her her literary reputation, and she also knew it could expose her and Una to an unpleasant scrutiny of their personal lives. Una did not hesitate. She told Hall to write what was in her heart. She too was tired of dissembling.

Hall sat down and worked in a fever she had never known before, staying up for days consecutively, smoking pack after pack of cigarettes. She completed the final chapter of *The Well of Loneliness* in April of 1928. It was a bildungsroman about a well-born, statuesque lesbian named Stephen Catlin. In many ways it was a piece of straightforward propaganda for the rights of the inverted, with all of the lecturing and dryness that it involved. Several publishing houses turned the book down because of the themes—not, they made clear, because of the execution, which most of them thought was rather good. Finally, after several months of shopping it around, a reputable publishing house, Jonathan Cape, agreed to take on the book.

Much thought went into the publishing process: the book was packaged in a sober black binding and plain jacket, and priced at twice the normal amount for a novel, to belie the natural sensationalism of the subject matter. The hope was that, in these circumstances, it could not be seen as a cheap, prurient book about sex. In addition, Hall had convinced the prominent sex theorist Havelock Ellis to write an introduction, giving what followed a gloss of scientific validity. Hall considered herself a "congenital invert" which was a phrase from Havelock Ellis's work; and she had long admired his work on the subject.

On its publication in the middle of June, the book received, at first, polite and largely positive reviews. Many critics from *The Saturday Review* to *The Sunday Times* admired the virtue and originality of the book, but felt its artistic power was compromised by its propagandistic aspirations. Others, like *The Daily Telegraph,* found it an unmitigated artistic triumph, and by the end of the first week, the book had sold out of stores. Somewhat to the surprise of everyone involved, the publication process seemed to be progressing smoothly and uneventfully. The world, it seemed, was ready for the inner life of a lesbian. But then, on Sunday, August 19, the *Sunday Express* ran a frothing editorial demanding that the book be immediately suppressed: "The decadent apostles of the most hideous and most loathsome vices no longer conceal their degeneracy and their degradation . . . the adroitness and cleverness of the book intensifies its moral danger . . . I would rather give a healthy boy or girl a phial of prussic acid than this novel." In response, Hall's publisher voluntarily submitted the book to the home secretary, and said he would abide by his recommendation.

In spite of its inflammatory subject matter, the book itself was fairly tame, and certainly not in any way sexually explicit. Hall's clever American lawyer, Morris Ernst, would remark in court: "If Stephen were a man the book would be merely another over-sentimental bit of Victorian romanticism. There can be no element in it that could bring a blush of embarrassment even to the cheeks of the complainant." To many of the book's more sophisticated supporters, the earnestness and dryness of the treatment were an obstacle to their enjoyment. In spite of the uproar created by its subject matter, Virginia Woolf confided to Ottoline Morrell: "The dullness of the book is such that any indecency may lurk there—one simply can't keep one's eye on the page."

Other prominent London writers had mixed responses to the book. Most of them supported Hall in the fight against censorship, but many were skittish about granting their imprimaturs to the book itself. H. G. Wells wrote that he could not testify as he was going abroad. Hugh Walpole agreed. Lytton Strachey had also agreed to testify though he wrote privately to E.M. Forster: "I suppose the book itself is pretty frightful." Virginia Woolf wrote to her sister in the country: "Most of our friends are trying to evade the witness box; for reasons you may guess. But they generally put it down to the weak heart of a father, or a cousin who is about to have twins." The members of Woolf's own social circle could not wholly support so unsophisticated and unironic a work, but they did not in principle believe in the suppression of literature.

On the day of the hearing, the Bow Street magistrates court had to place a sign on the door saying COURT FULL long before the proceedings began. All of London was consumed by the story, and pictures and cartoons of Radclyffe Hall flooded the morning papers. Hall arrived in the courtroom in a leather coat and a wide-brimmed blue hat. In the end, the defense had lined up fifty-seven distinguished writers, sociologists, and critics prepared to testify about the general worth and seriousness of the book, but the judge, Sir Chartres Biron, summarily ruled that their opinions would not be necessary. He announced that he planned to decide the question without hearing anyone else's opinion. At one point, when the judge began to criticize scenes from the novel involving a women's ambulance unit at the front, Radclyffe Hall finally stood up in her seat.

RH: I protest. I emphatically protest!

CB: I must ask you to be quiet.

RH: I am the author of this book.

CB: If you cannot behave yourself in court I shall have to have you removed.

RH: Shame!

At the end of the hearing, the book was banned from publication, and the judge ordered all existing copies be destroyed. He ruled from the bench: "Unfortunately these women exist, and the book asks that their existence and vices should be recognized and tolerated, and not treated with condemnation, as they are at present by all decent people. This being the tenor of this book I have no hesitation in saying it is an obscene libel— that it would tend to corrupt those into whose hands it should fall, and that the publication of this book is an offence against public decency, and an obscene libel, and I shall order it to be destroyed." After leaving the courthouse, Hall was greeted by emotional throngs of supporters, mostly women, who wanted to touch her and shake her hand. Leonard Woolf offered to take up a collection to defray her legal costs but Hall refused.

Hall's publishing house immediately halted publication, but they had already shipped molds of the type off to Paris, where the book was printed by the publisher Pegasus in vast quantities, and covertly shipped back to England for distribution. Before long, *The Well of Loneliness* had become an underground bestseller. Radclyffe Hall's book was now plastered across the windows of every bookstore in Paris. It could be found on news-vendors' carts in the streets near the crossings, and there was a black market trafficking the banned Cape edition. The book had become so infamous there was even a parody published: "The way to make a modern novel sell is/ to have a preface done by Havelock Ellis." Hall's previous books began to sell briskly as well. Her face was now so famous that people approached her in restaurants and cafés, and she could no longer move anonymously through the world. In some sense, however exhausting and demoralizing, the notoriety of *The Well of Loneliness* had achieved what respectful reviews would not: Radclyffe Hall had brought the world's attention to the cause of the invert. But she would never again write in her novels about lesbian love.

In private, John found the entire process draining. She was suffering from headaches and eye pain. To her, it felt like her lesbian friends were, for the most part, silent and unsupportive. She had many fans writing to her from all over the world, but many of those closest to her did not seem to appreciate her efforts to represent them. Many of them did not feel the need to be "represented." They found her portrait of lesbian life unnuanced and cartoonish, and John came away from the whole experience feeling oddly unappreciated.

Once the appeal and all the subsequent drama was over, John and Una fled to Paris with a maid and a cockatoo. Natalie Barney threw them an elaborate celebratory party, with tea and cucumber sandwiches. After the American obscenity trial, which was resolved in her favor, the two headed for St. Tropez for a long-anticipated rest. There they turned nut brown from the sun, swam naked, and lunched on lobster and white wine and strawberries, both of them regaining the sense of well-being and privacy they had lost.

For the rest of her days, John would be known as the author of *The Well of Loneliness*. But she was not entirely comfortable in the role of rebel and outcast. She did not take the pleasure that someone else might in the virulent opposition to her book. She did not thrive on controversy, was not fueled by it. She wanted her novel to be applauded as a brilliant and revelatory work of art, and she felt in the trilling twitter about its subject matter, that it was not. There was no doubt that the book had opened a conversation on its subject, but Hall was disappointed in the way that conversation unfolded: it had somehow devolved to the level of gossip and caricature.

Radclyffe Hall was also unhappy to be pitted against the government: unlike most of the writers and artists she knew, she had always considered herself patriotic and old-fashioned. She loved horseback riding and fine tweeds. Like many members of her class, Hall had been politically conservative all her life (a tendency that proved to be somewhat ironic, as it was the Labour Party who took up her cause during the uproar over *The Well of Loneliness*). In a sense it was this conservatism that tormented her: if she was truly a critic of the social order, she might have been more comfortable living outside of it.

In many ways what Hall craved was the comforting invisibility of traditional marriage. In her own memoirs Una wrote: "We desire order and fidelity and the privilege of a religious and legal bond." This does not sound like bohemianism, and it wasn't. When Una's daughter, Andrea, lived with a man she wasn't married to, both John and Una were extremely disapproving. They found her choice to remain outside of convention distasteful. Radclyffe Hall was reproducing a Victorian conception of love, in her own world of women: the man (John) had the power in the world, and the privilege to dabble in external relations, and the woman (Una) looked after the home. What was at stake for them was the replication of the old world. For all of their modernity, their lesbianism, this other world that shimmered in the distance bore a very striking resemblance to the world of the home ministers who had condemned them. Their dream was never radical: it was simply to live with impunity in the world of their fathers. Radclyffe Hall did not have any more enlightened or humane view of intimate relations to offer. Her radicalism, the isolated status her sexual preference had bequeathed her, was merely a matter of biology: she was in fact as blithe as a Victorian roué in her flight from monogamy.

4

IN SICKNESS AND IN HEALTH

In the years leading up to the Second World War, John and Evguenia's connection grew increasingly fraught. Theirs had always been a relationship that thrived on a certain amount of suffering, but now it had ratcheted up a degree, and John was left with an unmanageable amount of insecurity. She became frantic, and her desperation began to make matters worse. She wrote to Evguenia, on July 26, 1937: "Darling do you think that you really still desire me as a lover? Or am I now just Johnnie to whom you belong and who takes care of you? Do you want me physically as I want you? Tell me, tell me, my dearest." Evguenia swiftly reassured her, and they continued to sleep together as before, but John had detected a real strain of disenchantment. Evguenia was increasingly involved with her friends who were also Russian exiles in Paris. In November, they had an upsetting conversation in which Evguenia confessed to John that she was more "normal" than she had thought, that she was beginning to entertain vague thoughts of marriage. She also told John that she would no longer stay in the same town as Una for more than a brief visit.

When it seemed that Evguenia would not be coming to see them on Christmas of 1938, John was despondent. She told Una she didn't want to celebrate with the usual festivities. She was too unhappy to even think about Christmas. But when Evguenia wrote at the last minute to say that she was going to come after all, John suddenly arranged for all sorts of delicacies, smoked salmon, mince pies, plum pudding, and marrons glacés, along with other sweets and elaborate decorations. In spite of her anticipation, the visit turned out to be unpleasant for all of them. Evguenia enraged Una by commenting that Una always echoed John's opinions about everything. She seemed to have abandoned what little tact she had previously shown. She seemed to be courting some sort of explosion.

The hostilities between Una and Evguenia came to a head when Evguenia tried to tell Una that she should stop encouraging John to have cocktails. John's blood pressure was high and the doctors had urged moderation. As a trained nurse, Evguenia felt the need to protect John's health. She wanted to have a reasonable conversation with Una on the subject. Una tried to walk out of the room and Evguenia physically pushed her away from the door, so that she would be forced to hear her out. John demanded that Evguenia apologize, but she refused. She was no longer willing to play the penitent and petted child.

On this same visit, John reluctantly agreed to Evguenia's demand that they cease their sexual relationship. John was deeply upset, but she had no choice but to acquiesce. From this point on, they would be involved in an intangible, romantically charged, quasi-familial friendship, still central to both of them. John's love for Evguenia, which was already somewhat abstract given the constant geographical distance between them, would take on one more level of abstraction. John wrote to Evguenia that she noticed the moment Evguenia had fallen out of love, which she believed had occurred when she hurt her ankle some months before:

> I know these things for I myself have been a great lover—I have loved and then grown weary and bored and put an abrupt and brutal end to the thing just as you have done. Did I stop to consider the other person's pain? No I did not. Well, now perhaps I am paying for the past and the price is high. . . . I don't understand it, I ought to hate you, but instead I must love you.

John arranged for Evguenia to stay in the relative safety of England on a visa for foreign nationals with John as her guarantor. She believed this would give her some level of control over Evguenia's movements, and keep her safe from the hostilities erupting in Europe.

As the political drama unfolded, John and Una were encamped in relative luxury in the Imperial Hotel in Lynton, with a view of the sea. They had their gas masks and the canary with them. Evguenia fairly quickly took a job as a nurse in a neighboring town. John protested. Her eyes were bothering her and she wanted Evguenia to stay with them. But the prospect of living with John and Una in a remote country town seemed impossibly claustrophobic to Evguenia. She told John that she had to work. She was not willing to sit out the war. But in many ways, John was all Evguenia had. Evguenia cried when she left her and wrote to her every day.

During this period, John's eyes had become a substantial problem: her eyelashes had begun to grow inward, irritating her eyes and causing chronic infections. In September of 1941, she underwent a dubious and painful operation to repair them. While she was recovering, she could not read or write. As a result Una had to read aloud and write her letters to Evguenia, so they were often censored and altered.

At around this same time, Evguenia insisted on taking a typing course at Oxford, which John also protested, as she did when Evguenia eventually took a job typing for the Red Cross, and then with the BBC. John couldn't stand the idea that her Soulina was drifting around England, that she did not know where she was at all times. She fretted about Evguenia's health, about her going out in the cold without a raincoat and boots, and she worried about air raids. She told Evguenia that she wanted her to list her as her "next of kin" on any forms that she had to fill out. It may seem strange that this particular piece of symbolism was important to her. But she continued to think of Evguenia as part of her amorphous family and that fantasy mattered deeply to her. John's extravagant obsession with Evguenia now took the form of an obsession with her physical safety. Her letters to Evguenia during this period took on a very contractual tone, with details of her allowance, and the behavior expected, laid out methodically. If Evguenia did something to displease her, she enumerated her reasons, and docked her five pounds. If someone unfamiliar with their tangled relationship glanced at these letters, still peppered with affectionate nicknames and urgent, checked affection, one would get the impression that Evguenia was a prodigal daughter.

Throughout this stressful period, when bombs were falling, Hall was still pining for her "darling most chinky faced little tartar." Her health was faltering again, and she felt confined by Una's constant, watchful presence. On Christmas Eve of 1942, she wrote to Evguenia: "Try to remember that your John, once so active and all over the place, is in the Lynton Prison Camp asking you to feed it once in a while through the prison bars." Evguenia had planned to join them as usual at Christmas. But at the last minute, she had to cancel her visit. She had gotten a job in the Foreign Office, effective immediately, and her whereabouts were now a national secret. She sent John a pot of white heather and white chrysanthemums, which touched her enormously.

In March of 1943, John's health began a grueling final decline. Soon afterward she was diagnosed with colon cancer. Her symptoms were excruciating, and she was taking opiates to ease the pain. There is perhaps a hint of cruelty in Una's final dedication to nursing Hall. She wrote missives to Evguenia that were almost obscene in their humiliating detail. "She is terribly flatulent," she wrote, "with an absolutely unmanageable irregularity of her bowels." She had reduced Hall to a mass of unseemly symptoms.

Hall, meanwhile, was desperate to see Evguenia; she felt that a few hours with Evguenia was the only thing on earth that would cheer her up. "Oh how weary I am of these four walls," she wrote when she was able to, "& how I do long for a breath of fresh country air with Royal Chinkie Pig very pompous & self-important taking me for a walk!" John wanted Evguenia to remain in the same county, if not in the same town. Evguenia again refused, saying that she had to go where there was work. Una fired off a warning letter on the stress to her patient: "If the strain breaks her down & she dies it will be your doing & on yr. conscience all yr. life." But at the same time, Una sensed that she was beginning to win. She was fighting against Hall's persistent romantic attachment to Evguenia, a now wistful, disembodied desire, with her old weapon: her presence.

In the sickroom, Una had finally found her kingdom. She was finally able to control John, in every small, intimate particular, and she reveled in her task. She insisted on nursing John herself. While the doctors warned her to watch her own health during her twenty-four-hour vigils, she felt that she was thriving as never before. Her own health had never been better. And her opinion of herself was not low: "There was never an hour when I would not in my passion of love and pity and adoration have kissed the poor wounds that tortured and humiliated you even as the saints kissed the pitiful & wonderful wounds of Christ." She was almost unnaturally elated. She also engaged in games of competitive sympathy that Evguenia could never win. When Evguenia brought flowers, Una would outdo her by flooding John's room with pink rosebuds. And in the last phase of the illness, when Evguenia tried to visit, Una tightly controlled her access to John, claiming she didn't want to upset the patient. She allowed her rival to stand inside the room, directly inside the door, but if she tried to approach the bed, Una had her removed from the room.

Una later claimed that it was during this final, excruciating period that John truly grasped Evguenia's irrelevance and marginality. "Never in all our twenty-eight years together has she given me such perfect assurance that of everyone on this earth only I am necessary to her." In the sketchy, flagrantly dishonest biography of Hall she would later write, *The Life of Radclyffe Hall,* Una persisted in treating Evguenia as an interloper, a passing infatuation that had no lasting effects on their love. But the truth is that this interloping lasted for nine years, and it cannot be said to have no endurance or longevity; however turbulent, this was not a frivolous or fleeting attraction. In fact, there was no tangible evidence that John's devotion to Evguenia faltered at the end of her life. John continued to weave longing for Evguenia through the very last letter she was able to write: "The Christmas dinner was prepared in the wild hope that you would share it; we are having it in an hours time."

What happened next is a subject of dispute: whether Hall came to her senses and regained perspective in the dwindling days of her life, or whether she was manipulated, can only be a matter of speculation. But in the days before her death, a confused and weakened Hall made a rather remarkable change to her will, which had included a generous inheritance for Evguenia. It now read: "I appoint Margot Elena Gertrude Troubridge [Una's legal name] to be Sole Executrix of this my Will and Demise and Bequeath to her all my property and estate both real and personal absolutely trusting her to make such provision for our friend Eugenie Souline as in her absolute discretion she may consider right knowing my wishes for the welfare of the said Eugenie Souline."

After John's death, then, Una inherited everything she had: the houses in London and in the country, the jewelry, the paintings, the bank accounts, altogether amounting to an estate totaling more than one hundred thousand pounds, in addition to the royalties from Hall's books and the literary rights to all her works. Una was now a very rich woman. In an almost eerie way, Una stepped into John's life and took over her identity. She began to wear John's poplin shirts, dressing gowns, cuff links, and jodhpurs. She stopped dressing in the feminine way that she was accustomed to during John's life. She cut her hair short as Hall's had been. She stopped laying flowers on Ladye's grave on the anniversary of her death as she and John had always done.

There is no doubt that Radclyffe Hall's death restored her to Una in a way that nothing in life would have. Una wrote of the demise of her beloved: "Thank God you are safe, safe, safe." Hall's unruly attractions and intimate betrayals, her restlessness in Una's company had ended abruptly; all that was left was a blanched, whitewashed, ideal love. Even in a world where her relationship could not be officially sanctioned, Una had emerged, victorious, as "the wife." The million small domestic tasks she dutifully performed amounted to far more than the brilliance of feeling between John and Evguenia.

On John's deathbed, Una had promised John that she would destroy her own diaries, but she found herself unable to do so. She did, however, find the courage to destroy all of Evguenia's letters to John, along with John's unfinished manuscript, *The Shoemaker of Merino,* which she claimed that John had asked her to burn. As John was writing it, Una had urged her to destroy it. Always encouraging of John's literary efforts, she had told her this particular manuscript was worthless. Una believed that the work was too autobiographical—she thought it was about John's love for Evguenia—and would be destructive to her reputation if published.

Evguenia lost her job at the Foreign Office the day after John died because she had taken off too many days during John's final illness. She consulted lawyers and business managers involved in John's estate, but to no avail. In a legal sense, it didn't matter how devoted John was to her, or what level of financial security she had promised her. Their intense, physical entanglement, all of the love John had given her over nine years, amounted to nothing. In an official, public sense she was nothing to John. Una arranged for Evguenia to receive a small allowance, and begrudged her any more than that, even when she requested an extra sum of money to launch a boarding-house so that she could support herself. Evguenia eventually married a man, who was also a Russian immigrant, and lived with him in one small room.

Over the next decade, Una and Evguenia remained in a state of uneasy truce, with Evguenia's small allowance continuing to arrive, along with terse Christmas cards enclosing one-pound notes. In 1957, Evguenia wrote to Una to ask Una to pay her doctors' bills now that she too had cancer. She appealed to her on the grounds of John's affection for her. She reminded Una that shortly before John died, she had held both of their hands, on opposite sides of the bed, and told them it was her intention that both of them should live comfortably. Una responded angrily, telling her that she had fabricated this deathbed scene, and refused to pay the doctors' bills. Though she was about to die, Evguenia began to type out her letters from John for publication. They would tell her side of the story.

By this time, Una was spending most of her time in Florence, which she had always loved. She had found someone else to serve with her peculiar blend of fierce, grandiose self-abnegation. She had become an acolyte of the opera singer Nicola Rossi-Lemeni, attending all of his performances, managing his fan mail, helping him with publicity. She prided herself on the fact that he could not do without her. When he divorced his wife, she assumed even more importance for him. To the end of her life, she was a ferociously devoted, ambiguous maternal force. She rubbed his feet and sat with him in his bedroom until he fell asleep. As a token of her devotion, she gave him John's sapphire cuff links.

GEORGE GORDON CATLIN AND
VERA BRITTAIN

WINIFRED HOLTBY

> "One of the most rigid of traditions is that which regards
> marriage as a day-by-day, hour-by-hour, unbroken
> and unbreakable association . . . nothing could
> be further from the free, generous, and intelligent
> comradeship which is the marriage ideal of the
> finest young men and women of today."
>
> —VERA BRITTAIN, "ON SEMI-DETACHED MARRIAGE," 1928

1926. After a little more than a year, Vera Brittain's "semi-detached" marriage was in danger of becoming wholly detached. The ideals she and her accommodating husband, George Gordon Catlin, had painstakingly agreed to had lately begun to seem out of reach. In their rapid, skittish courtship, the young political philosopher had written to her: "I offer you, I think, as free a marriage as it lies in the power of a man to offer a woman . . . I ask you to give what you want to give, no more." Unfortunately in the first months of their marriage, these and other airy abstractions had been wrestled to the earth, and Catlin, at least, was frustrated. The richness and originality of "semi-detachment" seemed to confer its benefits only on Vera. Catlin found himself alone and depressed in a small, empty, third-floor apartment in Ithaca, New York.

At the age of thirty, Vera Brittain was a feminist, a pacifist, a journalist, and a novelist; she radiated an ambition that made itself felt as nervous charisma. Though she had not yet written the bestselling World War I memoir, *Testament of Youth,* that would make her famous, she tended to view her life on a grand scale. Her writing would include at least one-thousand-five-hundred pages of straight memoir, in addition to her autobiographical novel, autobiographical poems, and autobiographical articles. She seemed to find it nearly impossible to exhaust the literary possibilities of herself.

Her acquaintance with Catlin had begun with a fan letter he had written her after the publication of her first novel, set in Oxford, which was called *The Dark Tide.* He had also glimpsed her at debates at the university, though she had not noticed him. Vera was small, dark, and pretty. She had the romantic aura of someone afflicted by a mysterious sorrow. Her correspondence with Catlin continued for some time before they met. Vera was intrigued by Catlin's detailed appreciative criticism of her novel, and his smart, erudite letters began to spark her interest. He revealed his political ambitions, to one day be an elected official and try out his ideas, and sent a photograph that further intrigued her. When they finally met in person they went to a George Bernard Shaw play and took a walk through the park. Over the next two days, marriage was mentioned. A week later they went to Oxford together, and the river and cathedral began to work on her imagination, and she felt herself surrender to a new love. Vera would write wistfully to Catlin later about that day: "Why oh why can't one stay the same towards people? One perfect moment on the river—shy, a little embarrassing, but so exquisite. Stay there for ever, lovely moment, with all your possibilities, so much more exciting always than achievement! No—it has gone; it will never come back."

The serious political philosopher, thin as a reed and very stiff, wanted a woman as steeped in politics as he was and he had found one. On their honeymoon, while touring European cities, he interviewed various government figures for his work, and she did not find this unsettling.

Vera announced from the outset that she regarded the first year of marriage as an experiment. One of her main reservations was that she worried about marriage affecting her work. As a precocious eighteen-year-old, she had written in her diary about a "new era of companionship of woman, no longer the angel, set up on a pedestal, shut out of everything, & no longer the toy, the sort of soft cushion, or hot-water bottle, for the husband to soothe himself with after having spent the day seriously." It was her elaborately articulated position that a woman must be productive, and if that productivity was compromised by her domestic arrangements she had an obligation to change them.

In spite of her politically charged trepidation, Vera had, like an ordinary bride, sailed with Catlin, whom everyone called Gordon, to the United States where he was an assistant professor at Cornell University, and duly set up house in a small apartment on the top floor of a three-story building, but she was soon restless. She had the unsettling sense that she had returned to precisely the sort of cultural backwater she had grown up in and devoted her entire life to escaping: a small hill town in Derbyshire called Buxton. For the first time in her adult life she did not feel usefully occupied. She claimed that she could not find freelance work. She could not establish herself in America. She had gone from being a working journalist to a faculty wife pouring tea. While this was technically true, she was also having trouble concentrating on writing her next book. She couldn't think. The underlying problem was her sense of being exiled from London and the life she was building there. Perhaps most importantly, she missed her intimate friend and roommate, Winifred Holtby. "Gordon has never understood——I suppose in the nature of things he could not understand——how much I love you," she wrote to Winifred from her Ithaca apartment. The reality, which she only partially articulated, was that she found Catlin's company somehow unsatisfying. He ignored her or began to ostentatiously read his newspaper when she tried to talk about her ideas. He told her he didn't feel like talking and would have to "schedule" the conversation for later. It was Winifred, she believed, who created the perfect atmosphere for her writing.

Vera spent the summer stewing in misery, and in August they moved back to London. Vera did not return with Catlin when the semester started again in September. At first Catlin agreed that a temporary separation would be best. In theory, he was willing to accept the fact that she needed to be in England for her career, just as he needed to be in New York. But Catlin was soon writing to her in a state of leaden depression. He did not appear to Vera to be upholding the spirit of their agreement. She replied to one of his woeful letters: "Why should I have a sort of moral obligation to see that you eat enough? Much you would notice if *my* appetite showed a falling off! Why men should endow themselves with a monopoly in this kind of helplessness I really don't know!"

But in the end Catlin capitulated. The two remained apart until she came to visit him in the spring of 1927, with her mother in tow. The apartment felt smaller than ever, and the mood was volatile and tense. Vera's rather insightful mother, Edith, wrote to Winifred: "She will expect the 'mere man' to be what you are and have been to her and that is impossible." By summertime, when Vera was pregnant with her first child, she wrote to Winifred formally proposing the permanent establishment of a joint household. Catlin would teach half the year in the United States and travel for part of the rest of the year. Winifred would travel whenever she wished, and Vera would remain in their shared residence in London. They would all three share expenses. This was the culmination of the experiment that Vera labeled "semi-detached" marriage. Vera was exhilarated by their innovative arrangement. Why should a husband and wife, who mutually understood and respected each other, have to live together? Why should a freely united couple be tethered to a single household? Vera fired off a piece extolling the virtues of "semi-detached marriages" to *The Evening News*. Catlin, at first, was marvelous. He seemed to embrace her theories. He wrote to her: "What matters is not where you are, but what you are."

In many ways, their ménage did provide an ingenious solution to the problem raised by Vera's particular psychology, which required an intricate balance of attachment and independence. She and Catlin could pursue independent careers on separate continents, and travel on their own, and come together en famille for short stretches of time. And Winifred would be, as Vera put it, a second mother to their children. "Won't you feel the baby is yours too?" she wrote Winifred in the weeks before her son, John, was born. When her second child, Shirley, turned out to be blond, the two would joke that she had Winifred's hair. Both children adored their "auntie," and it did not seem to any of them unhealthy that the strain of the nuclear family was diffused onto more people, the work of the household approached with greater energy and creativity. As Vera herself pointed out, the unmarried Winifred was, in many ways, more temperamentally suited to the care of small children than Vera herself was. Vera, in fact, felt motherhood was not her "forte." Winifred, on the other hand, seemed to bring a natural levity to childcare. At one point when Vera was traveling, Winifred would write to her: "John today observed 'When are you going to get rid of that cold, Auntie?' (I've had a sniffle for some days) I replied 'As soon as I can.' John, contemplatively: 'Wouldn't it go quicker if you didn't talk so much?' (Screams of joyous laughter from Shirley; John continues to look bright and helpful.) . . . I love this dear household and its lovely children." When Vera and Catlin traveled on holiday to Portofino, where as Vera eagerly pointed out Elizabeth von Arnim had written *The Enchanted April,* Winifred oversaw the children and their nannies. For the bulk of the year, however, Winifred and Vera remained in London with the children.

John was somewhat confused by the family configuration. Vera reports, by way of charming anecdote, that her twenty-one-month-old son was fond of exclaiming: "I don't like my wife—I'll send him away because I want another woman." This surely was not an accidental or wholly benign interpretation of their arrangement. The child also, somewhat later, felt the need to ask his father, "Daddy, do you like me?"

Over time, Catlin interpreted the rubric of "semi-detached" marriage as license for affairs. In his wordy, opaque memoirs, he hints coyly at his extramarital adventures: "When a lady of charm takes the initiative by saying 'perhaps' it would be ungallant not to compliment her—and no small loss amid life's rarer pleasures." But Vera adamantly did not view those "rarer pleasures" as part of semi-detachment. For her, the geographical distance was richly repaid by the compensations of her platonic intimacy with Winifred. When Catlin wrote to Vera that he was considering one such dalliance, in the winter of 1929, she was extremely distressed. She did not feel that she could expressly forbid it, given the unusual freedom she herself had requested and seized, and yet she was deeply threatened by the possibility of her husband ensconced with another woman on the other side of the Atlantic. She was in the midst of reading D. H. Lawrence's *Lady Chatterley's Lover*. She understood, at least in theory, the power of sexual attraction. She responded by telling him to do whatever was necessary for his "health," as if sex, like exercise, were a matter of physical well-being. She also wrote to ask him if he thought that she was frigid, which he reassured her that he did not.

In their transatlantic exchange over this delicate topic, Vera characteristically retreated to politics. She wrote to him: "The thing I perhaps fear most is something that might smirch or spoil or render less dignified or in any way cheapen our relationship, not only in our eyes but in the eyes of the world. Our work—at any rate my work—depends largely for its success, not only upon the fact that we are ideally happy together, but that we are known to be so. If it sounds arrogant to say that the success of our marriage matters to the world, to society, to politics, to feminism, I can only reply that it is the kind of arrogance that one ought to encourage in oneself."

As they struggled to define their relationship, Vera was writing a utopian book in the spirit of H. G. Wells called *Halcyon: Or the Future of Monogamy*. The premise of the whimsical little book was that a woman academic from the twenty-first century writes a "history of monogamy." What this faux history reveals is that in the future, when women had obtained the same basic rights as men and everyone had the freedom they needed, they would be monogamous by choice. Promiscuity would be a thing of the past, a product of twisted Victorian values that forced sexual attraction underground. Unlike many of the progressives writing on marriage, Vera was in favor of monogamy. Vera had intended *Halcyon* to be part of a larger book on marriage, which she never ended up producing. At one point, Vera wrote to Catlin in a rare moment of vulnerability: "It seems hopeless to write about sex and marriage when I don't know what I really think . . ."

Theirs was a densely complicated marriage with more than two people involved. There had always been other figures, ghostly and real, enfolded in their relationship: Winifred, for one, and Vera's dead fiancé, Roland, for another. Vera did not view marriage as imposing a monopoly on emotional intensity. She was a highly romantic creature who seemed to idealize and mythologize every relationship in her life but her marriage. If Catlin felt rejected by Vera's clever, modish rhetoric of "detachment," it would take him years to fully articulate his objections.

2

ROLAND

"When the great war broke out," Vera wrote, "it came to me not as a superlative tragedy, but as an interruption of the most exasperating kind to my personal plans." At nineteen, with the country on the brink of war, Vera managed to be both frivolous and ambitious, intellectually driven and girlish. She wrote poems with names like "Fragment of a Soliloquy on an Unpleasant Evening"; she played tennis; she toyed with the affections of neighborhood boys. Her diaries could have been written by a smart, provincial Jane Austen character. And yet, she was remarkably driven: she slaved over her books to prepare for the examinations for Oxford, which was considered extremely eccentric for a girl in her small town. Though she came from a fairly conventional family, with a father who ran a paper mill, she had always been literary and rebellious, memorizing Longfellow poems when she was eight, and later engaging in what she called her "warfare against Buxton youngladyhood." She was not content to do what was expected of her; instead she was striving for some form of greatness. She wrote about her eighteenth year: "I shudder to think how I have thrown a year away—save in experience, which one cannot throw away—how little I have read, & written practically nothing, how unenergetic, unenterprising I have been." In her diaries, she analyzed every single thing that happened to her with unusual thoroughness and with the grandiosity one would expect from that stage of life, a grandiosity she somehow sustained for decades.

In the spring of 1914, her brother Edward brought home a

member of his close-knit group of friends from his school, Uppingham. Roland Leighton was brooding, brilliant, arrogant. He took home nearly all of the academic prizes at their school. Like Vera, he was determined to be a famous writer. His mother was a successful author of Edwardian romances, and his family had a bohemian, ramshackle ambience which Vera, who disdained her ordinary, bourgeois origins, greatly admired. Vera particularly enjoyed teasing her brother's handsome new guest for taking himself so seriously. She pointed out that he didn't respond to nature in a spontaneous way, but instead pretended to like it because he thought liking nature was a literary attribute. The two spent hours one afternoon sitting on a sawed-off tree trunk near her house, deconstructing each other's personalities, engaging in the aggressive banter that remained their characteristic mode of flirtation. She mocked him for his "Quiet Voice," the serious, condescending tone he would assume when speaking about important subjects, and he seemed to enjoy the mockery. They both felt, for the first time, known.

But as the young men of her acquaintance began enlisting for the war, there was suddenly no time for ordinary, meandering infatuation. In the weeks before he left for the army, Vera went from moderately intrigued by Roland to deeply in love. By the time they went through their obligatory farewell on a railway platform, they had already exchanged photographs. World events had defined their relationship for them. Every minor fluctuation of emotion occurred against the backdrop of mortal danger, with the extremes of war amplifying the usual drama of young love.

In truth, once the seriousness of the situation became clear,

Vera, Roland, and their friends were, on some level, invigorated by the prospect of war. She would later write: "It is, I think, this glamour, this magic, this incomparable keying up of the spirit in a time of mortal conflict, which constitutes the pacifist's real problem—a problem still incompletely imagined, and still quite unresolved . . . The challenge to spiritual endurance, the intense sharpening of the senses, the vitalizing consciousness of a common peril for a common end, remained to allure those boys and girls who have just reached the age when love and friendship and adventure call more persistently than at any later time."

Before Roland went off to the army, the two met in London with a chaperone, Vera's Aunt Belle. They were still following traditional courtship rules; the morals governing the behavior of young people had not yet been relaxed by the war. At first, sitting awkwardly in a tea shop, they were extremely shy and utterly incapable of carrying on a conversation. But after a few hours together, they began to warm to each other and launched into a discussion of how they would like to be buried (she wanted to be burned on a pyre like Achilles, and he wanted to be set adrift on a flaming boat like the Vikings). Vera's aunt was not pleased by this turn in the conversation. The next night he swept her off to the theater to see *David Copperfield* and brought her a bouquet of tall pink roses with a tinge of orange. The war, at this point, was still a glorious abstraction to both of them. Roland, like her brother, whom Vera herself encouraged to enlist, was hungry for battle. He declared that he did not want to "play" soldier. He said that he would hate to go through the war without getting wounded.

Roland left for the front at the end of March of 1915. In the beginning he slept on straw on the floor of a French farm-house, near the border of Belgium, but soon afterward he was sent into battle. He wrote from the trenches of Armentières: "It is a beautiful sunny day today, and it seems a pity there should be such a thing as war. Summer & trenches don't go to-gether somehow." He wrote sharp, eloquent letters to her while German bullets skimmed the sandbags covering the roof of his dugout. By May, the first man in his regiment was killed, and Roland, who found him lying very still at the bottom of a trench with blood trickling down his cheek, gathered the con-tents of his pockets—a torn letter, a pencil and a knife, and a piece of shell—and wrapped them in a handkerchief to send back to his loved ones.

Roland sent Vera fairly accomplished poems about the war, along with the violets growing on the roof of his dugout in France. "I am coming back, dear," he wrote. "Let it always be 'when' & not 'if.' The day will come when we shall live our roseate poem through." At other times he was too over-whelmed to send her more than a terse few lines, obliquely re-ferring to his movements to make it past the censors. Vera, meanwhile, was troubled by the fact that when she closed her eyes she was unable to picture his face.

Their physical relations were innocent in the extreme. When they finally saw each other unchaperoned for the first time, when he was on leave, they shook hands. In another of their rare, private moments in her parents' house, he draped his arm on the sofa, above her shoulders. These chaste mo-ments are described by Vera with a certain romantic intensity, but there was a quality of stilted yearning to all of their physi-cal relations. When Roland finally kissed her, Vera made a joke about how inexperienced he seemed. The fact was that neither of them was entirely comfortable with the idea of sex. For all of their sophistication in other areas, they were both still quite childlike. She recounts in her diary a talk she had with her mother directly before the war: "On the way to golf I induced mother to disclose a few points on sexual matters which I thought I ought to know, though the information is always intensely distasteful to me & most depressing—in fact, it quite put me off my game."

In the summer, Vera left Oxford to become a nurse. Now that the war seemed like it was going to last, she no longer felt she could devote herself to her studies in good conscience. She had been reading Plato and wandering by the river, while the boys who should have been there with her were sleeping in their uniforms, unwashed, unshaven, in the trenches in France. Vera threw herself into the hard work of nursing with characteristic zeal. Her days were taken up with bandaging amputated fingers, rubbing ointment into frostbitten extremities, and fetching warm drinks. In her spare time, she scanned the casualty lists in the newspapers and waited for the post. "I never thought I should say to anyone such things as I write to Roland," Vera confided in her diary. In some sense the urgency of war opened up new possibilities for intimacy, as all decorum, all reserve between them had broken down.

Even though Vera eschewed many of the values she grew up with, she was still a cossetted child of the comfortable middle class, and she now found herself living in unheated, shared rooms in London and walking to work through the cold, to begin a long day of hard, physical labor. Nursing, in its sheer, exhausting drudgery, was distracting: she could only think about the next task she had to perform. Only at the hospital had she begun to know men's bodies. Before that, she writes, she had never thought of men unclothed, had never seen any part of them but their faces. But in the hospital she was suddenly performing all manner of intimate tasks, and as she ministered to their lean naked bodies, she told herself that she was nursing Roland "by proxy." She felt that she was learning the specifics and beauty of the male form in a way that deepened her experience of love.

Though Vera spent much of her time agonizing over Roland's safety, and though she did love him with the obsessive fierceness of first love, there was undoubtedly a part of her that was storing everything she experienced for later use. She recorded the minutiae of daily life in a more ambitious spirit than that which infuses most schoolgirl diaries. One evening, she wrote with the unseemly self-consciousness of a budding writer: "I sat up till 1:30 reading my own letters. It was so interesting reading side by side mine & the answers to them from him. There is first-rate material there for an autobiographical novel."

In the beginning, both Roland and Vera had resisted labels for their relationship, preferring instead the "thrilling, indefinite glamour" of living outside accepted categories. But when Roland returned for a few days in August, they became engaged. Afterward, they went shopping in London, him for a knife, and her for a nurse's uniform. She refused to wear an engagement ring, which might connote ownership; but secretly she was thrilled by the prospect of spending her life with him. Her diaries reflect the usual solipsism of that period of life, as she laughs at "the world's ignorance of the meaning of a love like mine." In September, he sent her a letter with the words *hinc illae lacrimae,* which was their code to get past the censors for his entrance into one of the worst battles of the war, but he emerged without harm.

Even as Roland rose in rank, becoming acting adjutant of his battalion, the war blasted his emotions and made his life at home seem unreal. He wrote: "I feel a barbarian, a wild man of the woods, stiff, narrowed, practical; an incipient martinet perhaps—not at all the kind of person who would be associated with prizes on Speech Day, or poetry . . . Do I seem very much of a phantom in the void to you? I must. You seem to me rather like a character in a book or someone whom one has dreamt of and never seen." Vera was angry at being abstracted and dismissed and fired back: "Most estimable, practical, unexceptional adjutant, I suppose I ought to thank you for your letter, since apparently one has to be grateful nowadays for being allowed to know you are alive. But all the same, my first impulse was to tear that letter into small shreds, since it appeared to me very much like an epistolary expression of the Quiet Voice . . ." He wrote back, chastened: "Dearest, I do deserve it, every word of it and every sting of it. 'Most estimable, practicable, unexceptional adjutant' . . . Oh Damn! I have been a perfect beast, a conceited selfish, self-satisfied beast. Just because I can claim to live half my life in a trench, and might possibly get hit by something in the process, I have felt myself justified in forgetting everything and everybody except my own Infallible Majesty."

In December of 1915, Roland writes to her that he has been given six days' leave. She tells herself that during these few days they will finally get married. The morning of

Christmas Eve, she has her hair washed and done in a shop near Victoria. She spends Christmas Eve filling red gift bags for the men with sweets and nuts, in a pleasant haze of expectation. On Christmas Day, she cheerfully travels to Brighton where her parents are on holiday. She looks out at the gray, choppy waves and hopes that he is not having a rough crossing. Then on the morning of December 27, she dresses with great excitement in a pale blue crêpe de chine blouse. And she hears the phone ring. She runs to pick it up and revel in the sound of his voice, but it is his sister, Clare, saying that their family had a telegram. Vera hears the words, read aloud, through the phone line: "T233 regret to inform you that Lieut. R. A. Leighton 7th Worcesters died of wounds December 23rd. Lord Kitchener sends his sympathy." He was shot performing a routine check of a length of barbed wire in the moonlight. Apparently the soldiers his platoon had relieved in this particular stretch of the front had forgotten to inform their successors that German snipers had a habit of shooting at that particular stretch of barbed wire at night. He died twenty-four hours later of wounds. His death seemed to Vera unheroic, unnecessary, routine, and in this, more brutal.

To the twenty-year-old Vera, it felt that her entire future was blotted out. She had lost the one man on whom her happiness depended. But how well did she know him? They had an unusually well-developed intellectual rapport and, certainly, a more interesting, substantive love affair than most people their age. But they had spent, cumulatively, about seventeen days together. Some of the times they saw each other they were slightly awkward and prickly, with a misplaced sharpness. In spite of their fluent, playful, writerly letters, it is impossible to know if a marriage between these two very young people would have been happy. It is conceivable that their very similarities—their voracious ambition, their arrogance—would have created difficulties at some later point in time. It is possible that over the years their jubilant, articulate teasing, their gift for comically deflating each other, would have hardened into sharper criticism and intolerance. But to Vera, the relationship, now an idea of a relationship, was suspended in a state of immutable perfection. While Roland was at the front, she had confided in her diary that her greatest desire was suddenly, "not to astonish the world with some brilliant and glittering achievement, but someday to be the mother of Roland Leighton's child." And yet, of course, he was forever frozen as a beautiful young man, in the unattainable netherworld of death. Severed at a stage of unconsummated longing and novelty, the relationship would remain forever the central articulation of passion in Vera's life.

For the next years of the war, Vera devoted herself to nursing. On some level, she didn't want to feel better, because to feel better would be to forsake Roland. She wrote rather wisely: "If the living are to be of any use in this world they have to break faith with the dead," and for a long time she was unable to take this step. Still in a numbed state of anguish, she was transferred to St. George's Hospital in Malta. She loved the dramatic cliffs and white beaches and glittering purple ocean, even in her misery. She found the hard, physical work soothing and the outdoor life restorative. The photographs of her from the period show her browned and healthy in her elaborate nurse's uniform.

In the aftermath of Roland's death, Vera had grown closer

to Edward and Roland's other friends Geoffrey and Victor and she wrote to them and sent them cigarettes. She worried about all of them and tracked their movements through the various danger zones of Europe. Edward, her gentle musician brother, had fought in the battles of Ypres and the Somme, and was awarded a Military Cross for bravery. And then, that April she received bad news: Victor had been seriously wounded. He would almost certainly be blind for the rest of his life. And at around the same time, she was cabled the news that Geoffrey had been shot through the chest at Monchy-le-Preux. Somehow this last blow made it impossible for her to continue as she was. She felt that she had to see Victor. And she applied for a leave to return to England in order to devote the rest of her life to his care. In the long-ago days of their courtship, she and Roland had been astonished by an advertisement in the Agony column of the paper which read as follows: "Lady whose fiancé died in the war seeks officer, wounded, or blinded, to care for." Together she and Roland had speculated on what deep nihilism could have motivated this woman to take out this advertisement, what absolute disregard for the usual selfish concerns of happiness and love. But now Vera felt in herself the same impulse. She did not love Victor, but she wanted to marry him and nurse him, nonetheless. No man, she felt, would ever matter to her more than any other. Her personal life had become that abstract: she needed to nurse a soldier, in the most generalized form. The prospect seemed to her at the time to provide sufficient purpose for the rest of her days. As it turned out, Victor died in the hospital before she had a chance to declare her intentions. By the end of the war, Edward, who had been fighting in Italy, was also dead.

The war had been an event so cataclysmic and intense that amidst the jubilation of armistice, life as she now understood it seemed over. "How trivial my life has been since the war," she wrote. "How can the future achieve through us, the sombre majesty of the past?" Her romantic life certainly, seemed to have reached its highest pitch. She would never again feel "the invading passion that for me had burnt itself out, once and for all, in 1915." Now she could only hope for "the loyal, friendly emotion which arises between mutually respectful equals of opposite sex who are working side by side for some worthwhile end." This dreary, workmanlike conception of love is what she was left with after what she called the smashup of her youth. She was too tired for love.

In the aftermath of the war, the British newspapers were filled with discussions of the plight of the "superfluous woman": so many young men had died that there was a surplus of marriageable women who would not be married. Vera claimed to consider herself one of them, even writing a poem, "The Superfluous Woman," about how the best men of her generation had been killed in the war. But, in fact, she had always had admirers and had even had a fleeting engagement at Oxford in the dark, confused years after the war.

Vera took her degree and moved to London in 1922 to embark on her journalistic career. She was twenty-nine, living with Winifred Holtby and their pet tortoise, Adolphus, in a tiny ground-floor studio in Bloomsbury, divided with curtains. Together they taught, and lectured, and made a little money through freelance journalism. Then they would meet at the end of the long workday for a dinner of eggs and cheese prepared on their hot plate, to mull over everything that had happened

274 · Katie Roiphe

to them. Later they moved to the top-floor apartment where
the sun flowed in through drafty skylights. Winifred finished
her first novel, *Anderby Wold,* in the spring. Ironically, the romantic passion Vera claimed to have renounced after the war
was now transferred to friendship: it is her relationship with
Winifred that seemed freighted with some of the obsessive intensity of her earlier love. The two traveled to France and Italy,
visiting Roland's and Edward's graves, traveling third class,
staying in shabby inns, in what both claimed to be the most
perfect holiday of their lives.

In autumn of 1923, after the publication of her own first
novel, *The Dark Tide,* Vera received the fan letter from the
young political philosopher that would end in marriage. Her
new husband had reassured her that he would be the generous,
respectful partner she had dreamed about, granting her all of
the space and independence she required. Vera put off her ap-
prehension about marriage onto the politics of it: she claimed
that she was worried that domestic responsibilities would im-
pinge on her work, which no doubt she did. But she also must
have worried that this new relationship seemed paler than her
vivid love for Roland. What living man could compare to the
quintessential romance of a dead poet-soldier? Also, she barely
knew Gordon Catlin, and had spent less time in his physical
presence than she had with Roland. She joked about how like
her it was to become engaged to a man who was about to sail
off to another country, even when there *wasn't* a war.

After she agreed to marry him, Vera was beset by dreams
that Roland had not died, but had instead been missing all
along, and resurfaced, wanting to marry her. In real life, she
wavered, and Catlin, now painfully in love, appealed to

Winifred: "If Vera breaks off the engagement it will be the greatest disaster that has ever happened to me, and I do not know how I will survive it." Vera was also worried about how she was going to sustain the closeness to Winifred that she depended on. In the weeks after her engagement she sent off a letter to her: "Dear Winifred, I shall never be parted from you for very long. I never can be."

Winifred herself was nearly as wrapped in the idealized romance of the story as the principals. With her usual generosity, she was happy for Vera, and she seemed to take some of that happiness for her own. And yet, some small side of her stood apart with the ironic perspective toward love she had assumed in the past few years. She wrote to a friend: "G. is back. This is the most charming love story that I have yet encountered. When I saw him yesterday, slim, charming, brilliant, with his blue eyes ablaze with happiness, and his arm across the shoulder of his little love, I almost believed that the romance of fiction was less perniciously untruthful than I had thought." She was *almost* but not quite convinced of their happiness.

Brittain resolved to keep her own name, which was a fairly radical gesture at the time. But the wedding itself was surprisingly traditional. The couple took out an announcement in *The Times* of their engagement. Vera had also remained a virgin, despite Catlin's pressure. Her attitude toward what she referred to as her "purity" was surprisingly old-fashioned for a modern, independent woman. Though she had gained familiarity with men's bodies as a nurse during the war, and had, according to her own account, lost the Victorian modesty of her childhood, she did not feel sufficiently adventurous to lose her virginity to her fiancé.

They were married on June 27, 1925, at St. James's Church on Spanish Place, seven years after the war ended. Vera wore an ivory satin dress and tulle veil decorated with orange blossoms. The groom was tall, elegantly scrawny, and blue eyed. His shirt gaped slightly at his neck. He looked like a boy draped in a man's suit. One of his friends told Vera that he had always viewed Catlin as a natural bachelor and a monk. If this characterization disturbed her in any way, she never let on. The sky was pearl gray with sunlight breaking through. And as Vera walked down the aisle, she carried the same tall, pink, slightly orange-tinged roses that Roland had brought her on several occasions. She felt certain Catlin would understand the necessity of the gesture.

3

WINIFRED

As it happened, Winifred's date for Vera's wedding, Harry Pearson, had simply not shown up at the ceremony. That is, he had opened the door, glanced in, and then walked away without saying anything to anyone because the wedding looked too posh. Winifred, meanwhile, felt like a "stuffed amazon" in her bridesmaid's blue and mauve dress and elaborately feathered hat. And as she walked in, she had overheard one of the wedding guests speculate that she was the mother of the bride, even though she had just turned twenty-seven, and was, in fact, four years younger than Vera.

When the wedding was over Winifred returned to the hotel where the reception was held to retrieve a pair of gloves that Catlin had accidentally left behind. This would be the first errand in what would prove to be a pattern of quasi-familial devotion to the couple. On their wedding night Catlin wrote to Winifred: "You were, I think, almost more indispensable to the wedding than the bridegroom himself."

As Vera left for her honeymoon, she felt herself near tears. She had the pressing, irrational sense that they should be taking Winifred along with them. In the years since they had been at Oxford, she and Winifred had been inseparable—living, working, lecturing, and traveling together; it felt strange to experience something as monumental as a honeymoon without her. Who was she going to talk about it with? And, as Vera and her new husband wound their way through Vienna and Budapest, Vera's letters to Winifred were filled with emotional infidelity of an exquisite, most likely manipulative variety: "I still have the persistent feeling that my beloved husband is a mere accessory and that you, not him, belong to the real essentials of life."

If it had long been understood between them that Vera was the attractive one and Winifred the plain one, the distinction is not immediately apparent in their photographs. Winifred has waving blond hair, bright blue eyes, a strong smile, and the large frame of a Yorkshire girl raised on a farm, with the healthy appeal of a girl extremely comfortable on a horse. If there was an awkwardness to her appearance, it lay in her largeness, or in her feelings toward her largeness. She did not carry herself with the same grace and confidence as Vera.

Winifred's penchant for extravagant, highly theoretical loves may not have enhanced her confidence in her own attractions. She spent her adult life at least half in love with Harry Pearson, who had blue eyes, long lashes, suntanned skin, and a cigarette perpetually dangling out of his mouth. He was charismatic, unreliable, original, maddening; but he had loved Winifred, in his way, since they played together as children. He too had disappeared into the army before he had a chance to go to Cambridge, and returned darker and damaged—"a casualty of the spirit," Vera would write. In between stints in the navy and in India, Harry would surface periodically in Winifred's life. They had occasional romantic interludes and an electric, intimate friendship. She thought of marrying him, but he remained, as she put it, "my-young-man-who-would-always-be-only-my-young-man." He seemed, at times, fairly attached to her, but he would not take any conventional steps toward consummating that attachment, even becoming briefly engaged to another woman, to Winifred's great dismay. He drifted in and out of her life with just enough regularity to maintain his emotional hold over her. Winifred dedicated her novel *The Land of Green Ginger* to him: "To a philosopher in Peshawar who said he wanted something to read."

If Harry remained her abstract romantic hero, Vera was, for most of her adult life, Winifred's true companion. The friendship contained such deep stores of sympathy, such constant, easy intimacy that in certain ways it did resemble a marriage. Catlin acknowledged this openly when he wrote to her: "I know, my dear Winifred, what I am stealing from you." And she responded in kind with the assurance, "When you have returned to England you will find I have effected a quite neat and painless divorce." It is certainly true that Winifred and Vera's correspondence is charged with an ardor usually reserved for lovers. But if there was an erotic undercurrent to the friendship, it was largely on Winifred's part. After Vera sailed for America, she wrote, with a kind of sensual longing for Vera's presence: "I am, as I said, very, very happy, but it's a sort of autumn empty happiness. I miss the feel of your fingers round my left arm when I walk through the evening streets, and the lamps are golden flowers among the sycamore trees." As if projecting her affection for Vera onto a more acceptably male form, Winifred more than once imagined herself in a love affair with Vera's dead brother, Edward. She often thought of his musician's ear when she went to a concert, and she imagined the two of them would have had a special understanding if he had survived the war. But it is nonetheless unlikely that any physical longing she may have felt for Vera herself ever rose to the surface. Winifred's views on lesbian relationships seemed to veer toward intolerance. In a revealing comment on the public spectacle of *The Well of Loneliness*, she wrote: "Radclyffe Hall has taught me a lot. She's all fearfully wrong, I feel. To love other women deeply is not pathological. To be unable to control one's passions is. Her mind is all sloppy with self-pity and self-admiration."

There were, nonetheless, many rumors circulating about their unorthodox arrangement when, in autumn of 1927, Vera moved back to London to set up house with Winifred. Their neighborhood, Chelsea, was home to many same-sex unions, and many of what Vera called their "over-sophisticated" neighbors read sexual attraction into their complicated ménage. In her published writing, Vera treated these rumors as a source of amusement. (She was, however, not insensitive to innuendo. When the time came to prepare her's and Winifred's *Selected*

Letters for publication, she removed the plentiful endearments.) In fact, Vera preferred to discuss their unusual household as a clever solution to a practical problem. How could she raise a family without compromising her work? How could she manage the responsibilities of a family without compromising her feminist principles? She preferred *not* to view their arrangement in emotional terms, though, of course, her attachment to Winifred, her inability to live without her, was the impetus for their unusual family constellation. She wanted a husband, and children, and Winifred; she wanted conventional family life, and she wanted unconventional freedom. Their joint household was for Vera, "the nearest thing to complete happiness that I have ever known, or ever hope to know."

When Catlin returned to Ithaca for his first fall alone, in 1927, Winifred cabled him: "Bon Voyage will keep good guard Winifred." Her good nature and innate generosity seemed, at the outset, to have diffused any of the natural rivalry that might have emerged between them. In her letters to Catlin, she referred to Vera as the "child," as if they shared a protective purpose in regards to a temperamental, if charming protégée. In some sense Winifred acted as Catlin's proxy. She bought Vera presents from Catlin, and Catlin often wrote to Winifred for advice about his marriage. At one point, Winifred joked to Vera that if Catlin were a Mormon they both could have married him. The fact that she felt she could make such a joke bespoke a fairly high level of comfort with the triangular situation on all sides. The natural tensions seemed at first to have been subsumed in the clear practical benefits of the arrangement. At one point, Winifred sent Catlin a letter describing how Vera looked sitting in a pile of her tiny new shoes and shoe boxes, opening one of Catlin's letters. She had positioned herself intimately inside the marriage, a narrator and observer of their love.

Meanwhile the small household buzzed along happily. Once John was born, a month early and quite small, the two women consulted a group of mothers called the "Chelsea Babies Club." There, in the company of other women in the neighborhood, they learned to feed and care for him. Winifred took care of him on the nurse's half day and pushed his perambulator to the nearby Kensington Gardens and Vera referred to her as "his discreet but devoted slave." In the meantime, they were busy writing articles for the *Yorkshire Post,* the *Manchester Guardian,* and *Time and Tide.* When Vera's daughter was born three years later, Winifred stayed up all night helping the nurse with the birth. And she remained involved in the mundane domestic work of child rearing for the rest of her life. She helped Vera bathe and put the babies to bed before rushing off to dinner engagements. Several of Winifred's many friends privately felt that Vera exploited her and that it would be better for Winifred's writing and peace of mind if she moved out of the busy house. But this view was too simple. Winifred herself drew something from the arrangement, from her semi-inclusion in the domestic largesse of Vera's life. If she could not marry herself, she would sample a little of what she called "the rich unrest" of family life. By this time, she knew that she was unlikely to have her own husband or children, and to a surprisingly successful extent, she would vicariously enjoy these experiences through Vera. In John's recollection of his early childhood, Winifred had more influence on him than anyone else.

As they ran their unusual household, Vera and Winifred were enjoying the literary world now that they had both launched successful writing careers. Winifred was a director of *Time and Tide,* a prominent newsweekly, and she met with writers like Rebecca West at their formal board dinners. At this point, she was more well-known than either Catlin or Brittain. At one of their lively parties, Vera and Winifred introduced Rebecca West to her husband, the banker Henry Andrews who was a friend of Catlin's from Oxford. He sat by her feet on a cushion the entire evening, and then offered to escort her home. They were worried he had annoyed Rebecca with his effusiveness, but she said that she enjoyed him—he was like a publishing blurb. At another one of their parties, they had invited black South Africans to mingle with their wealthy British supporters, and the exotically mixed guests spilled out into the garden on the warm summer evening, arousing the curiosity of the neighbors. Winifred was passionately, almost exhaustingly social. She had scores of intimate friends, all of whom seemed to demand special favors and attention from her.

In spite of her self-deprecation, Winifred was not unsuccessful with men. But for some reason, Harry was the only man she could take seriously as a lover. He held more physical fascination to her than any other man, and they were friends, dear, old friends, in a way she found deeply seductive. Winifred described their time together to Vera: "I am a fool to want more than I get from him. What I have is so gay, foolish & charming—something everyone needs—a frivolity, an enchantment, a relaxation. Then in his black moods, he revolts both against & towards me, does & does not want me." They slept together, one spring, when she had taken a cottage by the sea. This was entirely her doing: she had decided to abandon pride and convention and push their romantically charged friendship to a crisis. She was glad to have done it, and hinted later that rather than getting him out of her system, she had instead, gotten him *into* her system. But, somehow their sexual intimacy had not brought him closer to her, and he remained, in all respects, elusive. Winifred wrote: "It is like loving the dead to love someone you can't touch or help."

Winifred, as always, made light of her fundamental isolation. Whatever pain her relationship with Harry caused her, she would not allow herself to revel in self-pity. When Catlin, with dubious taste, confided in her about his own brushes with other women in the United States, Winifred wrote back: "Last week I broke a record by having two improper proposals & being kissed by three different men within twenty four hours . . . But really it is very tiresome that I feel less emotion than if I had been caught in a thunderstorm—some concern as to my clothes, some admiration of the elements in action, and complete mental detachment."

On a trip to the south of France in August of 1931, Winifred began suffering from crushing headaches. The pain was nearly unendurable, and even Winifred, who tended toward complete reserve and stoicism, showed the strain. When she returned the doctor recommended rest, but after a series of rest cures and nursing homes, the symptoms persisted. Even Vera, never one to be overly caught up with other people, noticed deep plum-colored circles under her eyes and a new yellowish pallor in her complexion. Over the next months, the usually vivacious Winifred was often overcome with weakness and paralyzed with headaches and elevated blood pressure. Her frenetic lifestyle did not allow for rest. Between her causes, her friends, her parties, her writing, and Vera's children, she had no time to lay languidly in bed.

In 1932, Winifred received the news that she had Bright's disease, which had already irreparably damaged her kidneys. The doctor predicted that she would not live more than two years, but she did not tell anyone about the bleak prognosis, even Vera. By this time, she was taking the crude drugs that were available to lower her blood pressure, but she was still feeling weak. She wrote to her friend Lady Margaret Rhondda, who was the founder of *Time and Tide,* with her usual buoyancy: "I still find it hard to believe that the feeling of extraordinary physical exhilaration, which makes me want everyone else to drink champagne at parties, in order to get near my own plane of natural stimulus, was simply the symptom of a disease . . . I have doubts sometimes whether *my* blood pressure which made me feel so enormously alive, and so avid of experience, is not the proper one, and this poor half stupefied condition to which they are reducing me may be a disease . . ."

Through her pain, Winifred continued to glow with the overanimation that her friends loved in her. If anything, her illness gave her a sense of urgency in cramming as many experiences as she could into the limited amount of time she had left. One afternoon, after Vera dropped her off at her nursing home for a rest, assuming she would go right to sleep, Winifred called up H. G. Wells instead and said that she did not have much longer to live, and she wanted the chance to get to know him. He immediately invited her to tea, which was an enormous success. He was as warm and brilliant a conversationalist as she expected. He later addressed his letters to her: "Dear Winifred Holtby/Importunate Woman."

Unaware of the extent of Winifred's illness—at least in part because Winifred was actively hiding it from her—Vera was deeply immersed in the book that would make her name: an autobiographical account of the war years, which continued to haunt her. She labored over it for more than three years. At times, she wished she could cut off all human relations but Winifred's so that she could be at her most productive. In her nascent memoir, Vera deliberately set out to represent a generation whose idealism and entire conception of love was blown up by the war. In order to re-create the lost years, she patched together entries from her journals, letters, poems Roland had sent her into a richly textured account of a woman's wartime experience. Her plan was to write history through the eyes of an ordinary person (though whether Brittain ever truly thought of herself as ordinary is certainly up for dispute). At one dinner party, she was discussing her work-in-progress, and an outspoken male friend said: "An autobiography! But I shouldn't have thought anything in *your* life was worth recording!" Another guest, Rebecca West, said sharply: "Why, because she was not a field marshal?" What Vera's male friend failed to see was that her very averageness was the genius and innovation of the book.

When *Testament of Youth* was finally finished, Catlin admitted its cultural importance. But he found the part at the end about her meeting him and their subsequent courtship "intolerable," and asked her to excise most of it, which she did with some protest. She tried to explain grandly that the section on their marriage was meant to represent the recovery of their generation, that they as a couple would stand in for Europe rebuilt, but she ended up reluctantly succumbing to his wishes, and the chapter on her relationship to him, in its published form, remains fairly skeletal.

Vera was concerned that she had waited too long after the end of the war to write her book, and the material would not seem fresh. But when the book finally appeared in the summer of 1933, it created an immediate sensation. Though many soldiers' books had already been published, hers was the first book about the war from a woman's perspective, and it captured the imagination of the British public, still reeling from the destruction of those years. With a dramatic telling of her personal story, *Testament of Youth* managed to evoke for an entire generation the violence done to their youth by the war. In its intimacy, the book had done what other war writing had not: it brought to life the complicated psychological damage done to those at home. In the months after it appeared, Vera reported gleefully that she was opening her fan mail surrounded by flowers, awaiting one of the many cocktail parties and luncheons and receptions that were thrown in her honor. She had finally achieved the fame she had expected and craved all of her life.

Catlin struggled with jealousy over her sudden, meteoric success. His academic career was stymied, his efforts to find an academic appointment in England had failed, and his political aspirations had, as of yet, found no outlet. While he was on a lecture tour, the wife of one of his hosts asked him if it made him feel bad to have such a successful wife, and he nearly stormed out of the lecture he was supposed to give. Privately, he admitted that the book, or rather the truths related in the book, were a source of enormous anguish for him. Vera had written plainly: "At the beginning of 1915 I was more deeply and ardently in love than I have ever been, or am ever likely to be." The world was captivated by her story of innocence lost and love mourned. But how was her own husband supposed to respond to that sentence?

The winter before the book made its public appearance Catlin wrote to her: "Your book, I think, is a very great, a very moving book . . . powerful, significant, important—for me it is oppressive also—to it I am an outsider, intruding, shame-faced, feeling very unworthy, painfully unworthy to the verge of tears. After all Roland is entitled to you; all that is beautiful in love is between him and you." Vera makes the rather extraordinary admission that she did not entirely notice this letter. She was distracted when it arrived. She was not feeling well at the time, she reports, she had some sort of stomach ailment. By the time she felt better, she had misplaced it in a pile of papers, or had filed it away somewhere, and she never replied to its substance.

4

MORE DETACHMENT

In September of 1934, Vera, in a black coat with gray fox collar, embarked on a lecture tour of the United States, sailing first-class on the proceeds of *Testament of Youth*. In preparation for the trip, she had her hair done, her nails done, her eyebrows plucked, and her face massaged. Vera was extremely invested in the commercial possibilities of the American market. She had left the children, as usual, in the capable hands of Winifred, who was at this point feeling somewhat better.

When Vera docked in New York, her boat was met by her American publisher at Macmillan, George Brett, and his wife, Isabel. He took her to see the cover of her book—red, with pretty gold script—filling the window of the publisher's Fifth Avenue office. When she wanted to buy a new blouse for the stifling New York heat, Brett swept her off to a department store and insisted on paying for it. He took her to lunch at the top of the Empire State Building. He took her out on his boat on the Long Island Sound at night. From the beginning, Vera was drawn to him, his handsomeness mingling with the peculiarly American whiff of success surrounding the *Testament of Youth*. He was her purveyor to the vast, exciting, fickle American public. She felt like a celebrity in New York, which to her mind was much more glamorous than being a celebrity in London, and George Brett was encompassed in the overflow of that feeling. He also represented a simpler, purer admiration than her own husband now felt for her: he had nothing but enthusiasm for her book. He was as interested in the minutiae of her success as she was.

Before Vera set off on her tour of twenty-five cities across the country, the Bretts invited her to their country house in Connecticut. A week later, she found herself dancing with George, and told Winifred that she found him more attractive than was entirely convenient. What did it mean for her to feel drawn to someone else? After years of hearing about Catlin's various attractions, she was finally tempted herself. As the tour continued, her interest deepened. From Virginia, she reported: "I could easily be a little in love with George Brett if I liked, but it probably wouldn't be a good idea." Winifred wrote back in her usual, reassuring vein, saying a little "sunlit flirtation" never hurt anyone.

Over the next months, Vera moved through American cities, staying in fine hotels, signing books, charming audiences. In her limited spare time, she read Winifred's homey letters in which Winifred continued to convey her visceral pleasure in the children's physical presence on the page: it was with something very close to a mother's love that she narrated the adventures of John, and "darling, silly, stormy Shirley." Vera met Catlin briefly in Washington where they toured around the monuments, and had an odd conversation about what truly constituted infidelity, before they parted and went their separate ways.

In the meantime, the American copy of the book was selling magnificently, and film rights were being discussed. Vera was beginning to feel the slight alienation from the subject matter that constant repetition brings, but she still took pleasure in being fêted in obscure American locales. And then, toward the end of the tour, Vera's relationship with Brett came to crisis: on the train to New Orleans, in his bedroom compartment, they had a confrontation in which they almost, but did not become lovers.

On the surface, Vera's self-sacrifice is somewhat hard to decipher. Why, when she knew Catlin had other affairs did she have qualms about succumbing? If she now felt the true "anguish" of love, as she said that she did, why didn't she feel called upon to act on it? Catlin was still confiding in her about his attractions to other women. He was threatened by her success, embittered about his own career, and had fallen into a stony depression that had made him even more unreachable than usual. While she was not in love with Catlin, in the usual sense, Vera felt a family connection to him now that seemed inviolable. But there was another factor at work: Vera had a lifelong distrust of what she had squeamishly referred to as "the physical aspects of love." She was not ready to surrender her powers of rational decision to the baser impulses. She had once written to Winifred that a night of physical love was not worth giving up one published article, and had admitted to Catlin that for her, her career had always come before sexual attraction. Was there something wrong, she had once wondered, that a person of her vitality had not been more interested in the erotic side of life? She knew Brett's wife, Isabel, as well, and the messiness of the situation did not appeal. Vera was, as always, concerned with what her life looked like from the outside. Whatever balance of romantic complexity she could tolerate, it did not include Brett, and a literal, physical affair.

Vera duly reported the culmination of this private crisis in her marriage to Winifred. She described herself as deeply in love and in anguish over the impossibility of the situation. How did one absorb this particular blend of pain? Winifred wrote back with her own deep understanding of sublimation: "My long & often painful experience has taught me this—that passion can become friendship. I don't say without heartache— yes, & physical ache . . . & I personally have never known it to be without some humiliation. That is a quality you have rarely had occasion to experience; but I assure you that one need allow it only to affect a very small area of one's consciousness." Winifred seemed to take Vera's situation seriously. But there was something disingenuous in Vera's narrative of self-denial:

she had not wanted to sleep with George with the physical ache that Winifred describes. In fact she seemed to have preferred the diffuse, romantic energy of unconsummated longing. Vera was, after all, a connoisseur of the missed opportunity, of the unfollowed through and unacted on. By now, this shadow of an involvement must have come to seem natural. There was another hidden presence in her marriage, an affair that might have been.

In August of 1935, Catlin fell ill with an obscure form of glandular poisoning, and Winifred took over the care of the children at the French seaside, so that Vera would be free to nurse him in their house in Chelsea. As always, Winifred downplayed her own illness, and described the children, browned limbs, sand pails, blue bathing suits, in great, vivid detail to Vera, adding "what an academic busybody I would be without them!" Vera thought nothing of imposing on Winifred. She did not take her health into consideration. She felt remorseful later, felt that she had taken advantage of Winifred's boundless generosity.

In September, Winifred descended rather quickly into the final stages of her illness. Vera was distraught. She cabled Harry, and he arrived at her bedside immediately. He was persuaded, with some pressure from Catlin, to make some sort of proposal. Winifred was now vague from morphine, but he nonetheless told her that he wanted to spend the rest of his life with her. She seemed pleased by their belated engagement, but it was hard to tell how pleased. To Vera, who had in some sense engineered this final moment, his intention to marry her was all-important, the resolution of a central love story, but it may not have meant as much to Winifred who with her wry take on human relations was no romantic, and in any event, had never been interested in comforting delusions.

On September 29, at dawn, Winifred died in the nursing home on Devonshire Street, at the age of thirty-seven, in a roomful of roses and books. There were bruises all over her body where the unsuccessful injections had been given. Vera was holding her wrist. Catlin was sitting on an armchair behind her in the darkened room. The night nurse cut off a lock of her hair and gave it to Vera. Both Vera and Catlin bent down to kiss her forehead, and went afterward, through the cool darkness of early morning to the Church at St. James where they had been married, to light a candle for her. Winifred had written: "I never feel I've really had a life of my own. My existence seems to me like a clear stream that has simply reflected other people's stories and problems."

In her published memoir, Vera duly reported her and Catlin's presence at Winifred's deathbed, a calm family to the end. Her deliberate emphasis was on the peace of the moment, the gentleness of Winifred's exit, and the tenderness and warmth of their life together. But Catlin's presence in the background of the scene seems to be more vexed than it would initially appear. After Winifred's death, he wrote to Vera with unaccustomed virulence: "You preferred her to me . . . It humiliated me and ate me up. That's why of course I could not read *South Riding* [Winifred's last novel] and probably never shall be able to do so."

In the days after Winifred's death, Vera set about her work as Winifred's literary executor. In her published memoirs, Vera does not allow her emotions to appear in any way immoderate. But her diaries are filled with raw, almost apocalyptic anguish.

She wrote in the days after Winifred's death: "Are children and books enough incentive for living?" In this first, dashed-off formulation of her grief, her husband was conspicuously absent as further "incentive for living."

Five years after Winifred's death, Vera published a slightly stiff memorial to their friendship, *Testament of Friendship,* a five-hundred-page tome in which Winifred appears to be a saint. ("Winifred deserves better," Virginia Woolf wrote.) It was true that Vera drained Winifred of her mischievousness; she took away the rogue and left the generous friend, the devoted reformer, the striving artist who dies young. Many of Winifred's friends objected to the tragic, strained portrait of her that emerged from its pages, to the resolute erasure of her quirkiness, her sense of humor, her vitality. But it was not possible for Vera to write honestly because the world came to her already mythologized; Vera had no choice but to write her heroes and saints. Her mind would not work any other way.

In the aftermath of Winifred's death, Catlin was in the middle of a tough race as the Labour candidate for Parliament in Sunderland. He had resigned from Cornell, on the strength of Vera's increased income, and had hoped, finally, to build his career as a politician. He needed to put his theories to practical use; he needed to redeem the cumulative disappointments of his career. But it didn't work out for him. He was badly beaten. He would never be the politician he had hoped, but it may have been some consolation that their daughter, Shirley Williams, would later become a member of Parliament and an important political figure in the Labour Party.

In his pompous and peculiarly tormented autobiography, Catlin is curiously silent on the subject of his marriage. He dismisses the whole topic with a terse statement that Vera had already said all there was to say on the subject. He writes, in one of the few freighted, highly ambiguous descriptions: "As time went on our affection grew even deeper in the companionship of a long life time . . . of the later years I can say, with Sir Winston about Clementine Churchill, 'we lived happily ever after.' " This grandiose and also fairly tepid endorsement of their life together left much unsaid. And when his son was a young man, Catlin advised him that it was better to let someone fall in love with you, than to fall in love with them.

Catlin's instinct all along seemed to be to keep his romantic disappointment to himself. In 1933, he wrote Vera a long letter which he then put away in a drawer and never sent. It included this passage: "It will not be, that which I have desired. I do not know certainly why, but it will not be. Perhaps your book explains it. Sometimes I half hope that you may find your Lewis [a reference to the lover in *The Fountain*] But I do not think you will, for all the secret is that you have found him, and lost him, and so keep him more than any living man will be kept." Vera did not discover the letter for many years, and in *Testament of Experience,* her last voluminous contribution to her autobiography, Brittain wrote about this as a "tragic undercurrent of personal misunderstanding" between them. She argued then that Roland did not, in fact, stand between them. She claimed that her love for Catlin enabled her to renew her commitment to life, after the devastation of the war, but his sense of an incompleteness in their love was clearly not pure invention. Vera had in her diaries written that "Winifred in dying took with her that second life that she initiated for me just after the war." And it is clear in her private writings that what second life she had is indeed owed to Winifred, not to Catlin. Vera was so completely focused on her own mythologies that she wrote, once, that Roland could have been John and Shirley's father. The idea that her offspring were specifically and genetically linked to their father, had no place in her mental universe. The marriage existed in shadows; it was less real to Vera than those imagined fertilities, those secret lushnesses of emotion of her own creation. She had imported Roland and Winifred into their marriage, had ingeniously crowded the field, and what happiness she and Catlin did find was not the ordinary sort.

In the thirties, Vera achieved the professional success she had dreamed about all her life. She had the comfortable life of family, and husband, and interesting friends, and yet she still missed the intensity of her wartime experience, of her anguished days as a nurse in Malta. In one of her romantic outbursts she writes in *Testament of Youth:* "I cry in my heart come back magic days! I was sorrowful, anxious, frustrated, lonely— but yet how vividly alive! Take away this agreeable London life, of writing, of congenial friends, of minor successes for which I fought so long and worked so hard, take away my Chelsea home . . . and give me back that lovely solitude, that enchanted obscurity, those warm shimmering mornings of light and color, those hours of dreaming in hot, scented fields." Some of this, of course, is posturing, and yet it represents the posturing of a truly romantic and self-dramatizing soul: Vera craved an intensity that doesn't exist in ordinary, settled life.

In some sense, the idea that her life was warped and derailed by the war was too easy, and too beautiful. *Testament of Youth* offered a neat, external, overarching explanation of her character that was suspiciously representative, suspiciously universal. Her elaborately preserved diaries raised more complicated questions: were her ideals shattered by the war, along with those of her entire generation, or was she already a demanding and prickly and unusual girl? The war provided, perhaps, too ready a metaphor. Was she haunted by the simulacrum of young love that could never be recaptured, or was she someone who would always have an ideal elsewhere; an unattainable someone, who would make ordinary run-of-the-mill intimacy with one person seem drab? Vera Brittain had some sort of multiplicity in her temperament, some mythologizing instinct that would not leave life to take its more mundane forms. She would continue to make her saints and heroes. She would continue to have one eye on her reflection in the mirror. She would continue to be "semi-detached" from everyone, and those that loved her would continue, extravagantly, to love.

POSTSCRIPT

I emerged from these stories with a certain amount of envy for
the articulate cocker spaniel in Virginia Woolf's *Flush*. I would
like to curl up on a rug and listen in the rooms I have described, the perfect innocuous observer; I would like to soak in
more. One could ask why this hunger for information, this almost unseemly need to intrude on the private spaces of a couple? I almost feel that if one could see them, the woman at her
dressing table, the man lingering in the doorway, the vagaries
of attraction would reveal themselves; the essential questions
emerging from these stories—why do people drift apart? why
do they stay together?—would resolve themselves. It is so
rare, after all, to glimpse the interior of a marriage. (With the
tabloid revelations that are the wallpaper of contemporary life,
we have the illusion of seeing inside marriages. But stories of
celebrity breakups in doctors' offices contain no information at
all: nothing of any substance is revealed, and the reading of
these articles remains ritualistic and unsatisfying.) And then
how much do we know about even our closest friends' marriages? We may have great, intimate conversations without ever
touching on the private terrain of our married lives. We may
complain about, say, a husband's failure to wake up in the

middle of the night with a baby, but how much do we communicate even the rudimentary workings of a marriage? Marriage is, almost by definition, an incommunicable state: it is so public, so official, so much about exteriors. And then, how can one begin to communicate something so intricate and unwieldy and complicated? To me, what is exotic and refreshing about the people in the pages of this book is how ardently they tried. What is striking is how much they managed to commit to paper: how much nuance, how much detail, how much emotional substance they captured in writing.

In part this was an era in which everybody recorded more permanently and profoundly their daily comings and goings; letters of the breezy, literary, comprehensive variety that most of the people in this book dashed off to even their most casual acquaintances were not uncommon. Now our most substantive communications are usually lost on e-mail, and most e-mails are not as carefully written or exhaustive as the letters written then; we use the phone instead, and our idle communications, our informative, revealing chatter is lost.

And yet, of course, many of the people in these pages went farther than the usual letters; they kept extensive diaries, or in some cases, published and unpublished memoirs in which their love affairs were chronicled, with varying degrees of frankness, along with the detritus of their days. Unlike the bulk of humanity, most of them were not content to let their private lives remain private. They were not content to leave thoughts unformed, feelings unaired, episodes unsorted through. Some may find the insatiable need to put everything into words bewildering: Why not be content to simply live one's life? Why should one's secret squabbles and elations find their way ⹀ words?

Some will find this impulse to preserve one's intimate married life in language somehow corrupt, somehow overly literary and self-conscious. And it seems to me that this is a legitimate point of view. Should love in its healthier forms be private, lost in the shadows of the bedroom? Is there something faintly exhibitionistic, something suspect, in the desire to express the innermost evolution of a relationship in writing? Personally, I don't think so. I think there is something interesting, and even admirable, in the impulse to fix the ephemera of strong feeling on the page.

What is the act of putting feelings into words? In part it serves to clear the mind, as H. G. Wells wrote of his detailed personal autobiography: "I want to get these discontents clear because I have a feeling that as they become clear they will either cease from troubling me or become manageable and controllable." Writing, then, is a therapeutic act, and an act of transformation: in the writing one masters the experience, one tames and controls it.

In fact, much of Wells's memoirs reflect an enduring faith in rationality, in the power of the intellect to subdue emotion, that is very much of its place and time. Over and over the couples in the pages of this book believed that if they labeled their relationship, whether it was a "modus vivendi," or a "semi-detached marriage," or a "child-love," they could control and organize their intimate lives. They believed in the power of the mind and will to exert influence on the rogue emotions of jealousy, disappointment, and rage; and in this their faith is

hey wanted to think their way through the
riage, to impose a new form on the mess of ex-
yet of course, the heart would do what it would:
would write despairing letters, George Catlin
wou... se to read Winifred's novel, Katherine Mansfield
would stew in jealousy over Princess Bibesco. Even Vanessa
Bell, one of the most dedicated proponents of this far-reaching
rationality would write, in one of her more difficult periods
with Duncan: "It is an odd disease we all suffer from and I see
one can't expect always to be rational." For the most part, their
determined and flamboyant efforts to control their feelings
and those of other people through words, through the sheer,
seductive force of reason, were destined to fail.

But what else is behind that desire to fix the minutiae of a
romance on the page, to love in *words*? For a certain type of person the words are inextricable from the experience; it is the
translation of ineffable emotion into language that makes it
real; it is words that distill the most delicate feeling, the most
elusive rapport between two people into something one can
see. And then, for some, this comprehensive recording is also
an effort to say to the indifferent universe, *Here I am,* like the
initials carved by children into trees and wooden desks. These
writers and artists want to understand, to explicate, to go deep
into that which is most interesting in their lives. They want to
be known.

Of course, the record available to biographers and other
rogue investigators such as myself is not objective or documen-
tary; in every description is the mind at work on its subject; in
every description the wild skewing of imagination; the famous

distortions and idealizations of love. In some way it is the distortions that are most interesting to me precisely because they are not isolated to writers, or to the period in time I have chosen: the imagination works on the most ordinary days in enormously powerful ways. The intricate construction of a personal life is fascinating to witness, to the extent that one can, in fact, witness it.

In some sense the beauty of fantasy, of "that best emotion," to use a Wellsian phrase, is itself an achievement: a work to be admired, like a well-wrought short story. Take for instance, Katherine Mansfield. In many ways, one can disapprove of her childish love, one can question her choice of men as one would in a therapist's office; but then one can also admire that emotion, pure, pounded out to a kind of airy thinness; that belief, that wild, unsensible feeling is itself a consummate act of imagination. It is the work the mind does on the sometimes unsatisfying raw materials of life. For some people, their loves, their ability to chisel and sustain an implausible fantasy about another person is a central manifestation of their creative mind.

And again, this sort of over-the-top romanticizing is not only the province of writers and artists. Even Vera Brittain's destructive, self-indulgent vision of her early love is itself more common than one would think. This is the experience informing popular romances like *The Bridges of Madison County*: the lost love that lingers, that infuses everything else. Brittain's personal mythologies may have been more fully narrated than nearly anyone's in history, but she is not alone in nurturing them. And here too is an act of the imagination set against the drabness of life. It may be that I am perverse in admiring this, and yet I do. This is storytelling in its most challenging medium: life itself. Like novelists, we are always inventing even in the course of drinking coffee over breakfast; we are living in the fictions that we create, like the air in a room.

It comes to me, reading even the most tormented diary entries, the most pained accounts of jealousy, the most troubled fragments of memoir: these are love letters. There is Vanessa Bell stepping into a bath while Duncan shaves at the sink; there are H. G. Wells and Rebecca West winding their way through Parisian streets, lost and arguing; there is Katherine Mansfield rushing to the French market to buy violets for Murry's arrival; there is Vera Brittain carrying the orange-tinted pink roses that Roland gave her, as she walks down the aisle to marry another man: These hours lived, painful, messy, exhilarating, richly chaotic, are another kind of art.

Perhaps, the easiest way to think of the prolific intimate record keeping of an H. G. Wells or a Vera Brittain or a Katherine Mansfield is to compare it to the more common instinct of keepsakes: one keeps a photograph, or a matchbook from a restaurant, or a piece of sea glass someone has given you. When Roger Fry scribbled his note to Ottoline Morrell and when Ottoline kept the penciled fragment somewhere tucked away in a drawer, their unexpected night together is not lost; his momentary, disoriented feelings are not lost: "Still all amazed and wondering and can't begin to think . . ." For both of them, that scrap will evoke a few hours of exhausted recollection, of ruffled, pleasant emotion, hours otherwise vanished in memory. So much is lost anyway, so much is forgotten, the feeling of newness in another person's presence, the particular fascination of a walk together in a strange city. As T. S. Eliot, a friend and acquaintance of many people in this book, wrote in his famous poem: "These fragments have I shored against my ruin." In some sense the instinct to record is the instinct to keep, to hold in a tangible way, these passing moments of heightened experience; it is the instinct not to die.

SELECTED BIBLIOGRAPHY

Alpers, Antony. *The Life of Katherine Mansfield*. London: Jonathan Cape, 1980.

Anscombe, Isabelle. *Omega and After: Bloomsbury and the Decorative Arts*. London: Thames and Hudson, 1985.

Baker, Ida. *Katherine Mansfield: The Memories of L. M.* London: Michael Joseph, 1971.

Baker, Michael. *Our Three Selves: The Life of Radclyffe Hall*. London: Hamish Hamilton, 1985.

Barney, Natalie Clifford. *Adventures of the Mind*. New York: New York University Press, 1992.

Beauchamp, Harold, Sir. *Reminiscences and Recollections*. New Plymouth, New Zealand: T. Avery, 1937.

Belford, Barbara. *Violet: The Irrepressible Violet Hunt*. New York: Simon & Schuster, 1990.

Bell, Clive. *Old Friends: Personal Recollections*. London: Cassell, 1956.

Bell, Quentin, *Bloomsbury*. London: Weidenfeld & Nicolson, 1968.

——— and Virginia Nicholson. *Charleston: A Bloomsbury House and Garden*. London: Frances Lincoln, 1997.

———, ed. *Julian Bell: Essays, Poems and Letters*. London: Hogarth Press, 1938.

———. *Virginia Woolf: A Biography*. London: Hogarth Press, 1972.

Bell, Vanessa. *Notes on Virginia's Childhood*. Ed. R. J. Schaubeck. New York: Frank Hallman, 1974.

———. *Sketches in Pen and Ink*. London: Hogarth Press, 1997.

———. *Vanessa Bell's Family Album*. Eds. Quentin Bell and Angelica Garnett. London: Jill Norman & Hobhouse Ltd., 1981.

Bennett, Arnold. *Arnold Bennett and H. G. Wells: A Record of a Personal and a Literary Friendship*. Ed. Harris Wilson. London: Hart-Davis, 1960.

———. *The Journals of Arnold Bennett*. Ed. Frank Swinnerton. London: Penguin, 1954.

———. *Letters of Arnold Bennett*. Volumes 1–3. Ed. James Hepburn. London: Oxford University Press, 1966–1986.

Bennett, J. G., ed. *Gurdjieff: Making a New World*. London: Turnstone Books, 1973.

Berry, Paul, and Mark Bostridge. *Vera Brittain: A Life*. London: Chatto and Windus, 1995. Virago, 2001.

Bishop, Alan, and Mark Bostridge, eds. *Letters from a Lost Generation: The First World War Letters of Vera Brittain and Four Friends, Roland Leighton, Edward Brittain, Victor Richardson, and Geoffrey Thurlow*. London: Little, Brown, 1998.

Brett, Dorothy. *Lawrence and Brett: A Friendship*. Philadelphia: J. P. Lippincott and Co., 1933.

Brittain, Vera. *Chronicle of Friendship: Diary of the Thirties, 1932–1939*. Ed. Alan Bishop. London: V. Gollancz, 1986.

———. *Chronicle of Youth: War Diary, 1913–1917*. Ed. Alan Bishop with Terry Smart. London: V. Gollancz, 1981.

———. *The Dark Tide*. 1923. Reprint, London: Virago, 1999.

———. *Halcyon: Or the Future of Monogamy*. London: Kegan Paul Trench Trubner & Co, 1929.

———. *Poems of War and After*. London: V. Gollancz, 1934.

———. *Radclyffe Hall: A Case of Obscenity?* London: Femina, 1968.

—————. *Selected Letters of Winifred Holtby and Vera Brittain, 1920–1935*. Eds. Vera Brittain and Geoffrey Handley-Taylor. London: A. Brown, 1960.

—————. *Testament of Experience: An Autobiographical Study of the Years 1925–1950*. London: V. Gollancz, 1957. Virago, 1979.

—————. *Testament of Friendship: The Story of Winifred Holtby*. London: Macmillan, 1940. Virago, 1980.

—————. *Testament of a Generation: The Journalism of Vera Brittain and Winifred Holtby*. Eds. Paul Berry and Alan Bishop. London: Virago, 1985.

—————. *Testament of a Peace Lover: Letters from Vera Brittain*. Eds. Winifred and Alan Eden-Green. London: Virago, 1988.

—————. *Testament of Youth: An Autobiographical Study of the Years 1900–1925*. London: V. Gollancz, 1933. Virago, 1978.

—————. *Wartime Chronicle: Vera Brittain's Diary 1939–1945*. Eds. Alan Bishop and Y. Aleksandra Bennett. London: V. Gollancz, 1989.

—————. *The Women at Oxford: A Fragment of History*. London: George G. Harrap, 1960.

Carpenter, Edward. *The Intermediate Sex*. London: Allen & Unwin, 1908.

Castle, Terry. *Noel Coward and Radclyffe Hall: Kindred Spirits*. New York: Columbia University Press, 1996.

Catlin, George Gordon. *For God's Sake, Go!* Buckinghamshire: Colin Smythe Ltd., 1972.

Catlin, John. *Family Quartet*. London: Hamish Hamilton, 1987.

Cavitch, David. *D. H. Lawrence and the New World*. Oxford: Oxford University Press, 1969.

Chalon, Jean. *Portrait of a Seductress: The World of Natalie Barney*. Translated from the French by Carol Barko. New York: Crown, 1979.

Clark, Ronald William. *Bertrand Russell and His World*. London: Thames and Hudson, 1981.

—————. *The Life of Bertrand Russell*. London: Jonathan Cape, 1975.

Cline, Sally. *Radclyffe Hall: A Woman Called John*. London: John Murray, 1997.

Coren, Michael. *The Invisible Man: The Life and Liberties of H. G. Wells*. London: Bloomsbury, 1993.

Darroch, Sandra Jobson. *Ottoline: The Life of Lady Ottoline Morrell*. London: Chatto & Windus, 1976.

De Charms, Leslie. *Elizabeth of the German Garden: A Biography*. London: Heinemann, 1958.

Dickson, Lovat. *H. G. Wells: His Turbulent Life and Times*. New York: Atheneum, 1969.

————. *Radclyffe Hall at the Well of Loneliness: A Sapphic Chronicle*. New York: Harper Collins, 1975.

Dunbar, Janet. *Mrs. G.B.S.: A Biographical Portrait of Charlotte Shaw*. London: George G. Harrap & Co., 1963.

Dunn, Jane. *A Very Close Conspiracy: Vanessa Bell and Virginia Woolf*. London: Jonathan Cape, 1990. Virago, 2001.

Edel, Leon, and Gordon Ray, eds. *Henry James and H. G. Wells: A Record of Their Friendship, Their Debate on the Art of Fiction, and Their Quarrel*. Urbana: University of Illinois Press, 1958.

Egan, Beresford. *The Sink of Solitude*. London: Hermes Press, 1928.

Ellis, Havelock. *Studies in the Psychology of Sex*. Philadelphia: F. A. Davis, 1910.

Feinstein, Elaine. *Lawrence's Women: The Intimate Life of D. H. Lawrence*. London: HarperCollins, 1993.

Furbank, P. N. *E. M. Forster: A Life*. London: Secker and Warburg, 1977.

Fussell, Paul. *The Great War and Modern Memory*. Oxford: Oxford University Press, 1975.

Garnett, Angelica. *Deceived With Kindness*. London: Chatto and Windus, 1985.

Gertler, Mark. *Selected Letters*. Ed. Noel Carrington. London: Hart-Davis, 1965.

Gillespie, Diane Filby. *The Sisters' Art: The Writing and Painting of Virginia Woolf and Vanessa Bell*. New York: Syracuse University Press, 1988.

Glendinning, Victoria. *Rebecca West: A Life*. London: Weidenfeld & Nicolson, 1987.

————. *Vita: A Biography of Vita Sackville-West*. London: Weidenfeld & Nicolson, 1983.

Gorham, Deborah. *Vera Brittain: A Feminist Life*. Oxford: Blackwell, 1996.

Griffin, Nicholas, ed. *The Selected Letters of Bertrand Russell*. Volumes 1–2. New York: Penguin, 2001.

Hall, Colin. *Garsington Manor*. London: New Pyramid Press, 1988.

Hall, Radclyffe. *Adam's Breed*. London: Cassell, 1929. Virago, 1985.

————. *The Forge*. London: The Falcon Press, 1952.

————. *Mrs. Ogilvy Finds Herself*. New York: Harcourt Brace, 1934.

————. *A Sheaf of Verses by Marguerite Radclyffe-Hall*. London: Chiswick, 1908.

————. *The Sixth Beatitude*. London: Heinemann, 1936.

————. *The Unlit Lamp*. London: Cassell, 1928. Virago, 1981.

————. *The Well of Loneliness*. London: Weidenfeld & Nicolson, 1928. Virago, 1982.

————. *Your John: The Love Letters of Radclyffe Hall*. Ed. Joanne Glasgow. New York: New York University Press, 1997.

Hall, Ruth, ed. *Dear Dr. Stopes: Sex in the 1920s*. London: Andre Deutsch, 1978.

————. *Marie Stopes: A Biography*. London: Andre Deutsch, 1977.

Hammond, J. R. *H. G. Wells and Rebecca West*. New York: Harvester Wheatsheaf, 1991.

―――., ed. *H. G. Wells: Interviews and Recollections*. Basingstoke: Pan Macmillan, 1980.

Hankin, C. A., ed. *The Letters of John Middleton Murry to Katherine Mansfield*. London: Constable, 1983.

Hart-Davis, Rupert. *Hugh Walpole: A Biography*. London: Macmillan, 1952.

Holroyd, Michael. *Lytton Strachey: The Years of Achievement 1910–1932*. London: Heinemann, 1978.

Holtby, Winifred. *Anderby Wold*. London: Bodley Head, 1923. Virago, 1981.

―――. *The Land of Green Ginger*. London: Jonathan Cape, 1927. Virago, 1983.

―――. *Letters to a Friend: Winifred Holtby*. Eds. Alice Holtby and Jean McWilliam. London: Collins, 1937.

―――. *South Riding*. London: Collins, 1936. Virago, 1988.

Hunt, Violet. *The Flurried Years*. London: Hurst & Blackett, 1926.

Huxley, Aldous. *Crome Yellow*. London: Chatto and Windus, 1921.

Hynes, Samuel. *The Edwardian Turn of Mind*. Reprint, London: Pimlico, 1992.

Jackson, Rosie. *Frieda Lawrence*. London: Harper Collins, 1995.

Keen, Annie. *Women and Marriage in Modern England*. London: Henry R. Drane, 1929.

Lago, Mary and P. N. Furbank. *The Selected Letters of E. M. Forster*. London: Collins, 1983–85.

Lawrence, D. H. *Collected Letters*. Ed. Harry Moore. Volumes 1–2 London: Heinemann, 1962.

―――. *Psychoanalysis and the Unconscious*. London: Heinemann, 1921–22.

————. *Women in Love*. Reprint, London: Penguin, 2007.

Lea, F. A. *John Middleton Murry*. London: Methuen, 1960.

Lee, Hermione. *Virginia Woolf*. London: Chatto and Windus, 1996.

Levy, Paul, ed. *The Letters of Lytton Strachey*. London: Viking, 2005.

Lucas, Robert. *Frieda Lawrence*. London: Secker and Warburg, 1973.

Macdougall, Sarah. *Mark Gertler*. London: John Murray, 2002.

MacKenzie, Norman and Jeanne. *The Life of H. G. Wells: The Time Traveller*. London: Hogarth Press, 1987.

Mannin, Ethel. *Young in the Twenties*. London: Hutchinson, 1971.

Mansfield, Katherine. *The Aloe*. London: Constable, 1930. Virago, 1985.

————. *Bliss and Other Stories*. London: Constable, 1920.

————. *Collected Stories*. London: Constable, 1945.

————. *The Dove's Nest and Other Stories*. London: Constable, 1923.

————. *The Garden Party and Other Stories*. London: Constable, 1922.

————. *In a German Pension*. London: Constable, 1926.

————. *Je Ne Parle Pas Français*. London: Heron Press, 1920.

————. *Prelude*. London: Hogarth Press, 1918.

Mantz, Ruth, and John Middleton Murry. *The Life of Katherine Mansfield*. London: Constable, 1931.

Marcus, Jane, ed. *The Young Rebecca: Writings of Rebecca West, 1911–1917*. London: Virago, 1982.

Marler, Regina, ed. *Selected Letters of Vanessa Bell*. London: Bloomsbury, 1994.

Maude, Aylmer. *Marie Stopes: Her Work and Play*. London: P. Davies, 1933.

McNeish, Helen, ed. *Passionate Pilgrimage: A Love Affair in Letters: Katherine Mansfield's Letters to John Middleton Murry from the South of France, 1915–1920*. London: Joseph, 1976.

Meyer, M. M. *H. G. Wells, and His Family (As I Have Known Them)*. Edinburgh: International Publishing Company, 1955.

Meyers, Jeffrey. *D. H. Lawrence: A Biography*. London: Macmillan, 1990.

———. *Katherine Mansfield: A Biography*. London: Hamish Hamilton, 1978.

Moore, James. *Gurdjieff and Mansfield*. Boston: Routledge, 1980.

Morrell, Ottoline. *The Early Memoirs of Lady Ottoline Morrell*. Ed. Robert Gathorne-Hardy. London: Faber and Faber, 1963.

———. *Ottoline at Garsington: Memoirs of Lady Ottoline Morrell, 1915–1918*. Ed. Robert Gathorne-Hardy. London: Faber and Faber, 1974.

Murry, John Middleton. *Between Two Worlds: The Autobiography of John Middleton Murry*. London: Jonathan Cape, 1935.

———. *Countries of the Mind: Essays in Literary Criticism*. London: Collins, 1922.

———. *Journal of Katherine Mansfield*. London: Constable, 1927.

———. *Katherine Mansfield and Other Literary Portraits*. London: Peter Nevill, 1949.

———. *Katherine Mansfield and Other Literary Studies*. London: Constable, 1959.

———, ed. *The Letters of Katherine Mansfield*. London: Constable, 1928.

———, ed. *The Letters of Katherine Mansfield. Volume 2*. London: Constable, 1928.

———. *Looking Before and After: A Collection of Essays*. London: Sheppard Press, 1948.

———. *Love, Freedom and Society*. London: Jonathan Cape, 1957.

————. *Reminiscenses of D. H. Lawrence*. London: Jonathan Cape, 1933.

Murry, Mary Middleton. *To Keep Faith*. London: Constable, 1959.

Needleman, Jacob and George Baker, eds. *Gurdjieff: Essays and Reflections on the Man and His Teaching*. New York: Continuum, 1996.

Nicolson, Nigel. *Portrait of a Marriage: Vita Sackville-West and Harold Nicolson*. London: Weidenfeld & Nicolson, 1973.

————, ed. *Vita and Harold*. London: Weidenfeld & Nicolson, 1992.

Ormond, Richard. *Una Troubridge: The Friend of Radclyffe Hall*. New York: Jonathan Cape, 1984.

Priestley, J. B. *The Edwardians*. London: Heinemann, 1970.

Ray, Gordon. *H. G. Wells and Rebecca West*. London: Macmillan, 1974.

Roche, Paul. *With Duncan Grant in Southern Turkey*. London: Honeyglen, 1982.

Rollyson, Carl. *Rebecca West: A Life*. New York: Scribner, 1996.

Russell, Bertrand. *The Autobiography of Bertrand Russell*. Three vols. London: George Allen & Unwin, 1967–69.

————. *Marriage and Morals*. London: George Allen & Unwin, 1929.

Russell, Bertrand, et al. *Divorce as I See It*. London: Noel Douglas, 1930.

Russell, John Francis. *Divorce*. London: Heinemann, 1912.

————. *Lay Sermons*. London: Thomas Burleigh, 1902.

————. *My Life and Adventures*. London: Cassell, 1923.

Santayana, George. *Persons and Places*. New York: Scribner, 1944–53.

Scott, Bonnie Kime. *Selected Letters of Rebecca West*. New Haven: Yale University Press, 2000.

Scott, Margaret, ed. *The Katherine Mansfield Notebooks*. Minneapolis: University of Minnesota Press, 2002.

Seacrest, Meryle. *Between Me and Life: A Biography of Romaine Brooks*. Garden City, New York: Doubleday, 1974.

Seymour, Miranda. *Ottoline Morrell: Life on the Grand Scale*. London: Hodder and Stoughton, 1993.

Shaw, Marion. *Clear Stream: A Life of Winifred Holtby*. London: Virago, 1999.

Shone, Richard. *Bloomsbury Portraits: Vanessa Bell, Duncan Grant, and Their Circle*. London: Phaidon, 1976.

Souhami, Diana. *The Trials of Radclyffe Hall*. London: Weidenfield & Nicolson, 1998. Virago, 1999.

Spalding, Frances. *Duncan Grant: A Biography*. London: Chatto and Windus, 1997.

———. *Roger Fry: Art and Life*. Berkeley: University of California Press, 1980.

———. *Vanessa Bell*. London: Weidenfeld & Nicolson, 1983.

Stopes, Marie Carmichael. *Married Love*. New York: J. T. Little and Ives, 1918.

Strachey, Lytton. *Eminent Victorians*. London: Chatto and Windus, 1918.

Sutton, Denys, ed. *Letters of Roger Fry*. Volumes 1–2. London: Chatto and Windus, 1972.

Tomalin, Claire. *Katherine Mansfield: A Secret Life*. London: Viking, 1988.

Troubridge, Una. *The Life of Radclyffe Hall*. London: Hammond, 1961.

Usborne, Karen. *"Elizabeth": The Author of Elizabeth and Her German Garden*. London: Bodley Head, 1986.

von Arnim, Elizabeth. *The Adventures of Elizabeth in Rügen*. London: Macmillan, 1904. Virago, 1990.

———. *All the Dogs of My Life*. London: Heinemann, 1936. Virago, 1995.

———. *The Caravaners*. London: Smith Elder, 1909. Virago, 1989.

————. *Elizabeth and Her German Garden*. London: Macmillan, 1898. Virago, 1996.

————. *The Enchanted April*. London: Macmillan, 1922. Virago, 1991.

————. *In the Mountains*. London: Macmillan, 1920.

————. *Mr. Skeffington*. London: Heinemann, 1940. Virago, 1993.

————. *The Solitary Summer*. London: Macmillan, 1899. Virago, 1993.

————. *Vera*. London: Macmillan, 1921. Virago, 1983.

Watney, Simon. *The Art of Duncan Grant*. London: John Murray, 1990.

Weiss, Andrea. *Paris Was a Woman: Portraits from the Left Bank*. Ontario, Canada: Pandora, 1995.

Wells, Amy Catherine. *The Book of Catherine Wells*. London: Chatto and Windus, 1928.

Wells, Frank, ed. *H. G. Wells: A Pictorial Biography*. London: Jupiter, 1977.

Wells, G. P., ed. *H. G. Wells in Love*. London: Faber and Faber, 1984.

Wells, H. G. *Ann Veronica: A Modern Love Story*. London: Fisher Unwin, 1909. Virago, 1980.

————. *Certain Personal Matters: A Collection of Material, Mainly Autobiographical*. London: Lawrence and Bullen Ltd., 1898.

————. *Experiment in Autobiography*. London: V. Gollancz, 1934.

————. *Marriage*. London: Macmillan, 1912.

————. *Modern Utopia*. London: Chapman and Hall, 1905.

————. *Mr. Britling Sees It Through*. London: Cassell, 1916.

————. *The New Machiavelli*. London: The Bodley Head, 1910.

————. *Passionate Friends*. London: Macmillan, 1913.

————. *The Time Machine: An Invention*. 1895. Reprint, Cambridge: R. Bentley, 1971.

————. *The War of the Worlds*. London: Heinemann, 1898.

West, Anthony. *Heritage*. New York: Random House, 1955.

————. *H. G. Wells: Aspects of a Life*. London: Hutchinson, 1984.

West, Geoffrey. *H. G. Wells*. London: Howe, 1930.

West, Rebecca. *Ending in Earnest: A Literary Log*. Garden City, New York: Doubleday, 1931.

————. *Family Memories: An Autobiographical Journey*. Ed. Faith Evans. New York: Viking Press, 1988.

————. *The Fountain Overflows*. London: Macmillan, 1957. Virago, 1992.

————. *Henry James*. London: Nisbet, 1916.

————. *The Judge*. London: Hutchinson, 1922. Virago, 1980.

————. *The Meaning of Treason*. Harmondsworth: Penguin, 1965. Virago, 1982.

————. *Rebecca West: A Celebration*. London: Macmillan, 1978.

————. *The Strange Necessity: Essays and Reviews*. London: Jonathan Cape, 1928. Virago, 1987.

Woolf, Virginia. *Carlyle's House and Other Sketches*. London: Hesperus Press, 2003.

————. *The Diary of Virginia Woolf*. Volumes 1–4. Ed. Anne Oliver Bell. London: Hogarth Press, 1980.

————. *Flush: A Biography*. London: Hogarth Press, 1933.

————. *The Letters of Virginia Woolf*. Nigel Nicolson, Ed. Vols. 1–6. London: Hogarth Press, 1975–1980.

————. *Roger Fry: A Biography*. London: Hogarth Press, 1940.

NOTES

H. G. WELLS

Central to my understanding of H. G. Wells's life is Norman and Jeanne MacKenzie's *The Life of H. G. Wells: The Time Traveler,* along with Gordon Ray's *H. G. Wells and Rebecca West,* J. R. Hammond's *H. G. Wells and Rebecca West,* and Lovat Dickson's *H. G. Wells: His Turbulent Life and Times. H. G. Wells: A Pictorial Biography,* which was edited by his son Frank Wells, was helpful in establishing the residences Wells inhabited, along with his appearance at various points in his life. Some of the details of his study and work habits were drawn from a memoir written by his children's governess, Mathilde Meyer, *H. G. Wells and His Family (As I Have Known Them),* a rather benign and unsensational portrait of the family, which was generally useful in chronicling the workings of the Wells's household. Sir Sydney Waterlow's diaries, housed in the Berg Collection of the New York Public Library, gave a lively perspective of what it was like to be a guest at Wells's home. In addition, it was intriguing to read Waterlow's various descriptions of Jane: "She looks as if she may have suffered; but she has plenty of spirit and individuality, & though she lets herself be ordered about to fetch and carry, & accepts as a matter of course his hurricane upsetting of domestic arrangements on any whim, she knows when & how to put her foot down." I found another useful glimpse of the

Wells's domestic life in a rhapsodic article on the subject in the *Bookman*.

This chapter is also indebted to Anthony West's riveting and strange biography, *H. G. Wells: Aspects of a Life,* which begins with the night of his own birth, and throughout which he refers to Wells as "my father." In spite of its admittedly subjective point of view, it is an insightful and well-written biography. It was he who wrote, memorably, that at the time the young Rebecca West met Wells he was shaped like a teddy bear. Anthony West's enormously bitter account of his childhood in *The New York Review of Books,* along with his searing autobiographical novel, *Heritage,* about being the son of an artistic mother, shed light on his early experience of unusual family life.

Much of my understanding of Wells's romantic philosophy came from an immersion in his novels, which do not necessarily stand the test of time. H. G. Wells's perspective on his vast number of romantic attachments was charismatically set out in *Experiments in Autobiography* and *H. G. Wells in Love,* along with his various elaborate ideas and theories about relations between the sexes. *The Letters of Arnold Bennett,* edited by James Hepburn, and *The Journals of Arnold Bennett,* edited by Frank Swinnerton also enhanced my understanding of Wells. Further insight into Wells's mind at work was provided by J. R. Hammond's *H. G. Wells: Interviews and Recollections*.

For my knowledge of Rebecca West's life I am greatly indebted to the superb biography *Rebecca West: A Life* by Victoria Glendinning, along with *Rebecca West: A Life* by Carl Rollyson. My sense of Rebecca West's state of mind emerged in part from several of her mesmerizing published articles, like "The World's Worst Failure" in the *New Republic,* January 8, 1916, and "I Regard Marriage with Fear and Horror" in *Hearst's International-Cosmopolitan,* November, 1925. Her spectacular essays collected in *The Young Rebecca,* edited by Jane Marcus, and *Rebecca West: A Celebration,* edited by Samuel

Hynes, also lent insight into her thought process. For this chapter, I relied heavily on the *Selected Letters of Rebecca West*, edited by Bonnie Kime Scott. My account of her trip to Spain with Wells is drawn largely from Rollyson and Ray's description. I should also mention that elements of Rebecca West's adult behavior came into focus when I read her *Family Memoirs*, and her autobiographical novel, *The Fountain Overflows*, in which her complicated relations with men can be traced back to her relationship with her charming, unreliable father.

As both Rebecca West and H. G. Wells were notoriously liberal with the facts, there are a few moments of difference in their accounts. Certain facets of their relationship were subject to particular mythologizing: like the lurid episode of Hedwig Verana Gatternigg, and the conception of Anthony West, for example. In each instance, I have chosen what to me seemed the plausible version, though there is some guesswork involved.

The Book of Catherine Wells, Jane's collected stories, was also critical in my view of Jane's character: "a woman puts her heart in a harness when she marries," she wrote, for instance, in one of her fictional pieces. And H. G. Wells's introduction to the collection was perhaps the most interesting piece of personal propaganda he ever wrote—which is saying a great deal, considering the sheer volume that exists. It was also interesting to read Jane Wells's letters in the Berg Collection, as they gave a sense of her in her capacity as Wells's business manager. Wells's letters to Violet Hunt, also in the Berg Collection, were intriguing in terms of understanding the workings of the affair. And several of Rebecca West's letters to Eddie Sackville-West fleshed out her version of her troubled relationship with Anthony. Many of the details from my description of Jane Wells's funeral come from Arnold Bennett's diaries, and from Janet Dunbar's *Mrs. GBS: A Memoir of Charlotte Shaw*.

KATHERINE MANSFIELD

Several biographies enriched my picture of Katherine Mansfield's life: Claire Tomalin's *Katherine Mansfield: A Secret Life,* Jeffrey Meyers's *Katherine Mansfield: A Biography,* and Antony Alpers's *The Life of Katherine Mansfield.* Also crucial to my understanding of her relationship with Murry was F. A. Lea's wry and readable biography, *John Middleton Murry.* Ida Baker's memoir, *Katherine Mansfield: The Memories of L.M.* was invaluable in providing her point of view, along with an interesting counterbalance to Mansfield's account of the years in question: In particular, Ida's description of her travels with Mansfield and the years of her illness were illuminating. John Middleton Murry's autobiography, *Between Two Worlds: The Autobiography of John Middleton Murry,* was enormously helpful in supplying his version of events, and in giving me some understanding of the way his mind worked.

Mansfield's incomparable journals were crucial in conveying her mood, especially for the period of her illness, along with her letters to her friends. I worked with several versions of her journals: those versions edited by John Middleton Murry in the 1930s, as well as *The Katherine Mansfield Notebooks,* edited by Margaret Scott. Mansfield's fiction also contributed to my understanding of her state of mind in the course of her relationship with Murry. The letters of John Middleton Murry were also invaluable in establishing the texture of their relationship during their many separations. I relied on both volumes of *The Letters of Katherine Mansfield,* edited by John Middleton Murry, and *Passionate Pilgrimage: A Love Affair in Letters, Katherine Mansfield's Letters to John Middleton Murry from the South of France, 1915–1920,* edited by Helen McNeish, and *The Letters of John Middleton Murry to Katherine Mansfield,* edited by C. A. Hankin. Also useful in providing background information was *The Life of Katherine Mansfield,* by Ruth Mantz and John Middleton

Murry. Mansfield's father, Sir Harold Beauchamp's memoir of his daughter, *Reminiscences and Recollections,* also proved a valuable source of background for her character.

Several of John Middleton Murry's letters in the Berg Collection displayed his enormous and resourceful capacity for self-pity—in particular his letters to Thomas Moult, which complained about his "chronic overwork" one paragraph after describing Katherine's wasting from her illness. I also found it interesting that he began his desperate letter from Paris to his sometime patron Eddie Marsh, "Darling." This brought home to me the fact that the particular blend of seductive neediness he showed to women also occasionally showed itself to men.

My description of the wildness at the Christmas party at the Cannan's was fleshed out by details from Sarah Macdougall's *Mark Gertler,* and *Mark Gertler: Selected Letters,* edited by Noel Carrington. For information on the Murrys' relationship with the Lawrences I relied, primarily, on several books: Robert Lucas's *Frieda Lawrence*, Jeffrey Meyers's *D. H. Lawrence,* and *D. H. Lawrence: Collected Letters,* edited by Harry Moore. D. H. Lawrence's letters to Katherine Mansfield include the remarkably hostile line: "I loathe you. You revolt me stewing in your consumption."

In order to understand the rather mysterious period of Mansfield's life when she fell under the influence of Gurdjieff, I relied on several sources on his thought: James Moore's *Gurdjieff and Mansfield,* and *Gurdjieff: Essays and Reflections on the Man and His Teaching,* edited by Jacob Needleman and George Baker, and *Gurdjieff: Making a New World,* edited by J. G. Bennett. Virginia Woolf's brilliantly variable recollections of her friend, including much nastiness, provided as always a crucial, vivid thread of information. Lytton Strachey's letters also proved useful in his wry, gossipy perspective.

My version of Ottoline Morrell and Murry's flirtation owes a great deal to Ottoline's memoirs; Murry was not always entirely forthright in his accounts of people being in love with him. Ottoline's observations of Mansfield and Murry in *Ottoline at Garsington* were also telling: "He seemed devoted to Katherine though she laughed at him and often got impatient with his vague whispy ways, and his queer blank way of looking out as if he saw nothing, or as if his eyes were turned in on himself. She seemed often as if she would like to shake him."

To me, the account of Murry's ultimate affair with Frieda Lawrence was fascinating, though clearly outside the purview of this chapter. I also found the story of Murry's next wife, Violet—a woman who bore a striking physical resemblance to Katherine Mansfield, who also died very young of tuberculosis—riveting. In some ways the implausible outcome shows how powerful and enduring romantic mythologies are, how they somehow manage to impose themselves on other people: It brings to mind the similar fact that Ted Hughes's second wife died in the same manner as Sylvia Plath.

ELIZABETH VON ARNIM

I am indebted, in this chapter, to Karen Usborne's biography, *"Elizabeth": The Author of Elizabeth and Her German Garden*. Elizabeth's elusive memoir *All the Dogs of My Life* helped provide much background, along with the Elizabeth books, each one elaborating her character. Her personality, with all of its electric contradictions, is evident in her fiction in ways that are not true of all writers. Her other novels, especially *The Enchanted April,* also enhanced my understanding of her perspective on love. Finally, Elizabeth's *Vera* gave much insight into her experience of her marriage, though, of course, it is a fictional version.

For Elizabeth's sojourn in the United States, her daughter

Liebet's biography, *Elizabeth of the German Garden,* published under the pseudonym Leslie De Charms, provided nearly all of the details. This affectionate but surprisingly balanced book also offered a thorough account of the decline of Elizabeth's marriage.

The Selected Letters of Bertrand Russell, edited by Nicholas Griffin, *Betrand Russell: A Life* by Caroline Moorehead, and *The Autobiography of Bertrand Russell,* also helped establish his role and perspective in his brother's courtship, marriage, and beyond. George Santayana's autobiography, *Persons and Places,* gave a remarkably sympathetic yet clear-eyed portrait of Earl Russell. At times, he seemed to be the only person on earth who was actually fond of the unfortunate earl. Earl Russell's own substantial memoir, *My Life and Adventures,* fleshes out his personal mythologies, though it does not shed much light on his marriage to Elizabeth as he managed to omit the entire episode. Other perspectives on Elizabeth came from the reminiscences of Huge Walpole and E. M. Forster.

H. G. Wells's autobiographical fragments published as *H. G.Wells in Love* provided some of the background for his affair with Elizabeth, along with his rather interesting view of her. It was there he wrote, "If little e had been God the Creator, there would have been no earthquakes, no tigers and no wars, but endless breezes and quite unexpected showers; the flora would not have been without its surprises, a trifle burlesque, but very delicately and variously scented." I also relied on Katherine Mansfield's letters and notebooks for her accounts of her growing affection for her cousin.

VANESSA BELL

My greatest debt here is to Frances Spalding whose excellent biographies of several of the figures in this chapter—her *Vanessa Bell,* in particular—were central to my research. My view of the dinner conversation described in the opening pages comes in large part from Duncan Grant's diaries, which appear in Frances Spalding's *Duncan Grant: A Biography,* as does much of his point of view of the relationship. (Certain other small details, like the taste of Vanessa's coffee came from Angelica Garnett's *Deceived with Kindness.*)

In this chapter, in particular, the next generation's reflections were useful in organizing my thoughts on Vanessa Bell's ménage. Quentin Bell's judicious and keenly observant writings were always valuable—I am referring in particular to *Bloomsbury Recalled,* and *Virginia Woolf: A Biography.* Throughout his writings, he is the shrewdest, most compassionate observer a mother could wish for: I can't think of another son as tolerant, intelligent and humble in the face of a previous generation's colorful behavior. A vivid portrait of Julian Bell, and his warm relationship with his mother, emerged from his letters and poems and writings, which I read in the Berg Collection. Finally Angelica Garnett's curious and angry memoir, *Deceived with Kindness,* provided an interesting foil to the general tendency to idealize life at Charleston, including my own inclination in that direction. I also found Janet Malcolm's superb essay on the subject in *The New York Review of Books* enormously helpful.

For the intricate relation between Vanessa Bell and Virginia Woolf, Jane Dunn's *A Very Close Conspiracy* proved an invaluable resource, as did Diane Filby Gillespie's *The Sisters' Art: The Writing and Painting of Virginia Woolf and Vanessa Bell.* Vanessa Bell's letters in the Berg Collection at the New York Public Library were illuminating, as was Regina Marler's *Selected Letters of Vanessa Bell. The Diary of Virginia Woolf,* edited by Anne Oliver Bell, and *The Letters of Virginia Woolf,* edited by Nigel Nicolson, along with Hermione Lee's spectacular biography, *Virginia Woolf: A Life,* proved rich sources for the elaborate, conflicted love between the sisters. I also found quite interesting Virginia's biographical sketch of Vanessa, and Vanessa's memoir, *Notes on Virginia's Childhood,* as well as the autobiographical pieces in Vanessa's *Sketches in Pen and Ink.* In addition, *The Letters of Lytton Strachey,* edited by Paul Levy, were a key source for this chapter.

Further insight into Duncan came from Simon Watney's *The Art of Duncan Grant*, and Paul Roche's recollections, *With Duncan Grant in Southern Turkey.* And my sense of Vanessa's artistic aspirations owes a great deal to Isabelle Anscombe's *Omega and After: Bloomsbury and the Decorative Arts.* I also found Richard Shone's *Bloomsbury Portraits: Vanessa Bell, Duncan Grant and Their Circle* enormously useful. Clive Bell's *Old Friends* and David Garnett's memoirs from the period provided other interesting background information. From his diaries in the Berg Collection, it was amusing to note Sydney Waterlow's account of Vanessa's bravado during a visit to the Bells in January of 1911: "Then to see Clive and Vanessa. V. wants to form a circle on the principle of complete freedom of sexual intercourse." Also informative on the subject of Vanessa's affair and friendship with Roger Fry were the *Letters of Roger Fry,* edited by Denys Sutton, Frances Spalding's *Roger Fry: Art and Life,* and Virginia Woolf's *Roger Fry: A Biography.*

My sense of place was for the most part informed by two striking books of photography: Vanessa's own photographs, collected in *Vanessa Bell's Family Album,* edited by Quentin Bell and Angelica Garnett, and *Charleston: A Bloomsbury House and Garden,* edited by Quentin Bell and Virginia Nicholson. Vanessa's starkly beautiful snapshots offer insight into the rhythms of life at Charleston—the meals eaten in the gardens, the children running naked or half-naked, the feel of extended family and perpetual houseguests flowing through the house. Often one sees a balding Clive in the background, seated deep in one of the odd angular wooden chairs, low to the ground, with a newspaper opened, as everyone else carries on. It is these images that brought to life for me the true and exotic feeling of comfort between this highly unusual couple.

OTTOLINE MORRELL

Ottoline's memoirs were central to my understanding of the years chronicled in this chapter: *The Early Memoirs of Lady Ottoline Morrell,* and *Ottoline at Garsington: Memoirs of Lady Ottoline Morrell, 1915–1918,* both of which were edited by Robert Gathorne-Hardy. Her memoirs also lent enormous insight into her romanticizing instinct, and the starry, good-natured lens through which she tended to view her friends. There are also moments in the memoirs of greater insight and sharpness than she is usually credited with. *Lady Ottoline's Album* gave me a great visual sense of Ottoline's guests, and Colin Hall's *Garsington Manor* helped establish the ambience of Garsington. I also found Ottoline's snapshots, many of which are in the collection of the National Portrait Gallery in London, enormously effective in capturing her milieu.

Most importantly, Miranda Seymour's engaging biography, *Ottoline Morrell: Life on a Grand Scale,* provided invaluable insight into her life and many details of her marriage. Also useful was a previous biography, Sandra Jobson Darroch's *Ottoline: The Life of Ottoline Morrell.* Virginia Woolf's piece on Ottoline's famous Thursdays in *Carlyle's House and Other Sketches* offered a memorable glimpse of Ottoline in her preferred role of hostess. I found that other people's views of Philip were also helpful: like Lytton Strachey's, as he was a frequent guest at Garsington, and Virginia Woolf's, as she was the object of one of Philip's more enduring and irritating infatuations.

My view of the evening Ottoline's relationship with Russell began emerged largely from the pages of Russell's autobiography: She is somewhat more circumspect in her own memoirs about the exact contours of the relationship. *The Selected Letters of Bertrand Russell,* edited by Nicholas Griffin, was another important source. In addition, I relied on several biographies for my understanding of

Russell: Caroline Moorehead's *Bertrand Russell: A Life,* Ray Monk's *Bertrand Russell,* Bertrand Russell's *The Autobiography of Bertrand Russell,* Ronald William Clark's *The Life of Bertrand Russell* and *Bertrand Russell and His World*.

Several of the satiric versions of Ottoline were useful, in grasping the nastiness so frequently aimed at her—Aldous Huxley's *Chrome Yellow* and D. H. Lawrence's *Women in Love,* in particular. Useful sources for her relationship with D. H. Lawrence were Jeffrey Meyers's *D. H. Lawrence: A Biography,* and Elaine Feinstein's *Lawrence and the Women: The Intimate Life of D. H. Lawrence*. Ottoline's friends' views of her were always interesting and almost universally inconsistent: particularly useful were the letters of Vanessa Bell, Virginia Woolf, Lytton Strachey, Mark Gertler, and Roger Fry.

RADCLYFFE HALL

My conception of Hall's life owes a great deal to Diana Souhami's remarkably balanced biography, *The Trials of Radclyffe Hall*. My portrait of Hall's romantic life is also indebted to several other biographies, including Michael Baker's *Our Three Selves: The Life of Radclyffe Hall,* which provided among other details the pleasing fact that Una read aloud to Hall from *Elizabeth and Her German Garden;* Lovat Dickson's *Radclyffe Hall at the Well of Loneliness: A Sapphic Chronicle,* and Sally Cline's *Radclyffe Hall: A Woman Called John*. Richard Ormond's biography of Una Troubridge, *Una Troubridge: The Friend of Radclyffe Hall,* provided an interesting perspective, if rather skewed toward Una's version of events. Also invaluable in establishing Una's perspective was Una's own self-glorifying memoir, *The Life of Radclyffe Hall,* in which her relationship with Hall emerges as the most ecstatic and noble union to ever have existed on earth.

Much of my information about Una and John's rarefied life in

Paris, their lesbian coterie, and the salons they attended where flower petals fell through skylights, came from several books about their social circle: Jean Chalon's *Portrait of a Seductress: The World of Natalie Barney, Between Me and Life: A Biography of Romaine Brooks,* and Andrea Weiss's *Paris Was a Woman: Portraits from the Left Bank*. Terry Castle's *Noel Coward and Radclyffe Hall: Kindred Spirits* also offered an interesting account of their social world.

For insight into *The Well of Loneliness,* and the stir it caused, I found the memoirs, diaries, and letters of many of the writers of the period useful, especially those of Virginia Woolf. It was also informative to read Vera Brittain's meditation on the case: *Radclyffe Hall: A Case of Obscenity?*

Because there were highly conflicting views of Hall's life—Was she in love with Evguenia? Why did she turn against her at the end? What was the nature of her relationship with Una?—I had to make a judgment using several different versions. Una's powerful mythologizing instinct complicated many accounts of the basic facts. In the end, Hall's own letters seemed to me to provide the most compelling evidence of the last years of her life and of her tormented but rewarding relationship with Evguenia Souline. In particular, I drew on *Your John: The Love Letters of Radclyffe Hall,* edited by Joanne Glasgow.

The Well of Loneliness and Hall's other novels and poetry, provided an interesting window into the precise nature of her romantic temperament, as did her more straightforward accounts in her letters: She was a highly expressive person, and there was not much left unvoiced in her yearnings and desires.

VERA BRITTAIN

My greatest source for the life of Vera Brittain was, of course, Vera herself. Her diaries, her published "Testaments," and her voluminous letters proved a rich source for nearly all of the events of this chapter. For anyone with an interest in the arcane workings of Vera Brittain's mind, the small differences between the *Chronicle of Youth,* her wartime diaries, and the more polished *Testament of Youth,* covering the same period, are enormously fascinating, as are the small differences between *Chronicle of Friendship: Diary of the Thirties* and her public "Testament" of the same period.

In addition, I found George Gordon Catlin's stiff and convoluted autobiography *For God's Sake, Go!* useful, in spite of his concerted effort to avoid the charged and difficult topic of his marriage. He is the one who related the sad detail of his own son asking, "Daddy, do you like me?" though to him it seemed to be a charming and whimsical anecdote of childish irrationality. Revealing, also, was John Catlin's curiously stunned memoir, *Family Quartet.* Like Angelica Garnett, he appears to be a very articulate person rendered somewhat hazy by the prospect of narrating his odd childhood. He did mention that he married young to escape the disorder of his youth, and to attempt some sort of conventional structure. As he explained: "A major motivation for marriage was the need to distance myself from my parents. I looked forward to a degree of domesticity which I had never known."

Deborah Gorham's *Vera Brittain: A Feminist Life* and *Vera Brittain: A Life* by Paul Berry and Mark Bostridge proved very good sources for the remaining biographical information that somehow eluded Brittain's own narrative instincts. For instance the tiny, revealing fact that she wrote to her mother, during the war, to ask if it would be "correct" for her to send cigarettes to Geoffrey and Victor, as she did to her brother—a question which in its very articulation suggests a blurring of the line between friendship and romance in her relation to these friends. The etiquette concern must be fueled by some ambiguity in her own mind: Were these friends of her brother's just friends? Though she was officially in a trance of mourning for Roland, her one true love, she was, at the same time, involved in quasi-romantic correspondences with several other boys. I was also influenced in my understanding of Vera during the war years by *Letters from a Lost Generation: The First World War Letters of Vera Brittain and Four Friends, Roland Leighton, Edward Brittain, Victor Richardson, and Geoffrey Thurlow,* which was edited by Alan Bishop and Mark Bostridge.

For the texture of Vera's friendship with Winifred, I drew on the collection of letters, *Selected Letters of Winifred Holtby and Vera Brittain, 1920–1935,* which were edited by Vera Brittain and Geoffrey Handley-Taylor. Both her and Winifred's intellectual pre-occupations were fleshed out for me in *Testament of a Generation: The Journalism of Vera Brittain and Winifred Holtby,* which was edited by Paul Berry and Alan Bishop. Winifred Holtby's *Letters to a Friend,* which were not letters to Vera, helped in illuminating her character; in particular her liveliness and sense of humor. Somehow the energy emerging from these pages reveals her in all of her quirkiness. Marion Shaw's biography, *A Clear Stream,* also provided a fuller, more balanced account of her life than Vera's fairly bloodless portrait in *Testament of Friendship;* it also offered more in-depth evidence of the particular nature of Winifred's relation to Gordon.

PERMISSIONS

Grateful acknowledgment is made to the following for providing the photos used throughout the book:

H. G. Wells. George C. Beresford/Getty Images.

Jane Wells. By permission of the University of Illinois Library at Urbana-Champaign.

Rebecca West. George C. Beresford/Getty Images.

Katherine Mansfield and John Middleton Murry. Alexander Turnbull Library, Wellington.

Elizabeth von Arnim. Courtesy of Virago Press and the Estate of Elizabeth von Arnim.

John Francis Stanley Russell. By permission of McMaster University.

Vanessa Bell. George C. Beresford/Getty Images.

Clive Bell. National Portrait Gallery, London.

Duncan Grant. Frances Partridge/Getty Images.

Ottoline Morrell. By permission of McMaster University.

Philip Morrell. National Portrait Galley, London.

Radclyffe Hall and Una Troubridge. Fox Photos/Getty Images.

Vera Brittain and George Catlin. By permission of McMaster University.

Winifred Holtby. By permission of McMaster University.

ACKNOWLEDGME[...]

I am deeply indebted to Phyllis Rose's incomparable *Parallel Lives* which inspired me in thinking about lives, including my own. Rarely does one come across a book so spectacular that it opens up a whole line of study. I am also grateful for the example of other elegant group portraits: my particular favorites are Rachel Cohen's *A Chance Meeting,* Alethea Hayter's *A Sultry Month,* Francine Prose's *The Lives of the Muses,* and Claudia Roth Pierpont's *Passionate Minds,* along with the classic in the genre, Lytton Strachey's *Eminent Victorians.*

I am also enormously grateful to the vast number of scholars who have written biographies and studies on the figures in this book, and edited their collected letters and diaries. As I have detailed in my endnotes, I have relied on the archival research and insight of many great works of scholarship that exist on these figures. It goes without saying that I could not have written this book without the excellent biographies and studies, and collections of letters, journals, memoirs, and writings on which I have based the bulk of my observations about the world of these marriages, along with the recollections and memoirs and collected letters of other people from the period. My own work was primarily an act of synthesis, of putting together different points of view and sorting through the details, to get at the stories I wanted to tell, and I would not have been able to attempt this work without the excellent scholarship that exists on these writers and artists.

ACKNOWLEDGMENTS

...ateful to the Literary Executors of the Estate of ... for permission to use quotations from Brittain's mate- ...this book (all quotations from Vera Brittain are copyright © ...he Literary Executors of the Vera Brittain Estate 1970). Grateful thanks also to the Estate of Vanessa Bell for permission to reproduce her material; all such material is © the Vanessa Bell Estate, courtesy of Henrietta Garnett. Excerpts from *Henry James* and *The Judge* by Rebecca West, *Rebecca West: A Celebration* by Rebecca West and edited by Samuel Hynes, and *Selected Letters of Rebecca West*, edited by Bonnie Kime Scott, are © by Rebecca West and are reproduced here by permission of PFD (www.pfd.co.uk) on behalf of Rebecca West. *Your John: The Love Letters of Radclyffe Hall* by Radclyffe Hall © Radclyffe Hall is reprinted by kind permission of A. M. Heath & Co. Ltd, Authors' Agents.

In addition I owe a great debt to the New York Public Library, in particular to Wayne Furman in Special Collections, and to the Allen room for a cubicle of my own, and to the Berg Collection for kind permission to quote from letters and other sources. I am indebted also to the librarians and curators who helped me obtain the photographs that appear in these pages.

I am also grateful to Susan Kamil, Suzanne Gluck, Matthew Martin, and Noah Eaker; to my family, Anne Roiphe, Violet Roiphe Chernoff, Becky Roiphe, Ben and Ella Gruenstein, Jean and the Herz-Roiphes, and Emily Roiphe, and to Radha Ramkissoon, Theodore Jacobs, Larissa MacFarquhar, Philip Gourevitch, Josh Pashman, Jon Jon Goulian, Elyse Cheney, Tad Friend, Harry Chernoff, Deb Kogan, Nuar Alsadir, Aleksandra Crapanzano, and Richard Kaye.

INDEX